Affordances and Constraints of Mobile Phone Use in English Language Arts Classrooms

Clarice M. Moran
Appalachian State University, USA

A volume in the Advances in Educational Technologies and Instructional Design (AETID) Book Series

IGI Global
PUBLISHER of TIMELY KNOWLEDGE

Published in the United States of America by
IGI Global
Information Science Reference (an imprint of IGI Global)
701 E. Chocolate Avenue
Hershey PA, USA 17033
Tel: 717-533-8845
Fax: 717-533-8661
E-mail: cust@igi-global.com
Web site: http://www.igi-global.com

Library of Congress Cataloging-in-Publication Data

Names: Moran, Clarice M., 1964- editor.
Title: Affordances and constraints of mobile phone use in English language arts classrooms / Clarice M. Moran, editor.
Description: Hershey, PA : Information Science Reference, 2021. | Includes bibliographical references and index. | Summary: "This edited book examines the use of mobile phones in the secondary English language arts classroom and discusses the affordances and constraints of the now-ubiquitous technology by examining learning outcomes, best practices, and practical applications for using mobile phones in ELA"-- Provided by publisher.
Identifiers: LCCN 2020026653 (print) | LCCN 2020026654 (ebook) | ISBN 9781799858058 (hardcover) | ISBN 9781799866688 (paperback) | ISBN 9781799858065 (ebook)
Subjects: LCSH: English language--Study and teaching (Secondary) | English language--Study and teaching--Technological innovations. | English language--Study and teaching--Foreign speakers. | Mobile communication systems in education.
Classification: LCC LB1631 .A356 2021 (print) | LCC LB1631 (ebook) | DDC 371.33--dc23
LC record available at https://lccn.loc.gov/2020026653
LC ebook record available at https://lccn.loc.gov/2020026654

This book is published in the IGI Global book series Advances in Educational Technologies and Instructional Design (AETID) (ISSN: 2326-8905; eISSN: 2326-8913)

British Cataloguing in Publication Data
A Cataloguing in Publication record for this book is available from the British Library.

All work contributed to this book is new, previously-unpublished material.
The views expressed in this book are those of the authors, but not necessarily of the publisher.

For electronic access to this publication, please contact: eresources@igi-global.com.

Advances in Educational Technologies and Instructional Design (AETID) Book Series

ISSN:2326-8905
EISSN:2326-8913

Editor-in-Chief: Lawrence A. Tomei, Robert Morris University, USA

MISSION

Education has undergone, and continues to undergo, immense changes in the way it is enacted and distributed to both child and adult learners. In modern education, the traditional classroom learning experience has evolved to include technological resources and to provide online classroom opportunities to students of all ages regardless of their geographical locations. From distance education, Massive-Open-Online-Courses (MOOCs), and electronic tablets in the classroom, technology is now an integral part of learning and is also affecting the way educators communicate information to students.

The **Advances in Educational Technologies & Instructional Design (AETID) Book Series** explores new research and theories for facilitating learning and improving educational performance utilizing technological processes and resources. The series examines technologies that can be integrated into K-12 classrooms to improve skills and learning abilities in all subjects including STEM education and language learning. Additionally, it studies the emergence of fully online classrooms for young and adult learners alike, and the communication and accountability challenges that can arise. Trending topics that are covered include adaptive learning, game-based learning, virtual school environments, and social media effects. School administrators, educators, academicians, researchers, and students will find this series to be an excellent resource for the effective design and implementation of learning technologies in their classes.

COVERAGE

- Classroom Response Systems
- Curriculum Development
- Bring-Your-Own-Device
- Collaboration Tools
- Educational Telecommunications
- Instructional Design Models
- Hybrid Learning
- Adaptive Learning
- Social Media Effects on Education
- Web 2.0 and Education

The Advances in Educational Technologies and Instructional Design (AETID) Book Series (ISSN 2326-8905) is published by IGI Global, 701 E. Chocolate Avenue, Hershey, PA 17033-1240, USA, www.igi-global.com. This series is composed of titles available for purchase individually; each title is edited to be contextually exclusive from any other title within the series. For pricing and ordering information please visit http://www.igi-global.com/book-series/advances-educational-technologies-instructional-design/73678. Postmaster: Send all address changes to above address.

Titles in this Series

For a list of additional titles in this series, please visit:
http://www.igi-global.com/book-series/

Teaching and Learning Practices That Promote Sustainable Development and Active Citizenship
Sandra Saúde (Polytechnic Institute of Beja, Portugal & CICS, NOVA University Lisbon, Portugal) Maria Albertina Raposo (Polytechnic Institute of Beja, Portugal & MARE, NOVA University Lisbon, Portugal) Nuno Pereira (Polytechnic Institute of Beja, Portugal) and Ana Isabel Rodrigues (Polytechnic Institute of Beja, Portugal)
Information Science Reference • © 2021 • 383pp • H/C (ISBN: 9781799844020) • US $185.00

Designing, Deploying, and Evaluating Virtual and Augmented Reality in Education
Gokce Akcayir (University of Alberta, Canada) and Carrie Demmans Epp (University of Alberta, Canada)
Information Science Reference • © 2021 • 404pp • H/C (ISBN: 9781799850434) • US $185.00

IT and the Development of Digital Skills and Competences in Education
Patricia Ordóñez de Pablos (University of Oviedo, Spain) Miltiadis D. Lytras (American College of Greece, Greece & Effat University, Saudi Arabia) and Xi Zhang (Tianjin University, China)
Information Science Reference • © 2021 • 332pp • H/C (ISBN: 9781799849728) • US $195.00

Fostering Meaningful Learning Experiences Through Student Engagement
Despo Ktoridou (University of Nicosia, Cyprus) Elli Doukanari (University of Nicosia, Cyprus) and Nikleia Eteokleous (Frederick University, Cyprus)
Information Science Reference • © 2021 • 325pp • H/C (ISBN: 9781799846581) • US $195.00

IGI Global
PUBLISHER of TIMELY KNOWLEDGE

701 East Chocolate Avenue, Hershey, PA 17033, USA
Tel: 717-533-8845 x100 • Fax: 717-533-8661
E-Mail: cust@igi-global.com • www.igi-global.com

Editorial Advisory Board

Table of Contents

Detailed Table of Contents

expand on the research regarding 24/7 accessibility in an online environment. The second author provides a particularly powerful voice in this chapter as a current pre-service teacher. His vignettes were used throughout the chapter to add a student perspective that is often omitted from the scholarship.

The purpose of this chapter is to discuss cell phones in the classroom before and after the pandemic. The author discusses the problematic history of cell phones in the classroom, and how teachers have struggled and fought against them, many times outright banning cell phones. Instead of this approach, the case is made for the need for students to learn how to use them, and why they are so useful in the classroom for both formative assessment and feedback. Next, this chapter discusses how the author leveraged cell phones during the period of crisis instruction at the end of the 2019-2020 school year. The author was able to launch and successfully complete a unit that combined social justice themes, graphic novels, and podcasting – all of which utilizing cell phones. Finally, specific tools, resources, and strategies are shared and discussed that were used during this time, with recommendations for the future of education no matter how it may look.

The study explored the use of mobile phones by the early childhood teachers of English language arts (ELA) in Nigeria. Descriptive survey design was used using an online survey to assess early childhood teachers' use of the mobile phone in their classrooms. Ninety-eight teachers who responded to the instrument online formed the sample for the study. The instrument entitled Mobile Phones in ELA Classrooms' Questionnaire (MP-ELA-CQ) was used to collect data for the study. Data were analyzed using percentage and Pearson Moment Correlation Coefficients. Results indicated that teachers—both preservice and in-service—need regular training in technology and education to help them effectively utilize mobile phones in their classrooms.

Foreword

"Classrooms don't often allow students to network with each other and with various tools and technologies and be rewarded for doing so, rather than being rewarded for individual achievement. Furthermore, classrooms tend to narrowly constrain where students can gain knowledge rather than utilize widely dispersed knowledge" (Gee, 2004, p. 89)

Across my time both as a student and an educator, various technology tools have received pushback from English Language Arts teachers. Perhaps they were viewed as disruptive to classroom practice, or perhaps they were viewed as not belonging in traditional, school-sanctioned literacy spaces. When I was a student, it was the traditional tools of pen and paper used to pass notes in a classroom. Of course, these were in direct conflict with the tools we needed to complete work assigned in class or to simply take notes. When I was an early-career teacher, it was virtual pet toys students brought to class, dinging with their reminders to feed, water, or play with the "pet." In season 3 of *Ozark*, the character of Ben is teaching adolescents when everyone's mobile phones start pinging with messages. As most teachers do, he becomes frustrated and walks through the student rows with the trashcan collecting the mobile phones. He then goes outside and runs them through the woodchipper. As teachers, it is easy to laugh at this scene and even applaud it, having felt this way when students have not engaged with our lessons. Maybe, though, it is teachers who need to change the positioning of their lessons in relation to students and engagement.

LITERACY AND EVOLVING TECHNOLOGIES

Literacy issues have remained at the forefront of education since the publication of *A Nation at Risk* (1983), and with decades of rapid technological advances, the implementation of technology has become a critical component of literacy instruction

(Baron, 2001; Reinking, Labbo, & McKenna, 2000; Reinking, 1997). With the continued integration of a variety of forms of technology in education, teachers often turn to various technology tools and the possibilities that they offer to serve as a focal point for implementing new strategies that include all students and leverage tools they already use. Mobile phones offer one such tool in that most students carry them like an extension of their hands. While ELA teachers primarily focus on traditional literacy activities such as reading and writing, mobile phones present an evolving technology through which students may engage in these activities. For decades now, teachers have used computers to enhance the teaching of key literacy activities such as reading, writing, and researching (Burke, 2001; Anderson-Inman, Horney, Chen, & Lewin, 1994), and mobile phones are, at their most basic level, a personal hand-held computer device.

However, in using technology tools, educators need to focus on the initial rationales for implementing those tools. For example, many literacy experts assert that teachers need to teach literacy skills in the context of technology in order to best prepare students to function as critical thinkers (Eagleton, 2002; Reinking, 1997). Mobile phones provide a key means of teaching literacy skills in a technological context because of their increased accessibility in both schools and homes. Not all students, though, have equal access to and experiences with mobile phones; therefore, teachers need to plan integrations of these tools that account for those constraints of inequity.

Myers (1996) points out that literacy "does not represent a distinction between print and nonprint practices" (p. 119). Literacy, instead, encompasses a set of socially and politically predetermined communication practices; it represents a communicative system within which people of a society communicate and through which they have a common means of understanding their world. New literacy practices are continuously introduced into a society's range of communication practices. Literacy, and therefore literate thinking, somehow extends beyond making sense of the printed text on the page, and teachers have a responsibility to prepare students to think critically about their world and the information it contains in a manner that helps them to successfully deal with the continuous introduction of new practices, such as mobile phones (Myers, 1996).

TECHNOLOGY AND ADOLESCENTS' LITERACY PRACTICES

The Twenty-first Century has witnessed the impact that new technologies have on literacy practices. Any new technology tools, such as the mobile phone, inevitably affect literacy practices. All literacy technologies adapt to the old ways of doing things, and they introduce new ways as well. Albeit a difficult notion to conceive of today, pencils, and consequently writing, were once presented as new technologies, posing problems to the conceptions of literacy similar to those currently posed by mobile phones. In considering the impact of new technologies on literacy practices, Chandler (1985) asserts the importance of remembering that all technologies of literacy are fundamentally "systems for manipulating symbols" (p. 4). In this context, then, the teacher's role shifts away from that of teaching students to manipulate symbols through various mediums and in various contexts. In recognizing the implications and possibilities that mobile phones as a literacy technology pose to education, teachers need to begin to focus on how they impact literacy practices so that they can then directly address those in the classroom (Baron, 1985; Chandler, 1985).

With these advancements in technology, students have moved past what Postman (1986) refers to as the typographic mind – the mind resulting from a word-based culture. With the onslaught of computers and related mobile technologies that put the world at our hands, we have become a more image-based culture. When students search for something or someone online, images appear at the top of the search screen. For decades, schools have operated within a word-based culture, privileging written texts. However, considering multiple modes of literacy and shifts in culture, requires that teachers shift their focus toward genres of text that also engage students with image-based culture. Kress (1999) points out that as visual language becomes more predominant in public modes of communication, "written language is being displaced from its hitherto unchallenged central position in the semiotic landscape, and that the visual is taking over many of the functions of written language" (p. 68). As Witte and I point out (2018), this shift in to image-based culture "requires that teachers consider how students read images in the classroom, address visual literacy, and use images to construct critical literacy" (p. 2).

Alvermann (2008) and Gee (2004) argue that too frequently schools overlook students' out-of-school literacy practices, shrugging them off as something done on their own and not sanctioned in school spaces. Mobile phones present exactly this type of out-of-school literacy practice for students. Alvermann points out that these "literacies [are] so powerfully motivating that young people are more and more willing to invest a substantial amount of time and effort in creating content to share with others online" (p. 9). Gee similarly argues "that people learn best when their learning is part of a highly motivated engagement with social practices which they value" (p. 77). It is, therefore, exciting to see a text which examines how mobile phones – a traditionally out-of-school literacy practice—are being leveraged in classrooms. Even when constraints are involved, the examinations of those in this volume demonstrate teachers stretch in considering shifts in our culture and literacy practices. This text highlights teachers examining the affordances and constraints of mobile phones in the classroom to open up more image- and technology-based literacy practices for students.

Jennifer S. Dail
Kennesaw State University, USA

REFERENCES

Alvermann, D. (2008). Commentary: Why bother theorizing adolescents' online literacies for classroom practice and research? *Journal of Adolescent & Adult Literacy, 52*(1), 8–19. doi:10.1598/JAAL.52.1.2

Anderson-Inman, L., Horney, M. A., Chen, D., & Lewin, L. (1994). Hypertext literacy: Observations from the Electro Text Project. *Language Arts, 71*, 279–287.

Baron, D. (2001). From pencils to pixels: The stages of literacy technologies. In E. Cushman, E. R. Kintgen, B. M. Kroll, & M. Rose (Eds.), *Literacy: A critical sourcebook* (pp. 70–84). Bedford/St. Martin's.

Burke, J. (2001). *Illuminating texts: How to teach students to read the world.* Heinemann.

Chandler, D. (1985). Computers and literacy. In D. Chandler (Ed.), *Computers and literacy* (pp. 1–11). Open University Press.

Dail, J. S., & Witte, S. (2018). Introduction: Positioning students as creators in the classroom. In J. S. Dail, S. Witte, & S. T. Bickmore (Eds.), *Toward a more visual literacy: Shiftingthe paradigm with digital tools and young adult literature*. Rowman & Littlefield.

Eagleton, M. B. (2002). Making text come to life on the computer: Toward an understanding of hypermedia literacy. *Electronic Literacy in School and Home: A Look into the Future, 6*(1). https://www.learntechlib.org/p/96737/

Gee, J. P. (2004). *Situated language and learning: A critique of traditional schooling*. Routledge.

Kress, G. (1999). English at the crossroads: Rethinking curricula of communication in the context of the turn to the visual. In C. L. Selfe & G. E. Hawisher (Eds.), *Passions, pedagogies, and 21st Century technologies* (pp. 66–88). National Council of Teachers of English. doi:10.2307/j.ctt46nrfk.7

Myers, M. (1996). *Changing our minds: Negotiating English and literacy*. National Council of Teachers of English.

Postman, N. (1986). *Amusing ourselves to death: Public discourse in the age of show business*. Penguin Books.

Reinking, D. (1997). Me and my hypertext:) A multiple digression analysis of technology and literacy (sic). *The Reading Teacher*, *50*(8), 626–643.

Reinking, D., Labbo, L. D., & McKenna, M. C. (2000). From assimilation to accommodation: A developmental framework for integrating digital technologies into literacy research and instruction. *Journal of Research in Reading*, *23*(2), 110–122. doi:10.1111/1467-9817.00108

Preface

This book arrives at a time when the world seems to have changed suddenly and dramatically. Like a seismic shift, the entire focus and paradigm of the world seems to have lurched into a new era—an era that is dependent upon digital tools to get anything done. In this new world, work is conducted almost entirely through digital platforms that allow virtual meetings and collaboration. School looks nothing like it did even five years ago, and the English language arts (ELA) classroom is a new realm where learning frequently takes place through online tools.

When Jones and Hafner (2012) applied the terms "affordances" and "constraints" to digital tools, they had no idea that the world would shift toward increasing reliance on technology. Yet, the notion that this technology has plusses and minuses was ahead of its time. Now, as we find ourselves learning and communicating in amazing digital spaces, we also find ourselves increasingly isolated and reliant on the technology for connection. Jones and Hafner (2012) wrote:

Tools enable us to do new things, think in new ways, express new kinds of meanings, establish new kinds of relationships and be new kinds of people. On the other hand, they also prevent us from doing other things, of thinking in other ways, of having other kinds of relationships and of being other kinds of people. (p. 5)

In other words, digital tools have ways of bringing us together and also of pulling us apart. This is especially true with mobile phones.

In the ELA classroom, mobile phones can provide students with a wide range of opportunities, or *affordances* (Liu et al, 2014). Students can use the camera to take photos or video, and they can use apps to edit those photos and video into digital compositions that often surpass written ones. They can access the internet and its buffet of options for writing, reading, listening, and speaking activities. They can pop the phones into virtual reality devices and inhabit three-dimensional spaces to increase the fluency of their writing (Moran & Woodall, 2019).

Yet, these ubiquitous mobile devices also confound teachers with their *constraints*. Classroom management is more difficult when students are tuned out and scrolling through Instagram (Burns & LoHenry, 2010), while basic applications like texting have seemed to hinder students' ability to write Standard English. There are also worrying trends that indicate students may exhibit addictive behavior when they are asked to withdraw from their phones (Mendoza, Pody, Lee, Kim, & McDonough, 2018; Tams et al., 2018).

According to the Pew Research Center (2019), more than 96 percent of Americans own a mobile phone, and more than 82% of high school students regularly use a cell phone. The use of those phones in the classroom is a controversial topic that has political ramifications. School districts in Alaska, California, and Florida have banned cell phones in the classroom (Lemieux, 2019; McGreevey, 2019; Ramos, 2019) in an effort to combat what administrators say is a distracted student population. In fact, the entirc country of France banned cell phones in schools in 2018 (Diebel, 2018). However, research has demonstrated that cell phones can have positive effects on learning outcomes and engagement (Thomas & O'Bannon, 2013). Teachers who use educational apps, social media, and gaming applications through mobile phones find that students are more engaged in course materials (Hegarty & Thompson, 2019).

This edited collection examines the use of mobile phones in the secondary ELA classroom and discuss the affordances and constraints of the now-ubiquitous technology. Through the research of practitioners and scholars, the chapters in this book examine learning outcomes, best practices, and practical applications for using mobile phones in ELA. It is a resource for inservice and preservice teachers, administrators, researchers, teacher educators, and those seeking to understand the current thinking on mobile phone use in ELA.

This book is divided into four sections, each with a specific focus on the affordances and constraints of mobile phones in the ELA classroom. The chapters in each section offer new research and insights into curricular implications of using mobile devices.

Section 1, "Mobile Phones and Digital Literacies," encompasses three chapters that address the practical applications of using mobile phones with a variety of digital platforms.

Chapter 1, "This Is Next Level: Combining Video Games With Literature to Promote Literacy," features instructional approaches positioning video games and literature as text sets that can promote reading and writing engagement in ELA. Grounded in digital literacies and text-based gameplay, this chapter showcases how a text set framework can offer literacy instructors multiple pathways for student engagement that leverage diverse learners' sociocultural meaning-making toward success in school. Recommendations are offered for teachers, including a series of pedagogical moves that can be implemented in secondary language arts classrooms, as well as affordances and challenges to smartphone-driven teaching.

Chapter 2, "Beyond Apps and Activities: Intentional Integration of Technology in English Language Arts Education," examines the importance of intentionally planning with an instructional framework to leverage the use of technology. The author provides an integration framework to support middle and secondary language arts teachers. The author shares how she has refined the process of using mobile phones in her classroom and shares the transformative power of deliberately planning for the use of technology: a practice that has improved her clarity and amplified student learning.

Chapter 3, "Reimagining Mobile Phones: Multiple Literacies and Digital Media Compositions," offers insights into Digital Multimodal Compositions (DMCs)--digital texts created through the use of various modes, including written text, audio, visual, and other interactive media. DMCs are an effective way to incorporate both mobile technology and multiple literacies into the curriculum in both face-to-face and virtual settings.

Section 2, "Mobile Phones and the COVID-19 Pandemic," addresses the ways in which teachers and teacher educators used mobile phones to enhance learning experiences in the ELA classroom during the pandemic shutdown in 2020. The successful application of these activities now can extend beyond 2020 into the future.

In Chapter 4, "The Role of Cell Phones in Online Learning, Connectivity, and COVID," the authors used the lens of COVID-19 to explore how mobile phones and general technological connectivity can be both a positive learning experience and contribute to connectivity fatigue and burnout for both teachers and students. The authors reflect upon their own experiences and conversations as well as expand on the research regarding 24/7 accessibility in an online environment.

Chapter 5, "Decriminalizing Cell Phones: Before and After the Pandemic," discusses cell phones in the ELA classroom before and after the pandemic. The author discusses the problematic history of cell phones in the classroom and how teachers have struggled and fought against them, many times outright banning cell phones. Instead of this approach, the case is made for the need for students to learn how to use them, and why they are so useful in the classroom for both formative assessment and feedback. Next, this chapter discusses how the author leveraged cell phones during the period of crisis instruction at the end of the 2019-2020 school year. The author was able to launch and successfully complete a unit that combined social justice themes, graphic novels, and podcasting--all of which utilize cell phones.

Chapter 6, "Early Childhood Teachers' Usage of Mobile Phones in English Language Arts Classrooms in Nigeria: Challenges and Prospects," features a study conducted during the COVID-19 pandemic. The study explored the use of mobile phones by the early childhood teachers of ELA in Nigeria. Descriptive survey design was used using an online survey to assess early childhood teachers' use of the mobile phone in their classrooms. Ninety-eight (98) teachers who responded to the instrument online formed the sample for the study. The instrument entitled, Mobile Phones in ELA Classrooms' Questionnaire (MP-ELA-CQ), was used to collect data for the study. Data were analyzed using percentage and Pearson Moment Correlation Coefficients. Results indicated that teachers—both preservice and in-service—need regular training in technology and education to help them effectively utilize mobile phones in their classrooms.

Section 3, "Mobile Phones and the Arts," looks at creative applications of mobile phones through the arts and pushes the envelope for using the devices in the ELA classroom.

Chapter 7, "Mobile Phones, Arts Integration, and English Language Arts," considers the affordances of smartphones as tools for arts integration in ELA classrooms. It discusses the importance of students as creators of content and how teachers may capture the social tools already within student possession to function as learning tools as well. Arts-based instruction is briefly discussed as an important element for students' full participation in the multiliteracies that make up much of communication in modern society. The chapter also includes specific ideas for students' smartphone compositions that teachers may consider.

In Chapter 8, "Music and Mobile Phones: How Students' First Space Mobile Phones Afford Third Space Opportunity," the author argues that mobile phones establish a private, first space where students interact both socially and academically as they appear as audience/observers and agents/creators. In addition to practical affordances, the author discusses social-emotional aspects of mobile phones as they have become part of students' first space, representing both culture and identity. The author argues that music, which exists in students' private first spaces, affords teachers an opportunity to establish and engage students in a neutral third space where meaning and knowing occur without scripts or strategies but rather curiosity, respect, and connection.

Section 4, "Mobile Phones in the Classroom," focuses on the issues and concerns that ELA teachers have about allowing mobile phones into the classroom. The chapters in this section provide insight and direction for using the devices without disrupting instruction.

Chapter 9, "Cell Phones and Classroom Management: Minimizing the Distraction of Cell Phones in the Classroom to Ensure Student Success," outlines and analyzes various classroom management strategies for teachers to regulate cell phone use. Beginning with the background of why cell phones are known to cause distractions in the classroom, the chapter then focuses on using both positive and negative reinforcement strategies for teachers to structure and encourage proper mobile phone usage. The author also includes the benefits and challenges imposed by various classroom management systems in order to guide teachers in making the right decisions regarding cell phone use in their classrooms.

And, finally, Chapter 10, "The New Normal is Cell Phones in the Classroom: A Twenty-Year Retrospective," compares and contrasts a classroom without student cell phone use in 2000 to the ubiquitous use of cell phones in today's classroom and society. The author shares lived classroom experience in the twenty years from cell phone infancy to usage by more than 90 percent of students in today's classroom. The author also provides insights into effective use of cell phones in the classroom and pitfalls that occur without well-planned instruction.

Although there have been many news articles, blog posts, and conversations about mobile phone use, there has been very little published research on the specific benefits and constraints of the devices in ELA. Much research has emerged involving the integration of technology and digital literacies in ELA, but mobile phone use as a discrete construct has not been explored widely. This book adds to the body of literature on mobile phone use in secondary classrooms in general and stand as a unique resource on mobile phones in the language arts curriculum.

Clarice M. Moran
Appalachian State University, USA

REFERENCES

Burns, S. M., & Lohenry, K. (2010). Cellular phone use in class: Implications for teaching and learning a pilot study. *College Student Journal*, 805–810.

Diebel, M. (2018). France cellphone ban takes effect as kids return to school without devices. *USA Today*. Retrieved from https://www.usatoday.com/story/news/world/2018/09/05/french-school-cellphone-ban-students-return-class-without-devices/1199937002

Hegarty, B., & Thompson, M. (2019). A teacher's influence on student engagement: Using smartphones for creating vocational assessment ePortfolios. *Journal of Information Technology Education, 18*, 113–159. doi:10.28945/4244

Jones, R. H., & Hafner, C. A. (2012). *Understanding digital literacies: A practical introduction*. Routledge. doi:10.4324/9780203095317

Lemieux, M. (2019). Alaska high school bans cellphones, and students are happy with the new rule. *Newsweek*. Retrieved from https://www.newsweek.com/alaska-high-school-bans-cellphones-students-are-happy-new-rule-1463700

Liu, M., Scordino, R., Geurtz, R., Navarrete, C., Ko, Y., & Lim, M. (2014). A look at research on mobile learning in K–12 education from 2007 to the present. *Journal of Research on Technology in Education, 46*(4), 325–372. doi:10.1080/15391523.2014.925681

McGreevy, P. (2019). More California students may be banned from using cellphones in school under new bill. *Los Angeles Times*. Retrieved from https://www.latimes.com/politics/la-pol-ca-school-smartphone-ban-20190320-story.html

Mendoza, J. S., Pody, B. C., Lee, S., Kim, M., & McDonough, I. M. (2018). The effect of cellphones on attention and learning: The influences of time, distraction, and nomophobia. *Computers in Human Behavior, 86*, 52–60. doi:10.1016/j.chb.2018.04.027

Moran, C. M., & Woodall, M. K. (2019). 'It was like I was there': Inspiring engagement through virtual reality. *English Journal, 109*(1), 90–96.

Pew Research Center. (2019). *Mobile fact sheet*. Retrieved from https://www.pewresearch.org/internet/fact-sheet/mobile

Ramos, J. (2019). Cell phones banned during class time in Sarasota County schools. *WFTS-Tampa Bay*. Retrieved from https://www.abcactionnews.com/news/back-to-school/cell-phones-banned-during-class-time-in-sarasota-county-schools

Tams, S., Legoux, R., & Léger, P. (2018). Smartphone withdrawal creates stress: A moderated mediation model of nomophobia, social threat, and phone withdrawal context. *Computers in Human Behavior, 81*, 1–9. doi:10.1016/j.chb.2017.11.026

Thomas, K., & O'Bannon, B. (2013). Cell Phones in the classroom: Preservice teachers' perceptions. *Journal of Digital Learning in Teacher Education, 30*(1), 11–20. doi:10.1080/21532974.2013.10784721

Acknowledgment

I would like to thank Appalachian State University and my colleagues and friends from Kennesaw State University for their help on this edited volume. In addition, I would like to acknowledge the patience and love of my husband, Tom, and children, Katie, Thomas, and Daniel.

Section 1
Mobile Phones and Digital Literacies

Chapter 1
This Is Next Level:
Combining Video Games With Literature to Promote Literacy

Rick Marlatt
https://orcid.org/0000-0002-2182-1655
New Mexico State University, USA

Magdalena Pando
https://orcid.org/0000-0003-3799-4339
New Mexico State University, USA

Miles M. Harvey
University of New Mexico, USA

ABSTRACT

This chapter features instructional approaches positioning video games and literature as text sets that can promote reading and writing engagement in English language arts. Smartphone-accessible games were recently combined with middle school literary assignments in an after-school esports club in which students who identify as English language learners expressed an increased interest in academic tasks that prioritized smartphone usage. Grounded in digital literacies and text-based gameplay, this chapter showcases how a text set framework can offer literacy instructors multiple pathways for student engagement that leverage diverse learners' sociocultural meaning-making toward success in school. Recommendations are offered for teachers, including a series of pedagogical moves that can be implemented in secondary language arts classrooms, as well as affordances and challenges to smartphone-driven teaching.

DOI: 10.4018/978-1-7998-5805-8.ch001

INTRODUCTION

English language learners (ELLs) require two conditions to acquire a second language, like English: 1) they must have English native speakers available to them, and 2) the instructional setting must bring ELLs and English speakers into frequent contact to make language learning possible (Wong Fillmore, 1992). Smartphones offer numerous platforms to help instructors of ELLs meet both of these conditions, including narrative-driven video games that can supplement literacy curricula through literary analysis and identity construction. Over 95% of teenage students in the United States have access to a smartphone for daily classroom usage, which affords literacy teachers myriad interactive voice and mobile messaging applications to enhance native language capabilities, while the intentional pairing of ELLs with language applications can also support standards-based development (Anderson & Jiang, 2018).

The National Council of Teachers of English (NCTE) (2020) recently revised its position on the role of English Language Arts (ELA) teachers in the education of ELLs "to reflect current knowledge on and best practices in English language learning and teaching in K-12 schooling in the United States" (para. 1). NCTE (2020) outlined specific emphases on a number of curricular models such as explicit teaching of academic language, vocabulary acquisition for development in reading and writing, and contextualizing notions of literacy assessment to more closely align with students' home language practices. However, for ELA teachers interested in using technology integration to engage ELLs, the position statement's recommendations regarding the integration of digital literacies are especially important, given their inclusions of multiple modalities, digitized texts, and multimedia. Increasingly, ELA teachers are prioritizing instruction and activities that position ubiquitous technology such as smartphones as a primary platform in the literacy instruction of ELLs in secondary classrooms.

This chapter features ELA instructional approaches pairing smartphone-accessible video games with classroom literature to promote reading and writing engagement for ELLs. Following a review of literature surrounding digital literacies and play, video games and esports are positioned as ideal platforms through which adolescents' social meaning making can enhance academic achievement. A conceptual framework for engaging ELLs that prioritizes linguistic accommodations and multimodal text sets is then offered, which is followed by a description of the authors' contexts and motivations. Suggested interventions for teachers in the form of individual lessons and a recommended unit overview are then presented. The chapter concludes with a summary of additional recommendations and best practices involving the use of smartphones in ELA.

BACKGROUND

ELLs, Digital Literacies, and Play

Best practices in the teaching of ELLs emphasize the importance of interactive approaches for promoting meaningful language learning opportunities (Cazden, 2001; Echevarría et al., 2013; Fisher & Frey, 2013; McIntyre, et al., 2010; Saunders & Goldenberg, 2010; Zwiers & Crawford, 2009). As the degree to which technology is more affordable and accessible for schools in the United States continues to increase, these aims can be supported by the affordances of technology-mediated instruction provided by digital devices (Moran, 2019). An asset-based perspective of digital literacies and play can enable intentional pairing of smartphone-based video games and classroom literature, which requires teachers' knowledge of ELLs' individual skill profile and English language proficiency to target specific language instruction (Echevarría et al., 2013) and literacy instruction (Uribe & Nathenson-Mejía, 2008). Integrating strategies of textual pairing with pedagogical moves involving technologies amplifies instructors' ability to work with ELLs on improving academic outcomes that leverage shared native language and literacy practices.

This chapter draws on a sociocultural view of literacy, emphasizing the socially situated contexts surrounding how adolescents construct meaning within communities that are rapidly evolving and increasingly digitized (Gee, 2010). Digital literacies account for the multiple connections contemporary learners make between cultural experiences and operations with texts inside and outside of school spaces (Lankshear & Knobel, 2008). By integrating digital literacies with curriculum and instruction, teachers position students to engage in literacy practices that are reflective of their unique aptitudes, helping them establish new ways of being readers and writers (Cope & Kalantzis, 2000). Extending the kinds of platforms through which students express their understanding is an asset-based positionality that is inclusive of diverse language and literacy practices that have often been overlooked in mainstream classrooms (Ladson-Billings, 1995).

Recent studies have demonstrated that allowing adolescents to engage in multimodal, digital play can be purposeful and productive in their academic development (Lewis Ellison & Solomon, 2018). Multimodal instruction affords learners multiple modes for engaging with texts, leveraging new meaning-making from content knowledge, and using a combination of literacy practices to accomplish academic tasks. Playful approaches to digital literacies also afford students opportunities to cultivate inclusive classroom communities with greater access to curricula and stronger links between subject matter and real world contexts (Price-Dennis et al., 2015). While the benefits of mixing play with reading and writing have been well-documented, standards-based procedures and high-stakes test preparation often leave little time for playful approaches (Portier, et al., 2019). Exploring the educational implications of a popular platform such as videogames answers the call from Rowsell et al. (2016) for educators to imagine our schools' literacy futures by reconceptualizing how and in what ways students from diverse linguistic backgrounds learn through technology.

Video Games and Esports

Gee (2003) argued that games afford learners pathways to success through adaptability and reflection, including "opportunities for learners to operate at the outer edge of their regime of competence, thereby causing them to rethink their routinized mastery and move, within the game and within themselves, to a new level" (p. 70). In literacy settings, scholars and practitioners have recognized the impact of students' gameplay on their identity and engagement with reading and writing (Gee, 2017). Video games represent a significant component of digital literacies, not only because they reflect properties of active learning, but also because their growing ubiquity offers a conduit for students between their social and school lives (Marlatt, 2020).

As the popularity of video games has increased with adolescents since the turn of the century, so has the number of esports organizations to which students belong in schools (Engerman & Hein, 2017). According to Atalay and Topuz (2018), esports encompasses platforms facilitating both the versions of traditional athletic games such as football and baseball, as well as internet community-based games such as Minecraft, Halo, and most recently, Fortnite. Allowing for a diverse social group of players, observers, and coaches, esports enable the ongoing development of skills and capabilities that mirror 21st Century learning (Canning & Betrus, 2017). When used to support the learning that occurs during the school day, esports clubs have the power to motivate students and enrich their educational experience (Mann, 2017).

Integrating extracurricular contexts of esports clubs with formal classroom curricula is a pedagogical move informed by research that acknowledges adolescents as social meaning-makers who are equal parts intellectually inquisitive and playful beings, as argued by Portier et al. (2019), who call for scholarship and practices "examining ways in which teachers can emphasize academics while maximizing play" (p. 18). Although learner-centered environments incorporating technology often diminish the need for lecture, digitized literacy practices emphasize the instructor's role as a creative designer (Bawden, 2008). Simply injecting video games into classrooms does not make students better readers or writers, and because academic achievement involving engagement, vocabulary transfer, and mastery should never be taken for granted, decisions about play and text sets should address specific classroom contexts (McTigue & Uppstad, 2018). For teachers of ELLs, the incorporation of video games in academic instruction should include intentional content and language planning for conceptualizing subject matter and engaging in language and literacy practices through play. Integration of video games for ELLs is also a culturally-responsive pedagogical move that prioritizes students' sense of belonging to a community (Gay, 2010).

While the ever-expanding technological landscape and digitized lives of contemporary students have required educators to reexamine traditional methods in how they can best support literacy practices, the need is perhaps greater than ever to remain committed to disciplinary pillars such as literary analysis and academic composition, while maintaining a thoughtful, asset-based perspective regarding digital literacies and the multiple texts students encounter and construct (Morrell, 2012). Such a stance is especially important in the service of students who have been historically marginalized due to backgrounds and experiences not represented in standardized curricula (Sleeter, 2005). Literacy teaching in the digital age continues to emphasize helping adolescents read and write about literature and exploring with them the power of texts to impact lives, empower identities, and shape the world (Rybakova et al., 2019).

CONCEPTUAL FRAMEWORK

SIOP-Driven Multimodal Text Sets

The Sheltered Instruction Observation Protocol (SIOP) Model (Echevarria et al., 2013) offers a framework to guide practitioners in their instruction of ELLs toward mastery across the academic domains of reading, writing, listening, and speaking (Kareva & Echevarria, 2013). Combining daily language objectives targeting background knowledge and vocabulary (Ellis et al., 1994) with aspects of effective teaching such as reading comprehension and cooperative learning strategies (August & Shanahan, 2006; Genesee et al., 2006), SIOP has become an essential paradigm for literacy and language programs in school districts across the United States. In their review of SIOP's applications in multiple educational contexts, Kareva and Echevarria (2013) posit, "With high quality instruction that includes linguistic accommodations, students have access to the core curriculum and learn the kind of academic language they need to be successful in school" (p. 239). Drawing from Echevarria et al. (2013), the Appendix features strategies and activities for teachers within SIOP's eight components. Interventions presented in this chapter follow the recommendations of Kareva and Echevarria (2013), who describe SIOP as a flexible tool for language and literacy development, conducive to various teaching styles, and "not a step-by-step process but a guide for effective lesson planning and deliver" (p. 240).

The SIOP approaches described in this chapter adopt the framework for text sets proposed by Lupo et al. (2018), who recommend building background knowledge around a target text with three bridges that offer visual, informational, and accessible connections. Text sets are student-centered collections that can be used as a scaffold toward more complex works of similar themes (Elish-Piper et al., 2014). By allowing students to access content comfortably, text sets offer pathways to standards-based academic achievement that are interdisciplinary and differentiated (Donham, 2013). At the middle level, text sets have been used in conjunction with literacy strategies to teach numerous concepts from ancient civilizations and natural resources to algebraic functions and Shakespeare. Pairing video games with classroom literature via smartphone applications also aligns with the multimodal text set framework posited by Hotch et al. (2018), who suggest teachers attend to motivation and engagement and prioritize student synthesis. Operating within these parameters can maximize the potential for text sets to engage adolescent readers and also illustrate purposeful navigation of learning objectives. Combining standards-based, culturally relevant texts into instructional sets designed to promote academic achievement through literacy practices in and out of school is especially important in serving ELLs, for whom "the cognitive and linguistic demands of learning through a second language are significant" (Kareva & Echevarria, 2013, p. 239).

CONTEXTS AND PREVIEW OF PRACTICES

This chapter features text set instructional strategies involving the pairing of video games with canonical and noncanonical texts aimed at secondary ELA environments. In an after-school esports club at a middle school located in a large city in the Southwest United States, ELLs in grades 6, 7, and 8 recently expressed increased interest and engagement in classroom literary assignments alongside a series of game-based analyses using their smartphones. Based on these interactions and observations, three teacher educators have outlined several text sets and accompanying approaches that secondary literacy teachers can implement in their curriculum, specifically targeted to support ELLs. Featured approaches are geared toward vocabulary enrichment, comprehension, targeted language instruction, intertextual connections, metaphor, symbolism, and more. Following descriptions of lesson designs and recommendations, the chapter will conclude with a summary of affordances and challenges brought upon by teaching and learning with smartphones. Rick is an ELA teacher educator interested in the possibilities of leveraging the sociocultural literacy practices afforded by contemporary meaning-making toward increased interest and success in school. Magdalena is a bilingual education and Teaching English as a Second Language (TESOL) teacher educator interested in connections between language, literacy, and culture. Miles is a teacher educator, middle school ELA teacher, and esports coach interested in gaming culture and its impact on classroom literacies.

In addition to his role as an 8th grade ELA instructor, Miles serves as the founder and sponsor of his school's esports club, the first of its kind in the state. Motivated by the goal of offering students place and space to engage in video game play, Miles opens his classroom after school each day to a diverse group of adolescents all interested in smartphone and console gaming opportunities. Initially brainstormed by Miles as a spinoff of the school's "Battle of the Books" competition, the organization's popularity has soared, and in only two years, its members in grades 6, 7, and 8 have participated in numerous teams and events with other clubs around the world, inspiring many local and regional schools to adopt esports. Most notably, the team made international news by hosting the first international *Super Smash Bros. Ultimate* tournament played and streamed live worldwide (Waldman, 2020). Like many esports coaches, Miles engages students not as a distraction from academics, but as a way of promoting academic success through literacy operations including reading, planning, digital writing, and video casting, in addition to 21st Century skills such as team-building and collaboration (Figure 1). The team is student-led; members write scripts, organize competitions, analyze footage, compose press releases, manage their Youtube channel, and provide play-by-play commentary on game casts, In recent collaborations in Miles' school (Harvey et al., 2020), the present authors noted that the esports team is comprised of a large number of ELLs, which mirrors the school's overall demographics. Many ELLs expressed heightened interest in classroom literature when presented with opportunities to infuse their gameplay with discussions surrounding characters, stories, and authors they had encountered in texts. Based on these observations, the authors drew from their background and expertise as literacy practitioner scholars to practicing pairing literature from students' ELA courses with their smartphone games such as *Clash Royale* and *Clash of Clans*. This work resulted in a series of instructional recommendations for teachers that showcase the interdisciplinary, multimodal possibilities of leveraging ELLs' interest in video games toward engagement with academic domains.

VIDEO GAME AND LITERATURE TEXT SETS

The following propositions for instructional pairings of video games with classroom literature are comprised of strategies designed to support the reading, writing, listening, and speaking of ELLs (Echevarria et al., 2013) and suggested according to the procedures recommended by Lupo et al. (2018). The implementations are organized into two sections. The first section outlines three lessons integrating the video game, *Minecraft* with young adult (YA) novels, *Brown Girl Dreaming* (Woodson,

Figure 1. Esports players compete against another team and stream their competition on Twitch.

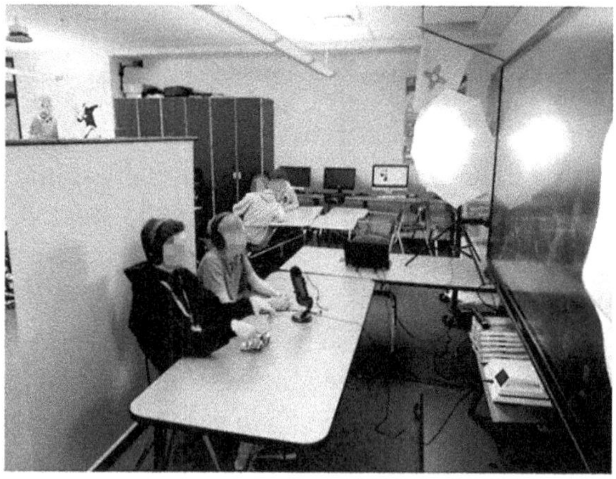

2014), *Cajas de Cartón* (Jiménez, 1997), and *The Outsiders* (Hinton, 1967). The second section offers a unit overview fusing the game, *Life is Strange* with the YA novel, *The Perks of Being a Wallflower* (Chbosky, 1999). Both sections begin with a scholarly overview of the featured game, including recent literature supporting its implementation in literacy settings, before moving into full descriptions of its role in supporting study around secondary level classroom texts.

Section One: *Minecraft* and YA Literature in ELA

Minecraft: Mining, Crafting, and Learning

Minecraft (Persson, 2011) (Figure 2) is a 3D generative environment in which players engage in constant construction of sequences and scenes using a variety of sculpting, digging, and crafting methods that help them cultivate life-worlds and collaborate with others to survive numerous perils (Gallagher, 2014). Though similar to other strategy games in its affordance of open-ended learning opportunities, Minecraft is comprised of numerous intricate capabilities that enable users to complete more complex tasks (Kenkel, 2015). A choice of gaming modes including Creative, Survival, and Hardcore options allow single or multiple players to create objectives, obtain necessary materials, establish sustainable communities, orchestrate defense systems, and more (Pike & Stuppy, 2015). Players can pursue interdisciplinary school-based activities by creating scale models, facilitating virtual tours, and constructing graphical representation of concepts, facts, and figures. Minecraft's classroom applications continue to expand throughout various content areas (Risberg,

2015). Model construction engages learners in scientific reasoning through which they are afforded space to explain their designs orally and in writing (Pando, 2019). Lorch and Mills (2016) argue that the game's complex visual structures are ideal for learning about DNA in chemistry units. The built-in ecology of the game and its aspects of physics can be used to enhance general scientific literacy (Short, 2012), and its navigation of geometric shapes can be useful in helping elementary learners understand mathematical concepts (Bos et al., 2014). Minecraft has also been integrated with art curricula to supplement instruction on visual aesthetics and imagery (Overby & Jones, 2015).

Figure 2. Minecraft is widely available on numerous devices including students' smartphones.

While Minecraft affords content area instructors numerous opportunities for specific standards-based curriculum and instruction, scholars have also alluded to the holistic approach many are taking with the game. A number of clinical trials have exhibited Minecraft's capacity for developing adolescents' sense of mindfulness (Butler et al., 2016) and shown implications for helping autistic learners practice socially connected behavior (Rutkin, 2016). The game's widespread applicability has spurred many schools across the United States to consider it a staple of its digital learning repertoire (Tromba, 2013). Regardless of its precise injection into academic operations, Lewis Ellison and Evans (2016) outline guiding principles for making Minecraft implementation an effective experience for all stakeholders: 1) ensuring that resources are situated as to induce the greatest benefit, 2) directing gameplay to target Common Core State Standards, and 3) emphasizing both large and small scale applications.

Marklund and Taylor (2016) mark two major obstacles teachers face when implementing Minecraft: "ensuring that game-based exercises remained focused on the taught subject matters, and the challenges of establishing and maintaining a sound technological infrastructure in which gaming sessions could be reliably conducted" (p. 132). Despite the game's contributions to personalizing learning by aligning students' sociocultural literacies with their standards-based academic expectations, Minecraft implementation is not without challenges. Instructors must maintain emphases on course content while facilitating an equitable learning experience through intentional steps in curricular design. These challenges are prominent in ELA where instruction is centered around central texts and interactions with texts are multimodal and multilingual.

Minecraft's role in literacy settings has increased dramatically in recent years, prompting ELA teachers to leverage gameplay toward enhanced literature study whereby students can re-enact scenes and develop plot narratives, assume character identities and interactions, articulate thematic elements through avatar embodiment, and produce multimodal compositions by manipulating texts and images (Saez-Lopez et al., 2015). Practitioners and scholars have successfully paired Minecraft with digital storytelling exercises (Lewis Ellison, 2017), positioned its adaptive imagery to inspire creative writing exercises (Trekles, 2012), engaged previously reluctant readers in literary analysis (Marlatt, 2018a), and helped adolescents describe their literacy identities (Marlatt, 2018b). As a platform, Minecraft is a culturally-responsive text that generates high levels of academic engagement by reflecting youths' contemporary meaning-making practices (Gay, 2010; Rezaiyan et al., 2007). The game's collaborative, task-driven layout aligns with the multilingual contexts of ELLs and ELA settings where language acquisition and diverse literacy practices are at play (Swier, 2014). Coupled with literature, Minecraft's blend of strategized action and spontaneous narrative can help illuminate reading and writing processes (Wernholm & Vigmo, 2015). In support of ELLs striving to utilize academic vocabulary, master literary concepts of characterization and conflict, and compose analytical responses to texts, Minecraft's adaptive, interactive learning principles help instructors actionize constructivist theory in conjunction with literature study (Schifter et al., 2013).

Pairing Minecraft With YA Literature: Three Instructional Approaches

The following instructional approaches position Minecraft as a central component of SIOP-driven (Echevarria et al., 2013), multimodal texts sets (Hotch et al., 2018; Lupo et al., 2018) through which ELLs can engage in literature study to demonstrate growth in the academic domains of reading, writing, listening, and speaking. Following a brief introduction in which each approach is summarized, a detailed SIOP-based lesson plan adapted from Echevarria et al. (2013) is provided. The authors have developed these lesson plan collectively through a combination of esports activities and ELAL literature study. Instructors are invited to utilize or modify these lessons as needed according to their classroom contexts.

Lesson One: Reading Comprehension

Minecraft offers teachers engaging alternatives to commonly-used instruments for gauging students' reading comprehension. Using Creative Mode, players have the autonomy to construct digital worlds from their own creative imaginations, an ideal platform to illustrate what they have read. In lieu of a vocabulary quiz to assess mastery of key terms or chapter tests for plot summaries, students can engage in scene recreation (Table 1). Given the opportunity to construct images and sequences while utilizing academic vocabulary on their own terms can position ELLs for success in comprehending texts and accounting for their understanding. Language and literacy accommodations are especially important in the contexts of multilingual texts that feature complex terminology for adolescent readers, such as *Cajas de Cartón* (Jiménez, 1997).

Lesson Two: Responding to Literature

Students are often asked to respond to literary elements such as theme, symbolism, characterization, and motifs by composing their own written responses. While expository writing can help ELLs articulate their engagement with literature, Creative Mode in Minecraft also positions adolescents for powerful responses to literature, especially in conjunction with stories told through remarkable imagery, such as *Brown Girl Dreaming* (Woodson, 2014). Table 2 transposes a paper and pencil prompt to the digital world of mining and crafting.

Lesson Three: Literary Analysis

Minecraft's Survival Mode thrusts players into conflict with a slew of nasty antagonists, including Creepers, Zombies, and Endermen. Navigating various social groups while constructing one's own identity is a common experience for adolescents, and one they can understand in the voice of Pony Curtis, the narrator of Hinton's (*The Outsiders*,

Table 1. Lesson plan for reading comprehension using Minecraft and Cajas de Cartón

SIOP Lesson Plan for Reading Comprehension
Lesson Title: Chapter Review **Content Standard(s):** CCSS.ELA-LITERACY.RL.8.10 By the end of the year, read and comprehend literature, including stories, dramas, and poems, at the high end of grades 6-8 text complexity band independently and proficiently.
Key Vocabulary: Summarize, Explain, Imagery, Synthesize, Articulate **Visuals, Resources, Supplemental Materials:** Minecraft on smartphone or classroom tablet and book
Connection to Prior Knowledge/Building Background: Students will utilize a mix of self-selected and teacher-selected vocabulary to help them facilitated their gameplay. They will focus on memorable scenes from the chapter and explain its sequences through showing and telling.
Content Objective(s): Students will demonstrate reading comprehension through scene recreation. **Meaningful Activities for Content:** Recreate five important scenes from the chapter using your vocabulary terms to help you construct what you remember reading. You will recreate scenes of your choice, including characters, settings, imagery, action, and more, as a way to demonstrate your understanding and to collectively summarize the story, especially your favorite moments. **Review/Assessment:** Ask students to clarify aspects of their scenes and invite them to share their knowledge of the story as it is exhibited in the scene recreation.
Language Objective(s): Students will recall their reading and summarize using vocabulary terms. **Meaningful Activities for Language:** Narrative your scene using appropriate vocabulary, explaining specific sequences of action, identifying characters and their traits and roles, and summarizing the story. **Review/Assessment:** Ask students to distinguish between story sequences, list important moments in the chapter and main ideas, and demonstrate their understanding of the text through dialogue.

(Jiménez, 1997)

1967) novel. This typical classroom text can be made more culturally relevant for ELLs, who can augment and extend the novel's tribal skirmishes between Socs and Greasers to the digital playground and beyond (Table 3).

Section Two: Unit Overview Pairing *Life Is Strange* With a YA Novel in ELA

Expanding Real Possibilities of Narrative in Digital Worlds

Smartphone games that are driven by narrative position players to engage in textual operations that mirror academic tasks. Teachers who wish to search for narrative-based smartphone games can locate them in their preferred online application market or website of their choice. The authors recommend identifying pairing possibilities by considering thematic connections between games and texts or linking titles based on similarities in content, topics, or storylines. Knowledge and skills outlined in academic standards can also serve as a starting point from which video games and literature can help students extend their understanding. Prioritizing the voices and experiences of adolescents helps guide instructors on making culturally relevant text set selections that are authentic and purposeful to the unit of study.

Table 2. Lesson plan for literary response using Minecraft and Brown Girl Dreaming

SIOP Lesson Plan for Responding to Literature
Lesson Title: Responding to Literature **Content Standard(s):** CCSS.ELA-LITERACY.RL.8.2 Determine a theme or central idea of a text and analyze its development over the course of the text, including its relationship to the characters, setting, and plot; provide an objective summary of the text.
Key Vocabulary: Elements of fiction, narrator, character, theme, symbol, plot, motif, foreshadowing **Visuals, Resources, Supplemental Materials:** Minecraft on smartphone or classroom tablet and book
Connection to Prior Knowledge/Building Background: Students will match their understanding of academic vocabulary with their own selections from the story. They will embody an element of fiction from the story by constructing scenes and engaging in sequences with a character of their choice.
Content Objective(s): Students will effectively and critically respond to literature. **Meaningful Activities for Content:** Select a character from the novel and pair it with a theme, symbol, or motif to demonstrate how your character embodies those elements through your gameplay. **Review/Assessment:** Ask students to narrate what is going on in their gameplay, specific to the actions and choices the character is making and how those operations represent the element of fiction.
Language Objective(s): Students will evaluate literary elements by embodying character identities. **Meaningful Activities for Language:** Justify the moves your character is making, discuss their interactions with other characters, evaluate their impact on the story and embodiment of themes. **Review/Assessment:** Ask students to clarify the identities of their characters, ask questions about their motivations and role-playing experience, have them infer larger implications beyond the text.

(Woodson, 2014)

Table 3. Lesson plan for literary analysis using Minecraft and The Outsiders

SIOP Lesson Plan for Literary Analysis
Lesson Title: Literary Analysis **Content Standard(s):** CCSS.ELA-LITERACY.RL.8.3 Analyze how particular lines of dialogue or incidents in a story or drama propel the action, reveal aspects of a character, or provoke a decision.
Key Vocabulary: Social groups, mobs, relationships, drama, conflict, plot, dialogue, incidents **Visuals, Resources, Supplemental Materials:** Minecraft on smartphone or classroom tablet and book
Connection to Prior Knowledge/Building Background: Students will translate their reactions to the text to analysis framed by their own experiences of navigating social groups as adolescents.
Content Objective(s): Students will engage in analytical interpretations of classroom literature. **Meaningful Activities for Content:** Select a social group from the novel and represent that group using a Minecraft mob. Students will each select a mob to represent a group from the novel and interact with other groups through gameplay in order to demonstrate real world implications of the central ideas. **Review/Assessment:** Invite students to scan their sequences and recall incidents from the text that prompted their interpretations, have them compare outcomes from the text to their own lives.
Language Objective(s): Students analyze the text through narrated gaming and academic dialogue. **Meaningful Activities for Language:** Articulate the relationships and interactions occurring between and among social groups by discussion the implications of identies, motivations, perceptions, and more. **Review/Assessment:** Ask students to locate specific information in the text that informs their interpretations and have them use ELA terminology to imply predictions for future readings.

(Hinton, 1967)

Although 95% of teenage students can access their smartphones during class daily (Anderson & Jiang, 2018), a number of strategies are available for students and teachers to use video games to experience literature. One strategy is to employ what the authors label as *Whole Group Gaming*, where one device is shared between the whole class. A smartphone can be used for the entire class, and one student or teacher can play while the others watch through projection. Another strategy that the authors label as *Small Group Gaming* uses one device for three to five students. This works well for literature circles or when there are a limited number of devices for students. For example, if there are four smartphones and twenty students, four groups of five could use a smartphone. In what the authors label as *Individual Gaming*, each student uses their own smartphone. Each method has its pros and cons, but they also serve their own purposes. *Individual Gaming* can take place autonomously and it allows for students to be in their own environment while sharing the same experience. Classroom common-devices such as iPads or tablets can help alleviate device discrepancies as well. Table 4 illustrates several recommendations for pairing smartphone games with literature in ELA. The authors caution instructors to consider prescriptions for their students cautiously; teachers are encouraged to approach curricular decisions critically and thoughtfully based on the contexts of their students.

Table 4. Narrative-driven smartphone games paired with classroom literature

Smartphone Game	Classroom Text
Sender Unknown: The Woods (DMP, 2017)	*Sherlock Holmes* (West, 2000)
Life is Strange (Dontnod, 2015)	*The Perks of Being a Wallflower* (Chbosky, 1999).
Come Home (Fulbright, 2013)	*Diary of Anne Frank* (Frank, 1947)
The Trace (Relentless, 2015)	*The Most Dangerous Game* (Connell, 1924)
Far from Noise (Batchelor, 2017)	*A Day Goes By* (Cengage, 2017)
80 Days (Inkle, 2014)	*Around the World in 80 Days* (Verne, 2014)
Old Man's Journey (Broken Rules, 2017)	*The Giver* (Lowry, 1993)

Pairing Life Is Strange With The Perks of Being a Wallflower

Pairing narrative-heavy smartphone games with classroom novels provides students with multimodal literacy experiences that are generative and interdisciplinary. One example can be found from pairing the game, *Life Is Strange* (Dontnod, 2015) (Figure 3), with the YA novel, *The Perks of Being a Wallflower* (Chbosky, 1999). These two texts can be taught together over the course of twenty-five school days as a unit of study. The game and the novel share coming-of-age themes and identify constructive content suitable for secondary students as readers/viewers follow teenage narrators who attempt to make sense of the world around them. Both texts use vignette scenarios and short stories to tell a bigger picture. The novel's main character guides readers through his journeys in and out of school via a series of letters in which he shares his battles with depression, struggles with making friends, and successes in finding himself. Similarly, the game's main character is faced navigating a number of trying issues, many of which contemporary adolescents face, including bullying, substance abuse, and understanding one's personal talents and finding purpose.

Figure 3. Menu screen for Life is Strange

Whereas the strategies presented in Section One largely targeted learners at the middle level, the following unit overview pairing *Life is Strange* with *The Perks of Being a Wallflower* is suggested for seniors in high school. The content in these texts necessitates a higher degree of maturity for audiences to navigate in comparison to *Minecraft* and its counterparts, and the range of secondary grade levels invoked is meant to provide instructors with a versatile gamut of instructional approaches. Instructors are encouraged to modify the following unit suggestions as they see fit and to adapt the speaking, listening, reading, writing, and gaming practices to meet the needs of their students. *Life is Strange* takes the average player approximately 13 hours to complete (Time to Beat, 2020) while *The Perks of Being a Wallflower* can generally be read in four hours (Reading Length, 2020). Based on these data, this unit accommodates 25 students for five weeks, meeting five days per week for one hour, and due to the texts' narrative complexities, recommendations are made based on students working in groups.

Smartphones in each group should have *Life Is Strange* installed, and students should each have their own copy of *The Perks of Being a Wallflower*. Each group's station should contain a printed list of assignments for the week, and they should also be uploaded to a centralized, smartphone-accessible location such as Canvas or

Google Classroom so assignments can transition between school and home. Activities should be centered around the exploration and juxtapositions made between the two texts. While the game takes considerably longer to complete than the novel, the unit is designed for concurrent textual study, and instructors have a great deal of freedom in how they can structure the unit. *The Perks of Being a Wallflower* contains 51 personal letters divided into four parts. Part I contains 10 chapters, Part II has 15, Part III includes 12, and Part IV has 14 chapters. Including the epilogue, the book runs just under 260 pages. Students are tasked with reading the novel and playing the game concurrently. Each week, students play for three days and should complete one episode from *Life Is Strange* in that time. During the other two days per week, students should read 25 pages from the book. Instructors are encouraged to add in their own in-class exercises for ELLs involving reading, writing, speaking, and listening activities throughout the unit. Classes can transition between group work and whole-class instruction as needed, and all approaches can be blended with current ELL programs or curricular models already in use.

There are a larger number of locations where instructors can locate strategy guides for smartphone games to aid in student's gameplay. Smartphone games like *Life Is Strange* come with instructions, but players often want more than simple directions on how to play, such as various story modes and extra narrative opportunities. Websites, online and print strategy guides, and supplemental information found in smartphone applications all provide additional resources for students. Game Pressure (2020) offers tips on how to get the most out of the game's literary experiences. Students can also find many YouTube videos that provide walkthrough guides. Table 5 illustrates an overview of the unit plan template.

ADDITIONAL RECOMMENDATIONS

The SIOP-based approaches for gaming-based literature in secondary ELA outlined in this chapter are offered as suggestions and not as prescriptive protocols. Numerous language and literacy strategies designed to engage ELLs can be implemented at any time and in myriad instructional contexts by instructors in a variety of ways that can align with school districts' wide-ranging expectations regarding literacy education. The flexible accessibility of SIOP approaches (Appendix) meshes well with constructivist learning environments because they afford teachers a menu of interventions on small and large scales for individual lesson sequences or full unit measures. Coupled with platforms many adolescents find engaging such as video games, the SIOP Model is versatile, serving as a "guide for effective lesson planning and delivery, a teacher self-reflection tool, and an instrument for observation of lessons by peers, school administrators, or university supervisors" (Kareva & Echevarria, 2013, p. 243).

Table 5. Unit Plan Template for pairing Life is Strange with The Perks of Being a Wallflower

SIOP Unit Plan for Literary Analysis
Unit Title: The Story of Us: Who We Are, Where We've Been, and Where We're Going **Content Standard(s):** CCSS.ELA-LITERACY.RL.11-12.2 Determine two or more themes or central ideas of a text and analyze their development over the course of the text, including how they interact and build on one another to produce a complex account; provide an objective summary of the text. CCSS.ELA-LITERACY.RL.11-12.5 Analyze how an author's choices concerning how to structure specific parts of a text (e.g., the choice of where to begin or end a story, the choice to provide a comedic or tragic resolution) contribute to its overall structure and meaning as well as its aesthetic impact. CCSS.ELA-LITERACY.RL.11-12.7 Analyze multiple interpretations of a story, drama, or poem (e.g., recorded or live production of a play or recorded novel or poetry), evaluating how each version interprets the source text.
Targeted Grade Level: 12th grade **Duration:** 5 weeks **Key Vocabulary:** Social groups, mobs, relationships, drama, conflict, plot, dialogue, incidents **Visuals, Resources, Supplemental Materials:** Student smartphones and/or classroom iPads or tablets, 25 copies of *The Perks of Being a Wallflower*, and school-supported learning management system.
Connection to Prior Knowledge/Building Background: Students will draw upon a range of sociocultural literacy practices to facilitate academic standards in ELA curriculum and instruction through the concurrent experiential study of narrative components within multiple texts.
Content and Language Objective(s): Situate the multiple experiences of coming-of-age in America within the multiple perspectives, genres, and narratives that account for how and why and where we tell our stories. Analyze elements of fiction through multiple texts and synthesize their collective implications for real-life choices and behaviors in society, utilizing academic vocabulary and skills. **Meaningful Activities:** Examine notions of narrative and identity functioning within texts through literary activities including literature circles, Socratic seminars, gaming, and reflective writing. Students can also engage in scene recreation, digitized chapter summaries, and multimodal character narratives.
Timeline: · Instructors begin each week with a face-to-face anticipatory set introducing the week's activities and highlighting academic vocabulary. Lesson should take approximately 20 minutes. · Small groups play *Life is Strange* and complete an episode over three days. · Students read 25 pages of *The Perks of Being a Wallflower* over two days in small groups. · Instructors assign a Canvas or Google Classroom activity for homework or classwork. · Instructors are encouraged to create an end-of-unit activity that brings both stories and students together in an engaging way. For example, students might create their own free YouTube music playlists for each main character in both texts. Students could pick out what songs on fit best with the characters' experiences and perspective of the world. Students could also share their playlists with their peers so they can listen to it as a group or on their own time. Students could write a compare and contrast essay about the similarities and differences between the music selected for each character. The culminating activity should be relevant for students. · Any and all modifications made from this example unit should be made accessible and impactful for ELL students and comply with current school or district protocol for ELL curriculum and instruction.

The authors acknowledge the time commitment necessary for planning and reflection necessitated by a shift from a lecture-driven, print-based ELA pedagogy to a more collaborative, digital environment that prioritizes play. Although the kinds of implementations outlined in this chapter require teachers to rethink and restructure how students engage in academic domains, this work is necessary for responding culturally and linguistically to diverse learners. ELA teachers are encouraged to approach multimodal text selection thoughtfully and to implement video games through a critical lens that considers academic standards and objectives. Before teachers lead their students into the digital worlds of smartphone-accessible games, they should reflect on what they want their students to gain from the experience and consider what connections gaming can offer to texts and literacy practices already functioning within their curriculum and instruction. Having a sense of these essential questions will go a long way towards establishing a consistent and successful gaming experience for learners. Brief surveys of students' familiarity with different games and platforms along with questionnaires inviting students to share their opinions regarding books and authors will inevitably produce a shared-power space where multiple texts and voices can be celebrated. As a final set of recommendations, Table 6 illustrates seven best practices for utilizing smartphone-accessible games in the ELA classroom.

Table 6. Best Practices for using Smartphone Games in ELA

1. It's OK to fail at first.	As with any other resource, practitioners must consider challenges with smartphone usage. Integrating games into teaching may take some time to become an efficient process.
2. Don't forget who is in charge	Define rules, expectations, routines, and procedures with smartphones from the outset, and hold students accountable. Your classroom will thrive within the limits you've constructed.
3. Management and Maintenance	Have students help by ensuring their smartphones are charged and updated with current application installments. Facilitate electrical cords, outlet proximity, and sanitation routines.
4. Immersion Before Mastery	Allow the smartphone game to do its thing. Allow students to play and build fluency at their own pace. Play the games on your own to develop your own competency as well.
5. Engagement Across the Board	Not all students have to be gaming at the same time. Feel free to mix things up. All students can be engaged at all times without having to fall into the dreaded pattern of busy work.
6. Aiming for Equity	Ensure that all students have a chance to game and engage actively in the classroom. Be creative with grouping and responsibilities to account for limited resources if necessary.
7: Shared-Power Stances	Listen to your students' suggestions. Allow their excitement and recommendations to filter into your curriculum and instruction. An environment of shared power is the objective.

CONCLUSION

This chapter featured a collection of instructional approaches pairing smartphone-accessible video games with classroom literature to promote reading and writing engagement for ELLs in the ELA classroom. Inspired by the authors' combined experiences in esports environments and literature study settings comprised of language learners, individual lesson sequences and unit overviews were provided in SIOP templates, including the implementation of several narrative-driven games and canonical and noncanonical texts for exploring academic domains in a culturally-responsive manner. A significant affordance in teaching through the use of smart phones is that teachers increase accessibility of instruction to ELLs to intentionally meet these two learning conditions that will address their content and language learning needs. Not all students have access to other technology devices such as laptops and tablets, however, there is abundant smartphone accessibility for teaching students and ELLs. By coupling smartphone accessibility and a text set framework in teaching, teachers are afforded with opportunities to provide ELLs with text sets through video games, literature texts, and other mobile applications to purposefully design instruction that targets both content and language development, while ensuring the collaboration and participation of ELLs through inclusive practices. ELLs benefit from opportunities to continue developing their language skills while learning content. Additionally, text sets afford ELLs with the scaffolding they require to assist with making content comprehensible, but also in constructing meaning as comprehensible output. Smartphones offer ELLs with sensory, graphic, and interactive supports that emphasize interaction and engagement and native language support when needed. The integration of video games with classroom curricula further motivates ELL collaboration and motivation.

ACKNOWLEDGMENT

The authors wish to acknowledge the Albuquerque Public School Educational Foundation for their generous support of esports facilities, which are utilized by students and helped to facilitate many of the authors' practices outlined in this chapter.

REFERENCES

Abrams, S. S. (2017). Emotionally crafted experiences: Layering literacies in Minecraft. *The Reading Teacher*, *70*(4), 501–506. doi:10.1002/trtr.1515

Anderson, M., & Jiang, J. (2018). *Teens, social media & technology 2018.* Retrieved from https://www.pewinternet.org/2018/05/31/teens-social-media-technology-2018/

Atalay, A., & Topuz, A. C. (2018). What is being played in the world: Mobile eSport Applications. *University Journal of Educational Research, 6*(6), 1243–1251. doi:10.13189/ujer.2018.060615

August, D., & Shanahan, T. (Eds.). (2006). *Developing literacy in second-language learners: A report of the National Literacy Panel on Language-Minority Children and Youth.* Lawrence Erlbaum Associates. doi:10.1080/10862960903340165

Batchelor, G. (2017). *Far from noise.* George Batchelor.

Bawden, D. (2008). Origins and concepts of digital literacy. In C. Lankshear & M. Knobel (Eds.), *Digital literacies: Concepts, policies, and practices* (pp. 17–32). Peter Lang.

Bos, B., Wilder, L., Cook, M., & O'Donnell, R. (2014). iSTEM: Learning mathematics through minecraft. *Teaching Children Mathematics, 21*(1), 56–59. doi:10.5951/teacchilmath.21.1.0056

Broken Rules. (2017). *Old man's journey.* Broken Rules.

Butler, D., Brown, M., & Criosta, G. (2016). Telling the story of mindrising: Minecraft, mindfulness and meaningful learning. *Proceedings from ITS, ICEduTECH, and STE '16: The International Conference on Internet Technologies & Society, Education Technologies, Sustainability, Technology, & Education.*

Canning, S., & Betrus, A. (2017). The culture of deep learning in eSports: An insider's perspective. *Educational Technology, 57*(2), 65–69.

Cengage. (2017). *A study guide for Luigi Pirandello's 'A Day Goes By'.* Cengage.

Chbosky, S. (1999). *The Perks of Being a Wallflower.* Pocket Books.

Cipollone, M., Schifter, C. C., & Moffat, R. A. (2014). Minecraft as a creative tool: A case study. *International Journal of Game-Based Learning, 4*(2), 1–14. doi:10.4018/ijgbl.2014040101

Cisneros, S. (1984). *The house on Mango Street.* Arte Público Press.

Collins, S. (2008). *The Hunger Games.* Scholastic.

Connell, R. (1924). *The most dangerous game.* Collier's.

Cope, B., & Kalantzis, M. (2000). *Multiliteracies: Literacy learning and the design of social futures.* Routledge.

Daily Magic Productions. (2017). *Sender unknown: The woods*. Daily Magic Productions.

Donham, J. (2013). Text sets, deep learning, and the common core. *School Library Monthly, 29*(6), 5–7.

Dontnod Entertainment. (2015). *Life is strange*. Dontnod Entertainment.

Echevarría, J., Short, D., & Vogt, M. E. (2013). *Making content comprehensible for English language learners: The SIOP Model* (4th ed.). Allyn & Bacon.

Elish-Piper, L., Wold, L. S., & Schwingendorf, K. (2014). Scaffolding high school students' reading of complex texts using linked text sets. *Journal of Adolescent & Adult Literacy, 57*(7), 565–574. doi:10.1002/jaal.292

Ellis, R., Tanaka, Y., & Yamazaki, A. (1994). Classroom Interaction, Comprehension and the Acquisition of Word Meanings. *Language Learning, 44*(3), 449–491. doi:10.1111/j.1467-1770.1994.tb01114.x

Engerman, J. A., & Hein, R. (2017). eSports gaming and you. *Educational Technology, 57*(2), 62–64.

Frank, A. (1947). *The diary of Anne Frank*. Contact Publishing.

Fullbright Company. (2013). *Come Home*. Fullbright Company.

Gallagher, C. (2014). *Minecraft in the classroom: Ideas, inspiration, and student projects for teachers*. Peachpit Press.

Game Pressure. (2020). *Life is Strange*. https://guides.gamepressure.com/lifeisstrange/

Gay, G. (2010). *Culturally responsive teaching: Theory, research, and practice*. Teachers College Press.

Gee, J. P. (2003). *What Video Games Have to Teach us About Learning and Literacy*. Palgrave MacMillan. doi:10.1145/950566.950595

Gee, J. P. (2010). A situated-sociocultural approach to literacy and technology. In E. A. Baker (Ed.), The new literacies: Multiple perspectives on research and practice (pp. 165–193). Academic Press.

Gee, J. P. (2017). Affinity spaces and 21st Century learning. *Educational Technology, 57*(2), 27–31.

Genesee, F., Lindholm-Leary, K., Saunders, B., & Christian, D. (2006). *Educating English language learners: A synthesis of research evidence*. Cambridge University Press. doi:10.1017/CBO9780511499913

Harvey, M. M., Deuel, A., & Marlatt, R. (2020). To be or not to be: Modernizing Shakespeare with multimodal learning stations. *Journal of Adolescent & Adult Literacy, 63*(5), 559–568. doi:10.1002/jaal.1023

Hinton, S. E. (1967). *The outsiders*. Viking Press.

Hotch, M. L., McCarty, R., Gurvitz, D., & Sitkoski, I. (2018). Five key principles: Guided inquiry with multimodal text sets. *The Reading Teacher, 72*(6), 701–710. doi:10.1002/trtr.1781

Inkle. (2014). *80 days*. Inkle.

Jiménez, F. (1997). *Cajas de Cartón*. University of New Mexico Press.

Kang, G. Y. (2018). Playing with digital tools with explicit scaffolding. *The Reading Teacher, 71*(6), 735–741. doi:10.1002/trtr.1672

Kareva, V., & Echevarria, J. (2013). Using the SIOP model for effective content teaching with second and foreign language learners. *Journal of Education and Training Studies, 1*(2), 239–248. doi:10.11114/jets.v1i2.173

Kenkel, D. (2015). Minecraft or mindcraft: Co-designing and co-learning in a virtual world. *Adminfo, 28*, 9–11. https://bcpvpa.bc.ca/wp-content/uploads/2015/12/Dec15Adminfo.pdf

Kress, G., & van Leeuwen, T. (2006). *Reading images: The grammar of visual images*. Routledge. doi:10.4324/9780203619728

Ladson-Billings, G. (1995). But that's just good teaching. The case for culturally relevant pedagogy. *Theory into Practice, 34*(3), 159–165. doi:10.1080/00405849509543675

Lankshear, C., & Knobel, K. (2008). Introduction: Digital literacies—concepts, policies, and practices. In C. Lankshear & M. Knobel (Eds.), *Digital literacies: Concepts, policies, and practices* (pp. 1–16). Peter Lang.

Lewis Ellison, T. (2017). Digital participation, agency, and choice: An African American youth's digital storytelling about Minecraft. *Journal of Adolescent & Adult Literacy, 61*(1), 25–35. doi:10.1002/jaal.645

Lewis Ellison, T., & Evans, J. N. (2016). "Minecraft," teachers, parents, and learning: What they need to know and understand. *School Community Journal, 26*(2), 25–43.

Lewis Ellison, T., & Solomon, M. (2018). Digital play as purposeful productive literacies in African American boys. *The Reading Teacher, 71*(4), 495–500. doi:10.1002/trtr.1657

Lorch, M., & Mills, J. (2016). How Minecraft could help teach chemistry's building blocks of Life. *Chemistry in Australia*, (Sep), 20–23.

Lowry, L. (1993). *The giver*. Houghton Mifflin Harcourt.

Lupo, S. M., Strong, J., Lewis, W., Walpole, S., & McKenna, M. C. (2018). Building background knowledge through reading: Rethinking text sets. *Journal of Adolescent & Adult Literacy*, *61*(4), 433–444. doi:10.1002/jaal.701

Mann, M. D. (2017). Increasing student motivation to learn by making computer game technology more engaging: Measurable outcomes that determine success. *Contemporary Issues in Education Research*, *10*(2), 117–120. doi:10.19030/cier.v10i2.9922

Marklund, B., & Taylor, A. (2016). Educational games in practice: The challenges involved in conducting a game-based curriculum. *Electronic Journal of e-Learning*, *14*, 122-135.

Marlatt, R. (2018a). Get in the game: Promoting justice through a digitized literature study. *Multicultural Perspectives*, *20*(4), 222–228. doi:10.1080/15210960.2018.1467769

Marlatt, R. (2018b). Literary analysis using Minecraft: An Asian American youth crafts her literacy identity. *Journal of Adolescent & Adult Literacy*, *62*(1), 55–66. doi:10.1002/jaal.747

Marlatt, R. (2020). Capitalizing on the craze of Fortnite: Toward a conceptual framework for understanding how gamers construct communities of practice. *Journal of Education*, *200*(1), 3–11. doi:10.1177/0022057419864531

McTigue, E. M., & Uppstad, P. H. (2018). Getting serious about serious games: Best practices for computer games in reading classrooms. *The Reading Teacher*, *72*(4), 453–461. doi:10.1002/trtr.1737

Moran, C. M. (2019, March 1). *5 reasons why virtual reality belongs in every classroom*. https://corwin-connect.com/2019/03/5-reasons-why-virtual-reality-belongs-in-every-classroom/

Morrell, E. (2012). 21st-Century literacies, critical media pedagogies, and language arts. *The Reading Teacher*, *66*(4), 300–302. doi:10.1002/TRTR.01125

Overby, A., & Jones, B. L. (2015). Virtual LEGOs: Incorporating Minecraft into the art education curriculum. *Art Education*, *68*(1), 21–27. doi:10.1080/00043125.2015.11519302

Pando, M., & Aguirre-Muñoz, Z. (2019). Engaging English language learners in model-based science instruction. In L. C. de Oliveira, K. M. Obenchain, R. H. Kenney, & A. W. Oliveira (Eds.), *Teaching the content areas to English language learners in secondary schools* (pp. 215–230). Springer. doi:10.1007/978-3-030-02245-7_14

Persson, M. (2011). *Minecraft*. Mojang Studios.

Pike, J., & Stuppy, J. (2015). *Use Minecraft to teach math*. http://www.iste.org/explore

Portier, C., Friedrich, N., & Peterson, S. S. (2019). Play(ful) pedagogical practices for creative collaborative literacy. *The Reading Teacher*, *73*(1), 17–27. doi:10.1002/trtr.1795

Price-Dennis, D., Holmes, K. A., & Smith, E. (2015). Exploring digital literacy practices in an inclusive classroom. *The Reading Teacher*, *69*(2), 195–205. doi:10.1002/trtr.1398

Reading Length. (2020). *The Perks of Being a Wallflower*. https://www.readinglength.com/book/isbn-1451696191

Rezaiyan, A., Mohammadi, E., & Fallah, P. A. (2007). Effect of computer game intervention on the attention capacity of mentally retarded children. *International Journal of Nursing Practice*, *13*(5), 284–288. doi:10.1111/j.1440-172X.2007.00639.x PMID:17883714

Risberg, C. (2015). More than just a video game: Tips for using Minecraft to personal- ize the curriculum and promote creativity, collaboration, and problem solving. Illinois Association for Gifted Children Journal, 44–48.

Rowsell, J., Burke, A., Flewitt, R., Liao, H.-T., Lin, A., Marsh, J., Mills, K., Prinsloo, M., Rowe, D., & Wohlwend, K. (2016). Humanizing digital literacies: A road trip in search of wisdom and insight. Digital Literacy Column. *The Reading Teacher*, *70*(1), 121–129. doi:10.1002/trtr.1501

Rutkin, A. (2016). *How Minecraft is helping children with autism make new friends*. https://www.newscientist.com/article/mg23030713-100-how-is-helping-children-with-autism-make-new-friends/

Rybakova, K., Rice, M., Moran, C., Zucker, L., McGrail, W., Mcdermott, M., Loomis, S., Piotrowski, A., Garcia, M., Gerber, H., Marlatt, R., & Gibbons, T. (2019). A long arc bending towards equity: Tracing almost 20 years of ELA teaching trends in CITE. *Contemporary Issues in Technology & Teacher Education*, *19*(4).

Saez-Lopez, J. M., Miller, T., Vasquez-Cano, E., & Dominquez-Garrido, M. C. (2015). Exploring application, attitudes, and integration of video games: MinecraftEDU in middle school. *Journal of Educational Technology & Society*, *18*(3), 114–128.

Schifter, C., Cipollone, M., & Moffat, F. (2013). *Piaget, Inhelder and Minecraft. Proceedings from*. The International Association for Development of the Information Society.

Short, D. (2012). Teaching scientific concepts using a virtual world—Minecraft. *Teaching Science*, *58*(3), 55–58.

Sleeter, C. E. (2005). *Un-standardizing curriculum: Multicultural teaching in the standards-based classrooms*. Teachers College Press.

Swier, R. (2014). Tasks for easily modifiable virtual environments. *The JALT CALL Journal*, *10*(3), 203–219. doi:10.29140/jaltcall.v10n3.176

Time to Beat. (2020). *Life is Strange*. https://howlongtobeat.com/game?id=21702

Trekles, A. M. (2012). Creative writing, problem-based learning, and game-based learning principles. *Proceedings of the International Society for Technology in Education.* https://pdfs.semanticscholar.org/730f/5b706aeb0ae26b4eb12e348ce0 04733557e2.pdf

Tromba, P. (2013). Building engagement and knowledge one block at a time with Minecraft. *Learning and Leading with Technology*, 20–23.

Uribe, M., & Nathenson-Mejía, S. (2008). *Literacy essentials for English language learners: Successful transitions*. Teacher's College Press.

U.S. Department of Education, National Center for Homeless Education. (2019). *Federal data summary: School years 2016-2017.* Retrieved from https://nche.ed.gov/wp-content/uploads/2019/02/Federal-Data-Summary-SY-16.17-Final published-2.12.19.pdf

Verne, J. (2014). *Around the world in 80 days*. Black & White Classics.

Waldman, B. (2020). Game, set…graduate! Schools diving into gaming as a source of education, not diversion. *Winnipeg Free Press.* https://www.winnipegfreepress.com/arts-and-life/life/sci_tech/front-hed-game-set-graduate-inside-hed-ready-to-learn-just-hit-play-567660792.html

Wernholm, M., & Vigmo, S. (2015). Capturing children's knowledge-making dialogues in Minecraft. *International Journal of Research & Method in Education*, *38*(3), 230–246. doi:10.1080/1743727X.2015.1033392

Wong Fillmore, L. (1992). Learning a language from learners. In C. Kramsch & S. McConnel-Ginnet (Eds.), *Text and context: Cross-disciplinary perspectives on language study* (pp. 44–66). Heath.

Woodson, J. (2014). *Brown girl dreaming*. Penguin Group.

APPENDIX: SIOP COMPONENTS AND STRATEGIES

Table 7.

Component 1 Lesson Preparation	• Add a glossary or word bank • Alternate materials • Differentiated instructions • Enlarge, adapted Text • Graphic organizers • Highlight essential vocabulary in text • Illustrate the text • Outline • Planning flow chart • Scaffolding • Simplified text • Task analysis/backwards planning • Timeline • Word association task
Component 2 Building Background	• Anticipation guide • Backwards book walk • Brainstorming • Carousel brainstorming • Charts of key information • Clustering/webbing/mapping • Concept definition maps • Contextualizing vocabulary • Corners • Exclusive brainstorming • Four corners • Four corners vocabulary • Idea wave • Identifying cognates • Insert method • KWL chart • Lesson connections • List/group/label • Most important word • Mystery word • Novel ideas • Open mind diagram • Opinion survey • Personal dictionaries • Predict-O-Gram • Predictions • Pretest with a partner • Questioning • Read my mind • Realia Photos and Illustrations • Signal Words • Snowballs • Story Impression Student Glossary • Student Journals • Surprise Book • Take Five • Treasure Hunt • Vocabulary Alert • Vocabulary Cards • Vocabulary Games • Vocabulary Self-Selection • Vocabulary Taboo • Word Generation • Word Map • Word Sorts • Word Splash • Word Study Books • Word Walls
Component 3 Comprehensible Input	• Adapted Dictogloss • Adapted Reading • Experience Approach • Bookmarks • Concept Personification • Role-Play • Everyone Gets a Chance • Fishbowl • Flip Books • Framed Outlines • Graphic Organizers ID relationships • Guided Listening • Homographs, Homophones, & Synonyms • Idiom Match-Up • Imaging • Information Gap • Instructions (1-way task) • Interactive Reading Guide • Mnemonic Strategies • Move It • One-Way Information Gap Question Task • Recast • Reformulation • Taped Text • Text Identification • Think Aloud • Two-Way Information Gap Task • Visuals • Vocabulary Cards
Component 4 Strategies	• Acting Out a Problem • Adapted Venn Diagram • Anticipation/Reaction Guide • Canned Questions • Categorize/Classify Chart • Category Sort • Cognates • Cornell Notes ("STARS") • Differentiated Question Prompts • Directed Reading- Thinking Activity (DRTA) • Frayer Model • GIST • Gloss • Group Assessment • Guided Note Taking • In-Text Questions • Interactive Reading Guide • KWL Chart • Note Taking • Pantomime, Role Play • Parking Lot • Plus-Minus Chart • PQRST • Progressive Maps • Question-Answer Relationships†©QAR® • Quick Draw • Quick Write • Reciprocal Teaching • Same-Different • Scanning for Details • Self Evaluation • Skim & Scan • SQP2RS • Stop & Think • Study guide • Summarize • T-Chart • Text Recall/Retell • Text Structure & Graphic Organizers • Think Aloud • Value Line • You're the Teacher
Component 5 Interactions	• Affinity • Card Games • Carousel • Clock Appointments • Clock Buddies • Co-op Co-op • Cocktail Party • Dinner Party • Fan & Pick • Find Your Match • Flash Cards • Four Corners • Frozen Moment • Gallery Walk • Give-one, Get-one • Great Performances • Group Reel • Group Response Board • Idea Wave • Information Gap • Inside-Outside Circle • Investigations • Is it Complete? • Jigsaw • Line-Ups • Lines of Communication • Literature Study Groups • Mine/Not Mine • Numbered Heads Together • Process Writing • Projects • Puppetry • Questionnaires & Interviews • Read-Around Groups • Reader-Writer-Speaker Response Triads • Roam the Room • Role Playing • Round Robin • Roundtable • Roving Reporter • Send a Problem • Snowball • Speedwriting • Stand Up and Share • Startling Statements • Story Summaries • Tableau • Take a Stand • Talking Chips • Talking Stick • Talmudic Pair Work • Think-Pair-Share • Think-Pair-Square • Think-Round Robin • Three Step Interview • Traveling Jigsaw • Writing Headlines • You Are There

continues on following page

Table 7. Continued

Component 6 Practice and Application	• Are You Sleeping? • Bingo • Card Games (student generated) • Circular Check • Concept Sketches • Cooperative Dialogue • Cooperative Graphing • GIST• Group Timeline • In The Loop• Information Gap• Learning Cell • Lines of Communication • Making Bigger Words • Numbered Heads Together • Pantomime-A-Tale • Pass the Picture • Piece O' Pizza • Poetry & Patterns • Posters • Role Play • Round Robin Writing • Send-A-Problem • Simulations • Text Recall • The Frame Up • Virginia Reel • Vocabulary Go-Fish • Zip Around
Component 7 Lesson Delivery	• ABC Summarize • Agreement Circles • Chunk & Chew • Diner Menu • Find Someone Who • Find The Fib • Four Corners (pick a Corner) • Give One, Get One • Headings & Questions • Idea Wave • Magic Buttons • Manipulatives • Procedural Knowledge • Quick Write • Response Cards • Response Frames • Secret Answer • Send a Problem • Stop that Video/DVD • Take A Stand • Thinking Maps • Transfer & Apply • TWPS • What Do You Know? • Whip-Around • Word Banks • Zip Around • Zip Line
Component 8 Review and Assessment	• 3-2-1 • Alternative Assessments • Carousel • Circular Check • Class Vote • Cloze Sentences/Text • Comprehension Check • Concentration • Dictogloss • Exit Slip • Fan & Pick • Find Someone Who • Find the Fib • Fist-to-Five Self-Assessment • Flash Cards • Hand Gestures • Image & Quote Cooperative Poster • Inside Outside Circle • Jumbled Summary • Mix & Match • Muddiest Point • Numbered Heads Together Review • Numbered Wheels • One-Minute Paper • Pair-Check • Performance-Based Assessments • Picture This • Posters • RAFT • Reel • Response Boards • Self-Assessment Rubrics • Share Bear • Sign In, Please • Signal Cards • Simultaneous Round Table • Startling Statements • Think Round Robin • Ticket Out the Door • Twelve Word Summary • Word Generation • Writing Headlines

Adapted from Echevarría et al. (2013).

Chapter 2
Beyond Apps and Activities:
Intentional Integration of Technology in English Language Arts Education

Maya Kristine Woodall
https://orcid.org/0000-0002-2711-8127
Georgia Public Schools, USA

ABSTRACT

This chapter examines the importance of intentionally planning with an instructional framework to leverage the use of technology. The author provides an integration framework to support middle and secondary language arts teachers. The author shares how she has refined the process of using mobile phones in her classroom. Initially, her focus was on trying new mobile applications in her language arts classroom by adding technology to existing lessons or adapting lessons to use with the mobile application. Next, she became more strategic, examining student thinking and actions throughout a daily workshop lesson and developing and applying a resource guide for mobile applications specifically geared for each lesson segment of class: opening, work period, and closing. No longer focused on application fit or application first, the author shares the transformative power of deliberately planning for the use of technology: a practice that has improved her clarity and amplified student learning.

DOI: 10.4018/978-1-7998-5805-8.ch002

INTRODUCTION

As a middle grades English language arts (ELA) teacher, I work tirelessly to tackle many challenges: creating relevant learning experiences, providing timely and effective feedback, collaborating with other teachers, gathering and using data effectively, preparing students for rigorous assessments, developing skills of critical literacy, building and maintaining a positive culture, keeping current on best practices, and tackling myriad other school and district requirements. With all these challenges, the thought of transforming daily digital distraction into effective instructional practice has not always been a priority in many ELA classrooms including mine. Of course, the 2020 global pandemic with forced distance learning has caused me to reexamine the need to leverage literacy and learning through digital learning available on any platform.

Re-examining instructional practice considering the pandemic begins with asking myself what elements of this pandemic pedagogy I need to retain to promote student success in and beyond the walls of my classroom. Being complacent or negative about integrating technology or simply using technology as a quick fill-in or review is clearly no longer enough; this fails to sustain engagement, foster communication, promote deep learning, or build independent learners. In this chapter, I will share my continued evolution with BYOT (Bring Your Own Technology) with cell phones, beginning with choosing mobile applications first and adapting lessons to fit the tool, to becoming a teacher connecting applications to a workshop model, and finally to a teacher applying a strategic instructional framework based on goals, pedagogy, strategy, and purpose to leverage learning. In sharing my evolution from a teacher engaging students through technology to a teacher intentionally planning for technology integration, my goal is to demonstrate how intentionally planned instruction that values pedagogy and practice over phones helps promote student success.

BACKGROUND

In the classrooms at my school, the inception of bring your own device (BYOD) was met with denial, fear, or enthusiasm. Thomas, O'Bannon, and Bolton, 2013 described cellphones as the "Swiss Army handheld multitool with computerlike capabilities" (p. 296). Initially, my primary focus in using mobile phones was using this multitool for engagement and fun. During this time, standing apart as an innovative and engaging teacher could be as simple as pairing students to use a phone to play a Kahoot review game or letting students use a search engine to answer a quick question. A 2013 survey of teacher attitudes towards mobile phones found that teachers saw using phones as positive for engagement and motivation and negative because of access problems and class disruption (Thomas et al, 2013).

During this time of flourishing technology, educational agencies began refining the concept of effective technology integration. AdvancedEd, a school accreditation organization, included the following concepts as important to measuring effective technology integration in schools: relevance, engagement, achievement, teacher empowerment, home and school communication, and accountability (Zucker, 2012). With these new standards in place, my district recognized the importance of empowering teachers to become technology leaders; this led to a lasting partnership with a local large university's iTeach program in a TechEd's initiative. As a part of the inaugural TechEds group, I vacillated between feeling overwhelmed and empowered. The mission of the PCSD TechEds is to promote transformative learning through blended/personalized learning (Barton, et al, 2020). During the 2014-2015 school year, TechEds gave me the opportunity to partner with teachers from all content areas from the middle and high schools throughout the district where we participated in six days of professional development, regular job-embedded coaching, and model technology visits. A portion of my training was designated for phones and BYOD. Through my TechEds experience, I learned how to develop BYOD routines, apply technology integration models, and vet and share mobile applications. In addition, I received personal coaching and was able to share my learning as a model classroom and participate in visiting other model classrooms.

The solid foundation of TechEds piqued my awareness of effective blended learning, but altering my practice has been a continually evolving process as I learn more about content, instruction, and technology. As an innovative and adventurous educator, I have found that my greatest challenge is when I encounter great digital tools as a way to slow down my impulsivity and excitement in trying the bright and shiny long enough to prioritize content and pedagogy to find ways to effectively leverage the tools. Kieschnick (2017) cautions teachers not to try too many tools at once. He advises teachers to begin with one tool and spend time acclimating yourself and students to that explaining that "slow, steady, and strategic wins the race" (p. 39). Educational technology specialist, teacher, and blogger Vicki Davis (2017) offers teachers similar advice with simple wisdom to "innovate like a turtle" (00:42-00:51).

Mishra and Koehler's (2009) Technology Pedagogical and Content Knowledge (TPACK) framework examines the complexities for effectively teaching with technology:

Underlying truly meaningful and deeply skilled teaching with technology, TPACK is different from knowledge of all three concepts individually. Instead, TPACK is the basis of effective teaching with technology, requiring an understanding of the representation of concepts using technologies; pedagogical techniques that use technologies in constructive ways to teach content; knowledge of what makes concepts difficult or easy to learn and how technology can help redress some of the problems that students face; knowledge of students' prior knowledge and theories of epistemology; and knowledge of how technologies can be used to build on existing knowledge to develop new epistemologies or strengthen old ones. (para. 10)

When first exposed to TPACK in TechEds, I applied technological knowledge to content knowledge, but I really did not understand how to combine current pedagogical knowledge to those to amplify learning. Kieschnick's Bold School Framework for Strategic Blended Learning (2017) has helped me become more successful in technology integration by providing an intentional and strategic framework that values learning goals, teaching strategies and technology tools. In addition, Monica Burns' (2018) approach emphasizing focusing on learning tasks before cellphone applications has offered me insight into how purposeful planning helps leverage technology use. Finally, applying TPACK requires continued adaptation as my understanding of language arts and literacy evolves.

When mobile phones or other technologies are part of my instructional routine, I must continue to learn and develop my expertise and understanding of content, pedagogy, and technology. In addition, I must challenge myself to continue to reflect and examine how these elements work together. In doing this, I will continue to develop a repertoire of practice to leverage the use of technology in my classroom.

MOBILE APPLICATIONS AS ADD INS

Enticed by educational technology and ELA blogs, "there's an app for that" was a call I could not refuse. While TechEds offered me a solid foundation, my excitement and impulsivity outweighed my technology pedagogy. Excited to engage students and try out innovative technology tools, I exposed students to several new mobile applications each month. In my excitement, I put the tool before the teaching and did not consider the impact this could have on student learning.

Throughout the year I learned about a variety of tools and techniques for integrating technology into ELA instruction. Inspired by the thought of engaging students with these tools, I would find ways to fit these applications into my instruction. I spent hours determining ways to engage students and use technology.

Tech savvy sixth-grade students were thrilled to try each new idea, often "app smashing," the process of using multiple applications to complete a task. Students who were less comfortable with technology, however, would expend their mental energy and class time mastering technology; as a result, these students would often change to a no-tech option after spending half the class time trying to figure out how to work the application. In the end, the quality of their work did not demonstrate their ability.

When I recognized the problem, I helped them work to become more assessment-capable and asked them to monitor their technology learning curve and make sure they spent more time showing their learning of content and less time learning how to use the application. In addition, I began differentiating to offer no-tech options for learning tasks. Still, even after the warning, my students would begin a task, determined to try and master a new application; however, oftentimes they would lose track of time and end up frustrated and unfocused.

As I evolved, I would differentiate ahead of time offering my students options: high-tech, some tech, or no-tech. Still, though, my instructional mindset was application first and instruction second.

My nuts-and-bolts focused administrator challenged me to shift my mindset by telling me that I chose the technology first and then plugged in content. At the time, his words upset me because I believed my instruction was innovative and engaging. Looking back, I realize he was right and that my integration lacked intentionality—my approach needed to shift.

MOBILE APPLICATIONS APPLIED TO DAILY LESSONS

Following my year in TechEds, I was invited to help with district curriculum planning and given the task of helping teachers integrate technology in ELA. thinking and planning for this task helped me develop a way of applying what I had learned in the TechEds program as I developed clarity and consistency for using mobile phones applications in class with a focus on examining looking at the instructional purposes each application could serve during lessons. To support language arts teachers, I connected workshop model instruction to applicable tools (as seen in Table 1) in a way that served me as well as others because this intentional application of tasks to tools helped me become more intentional in curriculum planning while also providing support to other teachers. Applying technology tools to my current instructional practice helped me develop protocols. In addition, using applications regularly ensured that my students' mental energy was focused more on content than on the tool.

While this framework helped me develop clarity and consistency, it did not aid in developing competencies that students need for their future. While my two Cs of clarity and consistency fulfilled my needs, they fell short of providing my students' needs. My two Cs were not among the Four Cs that the National Education Association (2012) outlines as important 21st century skills: creativity, collaboration, critical

Table 1. Applying Digital Tools to a Workshop Lesson

Tool With Description and Link(s)	Description	Workshop Applications
Answer Garden https://answergarden.ch/	An easy-to-use feedback tool Plant a question and invite participants to your AnswerGarden. Their answers will instantly form a growing word cloud.	Opening: engage students, brainstorming, pre-assess understanding, Ticket in the Door Workshop: collaboration, critical thinking Closing: get feedback, poll students, gauge understanding
Padlet https://padlet.com/	Padlet is an online interactive bulletin board (think Pinterest here) that you can use in a variety of ways.	Opening: Use Padlet to answer a single question or generate ideas. Workshop: Students can use Padlet to collaborate and present ideas. In Freeform view Padlet can be used with an interactive board to group like concepts. Students can also draft on their phones and post their writing on Padlet. Closing: Use Padlet to answer Essential Question. Use Padlet with differentiation with tiered questions.
Poll Everywhere www.polleverywhere.com	Poll Everywhere offers quick, animated videos on a variety of topics. Great tool for differentiation because videos simplify concepts to nuts and bolts.	Opening, Workshop, Closing: Any time you want to quickly get feedback on a question, Poll Everywhere is a great tool. You may ask open-ended questions or multiple-choice questions.
QR Code Scavenger Hunt https://www.classtools.net/QR/_	QR Code Scavenger Hunt lets you or your students create scavenger hunt quizzes using QR code questions while also allowing for movement. Note: no Wi-Fi connection needed with these QR codes.	Opening, Workshop, Closing: Use this at any point during the lesson to get formative data and to allow students to move and learn.

thinking, and communication. To truly integrate technology effectively, those four Cs needed to become a part of my repertoire of practice for integrating technology.

BUILDING REPERTOIRES OF PRACTICE

Integrating technology is a complex endeavor, requiring an understanding of content, pedagogy, and technology. While TPACK offers an integration framework; the nuances of integration are complex and evolving. This section provides frameworks with examples of how my practices continue to evolve. While I do not adhere rigidly to one model, I continue to develop ways to strategically integrate technology in a manner that values content, pedagogy, technology, twenty-first century skills, and teacher evaluation measures. As a ELA educator, I strive to teach in a way that draws from my evolving repertoires of practice. My goal is to share the tools I use based on research and practice in terms of content, pedagogy, and technology that informs my planning and practice in using digital tools and mobile phones to impact student learning today while also preparing them for their future success.

To reflect on my ongoing building of repertoires of practice, I will reflect on how I continue to evolve and build my repertoires of practice drawing from my own experiences and reflection. I will reflect on my collaboration with Moran using mobile phones and virtual reality (VR) to enrich ELA students' literary experiences (Moran and Woodall, 2019).

My students enjoyed diving in the setting of our novel using virtual reality. Students were better able to grasp the setting of the rural south during the 1960s. The beauty of enhancing the learning experience for students equaled the playing field and pairing students allowed all students access. No student was left behind due to a lack of prior knowledge of a time or space. All students could come together to experience the necessary backdrop for our novel. As I had predicted, there were a few hiccups in learning how to navigate through the VR, but my students soon picked up the needed skills to successfully navigate through the task. To gauge how students perceived the task, Moran I allowed and welcomed feedback on the task using anonymity to protect all responses. A vast majority of my students found value in the experience overall. The student interest and buy-in for the writing that followed the VR experience was evident.

Prioritize Learning Over Apps

The International Literacy Association (2018) maintains that "digital tools are secondary to the teacher's literacy and learning goals" (p. 2). When I reflect on the collaborative planning process for my work with Kennesaw State University English teacher educator Clarice Moran using virtual reality experience with the goal of determining if virtual reality (VR) could enhance the literary experience of secondary language arts students, I realize that our joint planning process effectively integrated technology in part because we prioritized my students' learning (Moran and Woodall, 2019). Had she approached me in my "Apps First" days, I would have asked her how she wanted to use VR and simply added in virtual reality with no concern to making connections to my upcoming unit. Moran was enthusiastic about incorporating virtual reality into my upcoming unit, and as we worked together, we prioritized student learning by using virtual reality to enhance my students' learning experience with narrative writing.

To continue to refine the work with narrative writing and virtual reality, I applied my work with Moran (2019) to Marilyn Burns' *Tasks before Apps* (2018) approach to improve clarity with plans that include what students should understand (learning goal), how I will know they understand (expectations), and what I would like to see students accomplish (student experience). Burns explains how this gives students a why and helps teachers keep priorities at the forefront of instruction. Here is my application of a VR lesson with her model:

- **Learning goal:** I can collaborate to create sensory notes that show the importance of both physical and geographical setting to use a launchpad for rewriting a key scene from *To Kill a Mockingbird.*
- **Partner Expectations:** One student views Google Expedition and narrates the experience by describing setting. Other student asks questions for sensory details and elaboration and writes down what partner says. Partners switch roles and repeat.
- **Learning Experiences:** I would like for students to work together to take descriptive and sensory notes depicting various physical and geographical settings that they can use as a launchpad to rewrite a key scene from *To Kill a Mockingbird.*

By shifting my instructional mindset to prioritizing the learning experience over the VR experience, students moved back and forth from the VR setting to their narrative scene with greater purpose and attention to detail. In fact, several students took it to a next level asking if they could research the Google Expeditions settings and find out more about their new setting to make sure their writing was reflective of this new setting.

Plan for Technology

While Burns' approach helped me improve previous lessons, Weston Kieschnick's (2017) Bold School Framework for Strategic Blended Learning has helped me consider how to plan for leveraging technology using high-impact strategies. His idea is to take tried and true strategies and apply those to digital tools. Of course, to leverage those strategies, effective planning is important. Kieschnick (2017) begins with goals that he aligns to high impact strategies. Then, he chooses digital tools, plans blended instruction, and self-assesses his plan with a framework.

In his (2019) webinar, Kieschnick applies his blended approach to content literacy where he leverages and amplifies the effectiveness of Reciprocal Teaching (see table 2). In this demonstration lesson, Kieschnick shows how to help students move in and out of technology through his bold and engaging poetry lesson. According to the International Literacy Association's (2018) *Improving Digital Practices for Literacy, Learning, and Justice* leadership brief, digital practices should help students develop fluidity:

The point to grasp is that digital and non-digital context for learning are not discrete... Our classrooms must move fluidly between the digital and analog worlds that we simultaneously inhabit...allowing us to move away from rote instructional practices that are anchored in individual apps and devices toward considering how today's professionals seamlessly produce, respond to, and coordinate work and personal activities across myriad devices, tools, and topics. (p. 3)

Kieschnick's (2017) blended approach helped me leverage high-impact strategies and helped students develop fluidity navigating between digital and non-digital texts, With his approach, the context is grounded in classroom teaching and learning. In the future, I would like to find ways to enable and empower students to become more self-directed, agentive and authentic while navigating between digital and non-digital contexts.

Test Your Integration

As illustrated in the previous section, Kieschnick (2017) applies Bill Daggett's Rigor and Relevance framework to self-assess his use of technology. Several models and frameworks exist to help teachers assess their level of integration. In addition to the previously mentioned TPACK model, TechEds exposed me to other models. One model that helps me assess how students are using technology is the SAMR ladder that moves from a basic level of substituting (S) a print assignment for a digital one to the complexity of creation or redefinition (R). Alex Oris (2020) offers digital tools to help teachers climb the SAMR ladder but cautions teachers, reminding them that the complexity does not reside within the tool itself but with what the student does with the tool.

When reflecting on the 2020 global pandemic, I recognized the inherent value in Burns' model of testing integration because her ACES framework demonstrates the practical skills needed to fully function in an asynchronous learning environment: access, curation, engagement, and sharing (p. 14). Burns keeps the ACES framework at her side when planning units to ensure she varies her tasks and provides students with important skills that can be applied using different applications (p. 14). I have provided examples and applications for using the ACES framework (Table 3) to create deeper learning experiences that make students more adept with technology.

Table 2. Weston Kieschnick's Bold School Framework for Strategic Blended Learning

Step	Key Questions	ELA Application
Identify desired academic outcome	What are the desired skills and priority standards?	Skills: Make inferences, analyze theme, closely read text Cite text evidence to support inference and analysis of text
Align goal aligned and effective strategy	What high-impact strategy will I use? What will students be doing? What will I be doing?	Reciprocal Teaching Predict, clarify, question, summarize
Choose digital tool	What digital tool can I use to elevate the strategy? How will the tools make me more efficient/effective? How will the tools increase student learning? Will these tools build on my skills or create barriers for my students or me?	Predict: Question/poll on www.menti.com Preview text/clarify unknown words: Use Google image search Summarize: What text says directly, inferences drawn from text, themes in text: Flipgrid Video
Plan blended instruction	How will I plan this lesson with rigor and relevance in mind?	Predict: Show image and have students answer a Menti poll using their phones. Preview/Clarify: Students scan poem and find words that they do not know. Students use a Google image search to find a visual for group-assigned term. Then, students share visuals and produce a 4-word definition. Read/Question: Students read texts and ask and answer questions. Deeper Analysis/Summary: 1-minute Flipgrid—each student makes a video of what the text says, inferences drawn, and applicable themes. Share videos as a class and evaluate best themes.
Self-assess plan/ progress with a framework	Are the learning tasks rigorous? Are the learning tasks relevant, so student will be able to apply learning beyond class?	Rigor: Students are engaged in deeper thinking and analysis. Relevance: Students are engaged in four habits of good readers.

Note: Used with permission from the author

CONCLUSION

My evolution as a language arts teacher has taught me the importance of effective technology integration, showing me technology is most effective when pedagogy, content, purpose, and strategy are prioritized (e.g., Burns, 2018; Kieschnick, 2017; Koehler & Mishra, 2019). Applying the lessons that tasks precede applications (Burns) and that technology can be a way of leveraging effective strategies (Kieschnick) has helped me to prioritize student learning over technology. Both Burns and Kieschnick have offered me valuable guidance for using technology with a focus on learning tasks, effective teaching, and effective integration.

Table 3. Monica Burns' ACES Framework

ACES Framework	Description	Examples/Applications
Access	Students locate online content to find information and connect with others.	WebQuest, Research, Discussion Boards
Curate	Students interact with digital resources related to content, interest, and need.	Diigo, Padlet, ScoopIt!, Flipboard, Symbaloo
Engage	Students build transferable skills using technology enabling them to create and collaborate.	Office 365, Google Suite, Padlet, Zoom Break Out Rooms, Flipgrid, Thinglink
Share	Students have an authentic audience, set a purpose for work, and connect to a wider audience.	Blogs, Podcasts, online pen pals, global reading or writing projects

Note: Used with permission from the author

As I reflect on my current practices teaching with technology, I realize that tasks and frameworks are limited in their value. While processes and frameworks have instructional value, I must use this knowledge to move forward not with applications or integration at the center but with students at the center. With my remote teaching experience during the global pandemic of 2020, I know that my students need to see how technology can foster positive connections, and I need integrate in ways that build their capacity to work independently across platforms. Most importantly, my integration of technology must involve building repertoires of practice that value authentic literacy, consider student interests, promote social justice, and build equity.

REFERENCES

Barton, J., Peek, N., & Crocker, B. (n.d.). *The TechEds Program*. http://pauldingteched.weebly.com/the-techeds-program.html

Burns, M. (2018). *Tasks Before Apps: Designing rigorous learning in a tech-rich classroom*. ASCD.

Davis, V., & Lang, A. (2017, January 27). *How teachers can find time to innovate*. Bam Radio Network. https://www.bamradionetwork.com/track/nefields-exposed-kids-naive-adults/

International Literacy Association. (2018). Improving digital practices for literacy, learning, and justice: More than just tools [Literacy leadership brief]. Newark, DE: Author.

Kieschnick, W. (2017). *Bold school: Old school wisdom plus new school technologies equals blended learning that works*. International Center for Leadership in Education.

Kieschnick, W. (2019, January 15). Supercharged literacy: Strategies and digital tools to support content area literacy [Video file]. *Brightcove*. Retrieved from https://players.brightcove.net/68348719001/default_default/index.html?videoId=5993548059001&elqTrackId=bf82fa7e05804fdba2698866a043bda2&elqaid=4046&elqat=2

Moran, C. M., & Woodall, M. (2019). "It was like I was there": Inspiring engagement through virtual reality. *English Journal, 109*(1), 90–96.

NEA. (2012). *Preparing 21st century students for a global society: An educator's guide to the "Four Cs"*. National Education Association.

Oris, A. (2020). *Integration - SAMR Matrix*. Integration - SAMR Matrix. https://sites.google.com/cftigers.org/techcoach

Thomas, K. M., O'Bannon, B. W., & Bolton, N. (2013). Cell Phones in the Classroom: Teachers' Perspectives of Inclusion, Benefits, and Barriers. *Computers in the Schools, 30*(4), 295–308. doi:10.1080/07380569.2013.844637

Zucker, A. (2012). *Using Digital Tools to Help Transform Schools*. AdvancedEd Source. https://www.advanc-ed.org/source/using-digital-tools-help-transform-schools

Chapter 3
Reimagining Mobile Phones:
Multiple Literacies and Digital Media Compositions

Monica B. Morall
Gwinnett County Public Schools, USA

ABSTRACT

As the number of students with access to cell phones increases, so do opportunities to bridge the technology divide that may exist among them. With the shift towards virtual learning gaining momentum, now is the time for teachers to increase their digital footprints in the classroom, and utilizing available mobile devices is one way to increase digital access for all. Coinciding with the ease of access to mobile technology is the growing research that supports the adoption of multiliteracies to foster readers and writers who can participate in and impact the world around them with nontraditional forms of communication. Digital multimodal compositions (DMCs) are digital texts created through the use of various modes, including written text, audio, visual, and other interactive media. DMCs are an effective way to incorporate both mobile technology and multiple literacies into both face-to-face and virtual curricula.

INTRODUCTION

For an abundance of reasons, many teachers feel anxiety when it comes to utilizing mobile technology (McGrail, 2005). Some fear a lack of knowledge might expose their inadequacies when it comes to the latest tools and resources. Some fear a lack of control over what content the students might be exposed to in the process. Still

DOI: 10.4018/978-1-7998-5805-8.ch003

others might just be stuck in patterns of familiarity and a "dispositional tolerance for uncertainty" when it comes to technology (McGrail, 2005, p. 10).

When I first entered the classroom as an educator over two decades ago, technology in the classroom was a new, and largely uncharted, territory. The first computer I had in my classroom in the late 1990s was not even connected to the internet, and was to be used primarily as a word processing device. My Title 1 school received a $1 million grant that paid for, what was then considered, a state-of-the-art computer lab, but students had very limited access to it. It took years before technology became the norm in education. As I have evolved as a teacher, I have increasingly incorporated technology into my instruction. Currently, my curriculum is about 80% technology-based, and that percent will increase substantially going forward as schools across the nation re-examine how virtual instruction can be delivered to students during uncertain times. My students' work is housed on a Google Drive and throughout the semester, they are perpetually in one stage or another of an ongoing multimedia project.

BACKGROUND

Teaching and Learning in a Digital Age

In the spring of 2020, many teachers became virtual learning experts, virtually overnight. Fortunately, in many schools across the nation, technology is now an integral part of the curriculum; however, for the student who does not have access to a computer and/or internet service at home, the technology gap widens the pre-existing achievement gap (Camera, 2020). The shutdown of schools emphasized just how important technology is to the education of the nation's students, but it also highlighted the disparities in accessibility that still exist in many parts of the nation. Though many students were on board and finished successfully, some teachers reported that the majority of their students stopped participating online, and many teachers never heard from some of their students again (Goldstein, Popescu, & Hannah-Jones, 2020).

According to the latest polls by Pew Research, approximately 12% of all students do not have access to a home computer (Auxier & Anderson, 2020). That may seem like a small number, but it translates to nearly 9 million students who are placed at a disadvantage. As the nation witnessed in the spring of 2020, ease of access for students to digital resources is a legitimate area of concern. Over a decade ago, Alvermann (2008, p. 15) asked, "Who gets to participate?" in digitized learning. While teachers sometimes take for granted that students have unlimited access to technology and data, it must be acknowledged that some students' access may be reduced to public computers, limited data plans, malfunctioning hardware, and/or outdated software.

Unfortunately, like most other deficiencies in education, and society as a whole, this technology gap adversely affects minority and marginalized children in disproportionate numbers, with 9% of Black children and 18% of Hispanic children lacking access to a home computer. This percentage skyrockets to a staggering 25% of students who are labeled as economically disadvantaged who do not have access to home computers (Auxier & Anderson, 2020). These students were effectively "academically quarantined" during this time period.

Cellphones in the Classroom?

Conversely, approximately 95% of teens reported having a smartphone or having access to one (Anderson & Jiang, 2018), and even though historically, minority students and students from low economic households have had less access to technology than their White, economically affluent peers, research shows that these students now have more access to technology via their mobile phones (Thomas & Munoz, 2016).

The Bring Your Own Device (BYOD) initiative that gained steam across the country in 2009-2010 was met with mixed reactions from teachers and administrators, alike. Originally viewed as distractions, electronic devices that were once banned from classrooms were now being welcomed with the aid of school-filtered networks (Simplicio, 2015). Mobile phone access provides a wide range of benefits including opportunities for differentiation and ease of sharing information (Thomas & Munoz, 2016). Many teachers find the use of mobile phones to be useful when allowing specific technology support during supervised or extended practice (Price & Nelson, 2014). Allowing students to use their own devices allows them to conduct research, participate in audience response systems and interactive assignments, play educational games, store assignments, interact with students globally, and limit distractions with earbuds (Bruder, 2014).

While the implementation of mobile devices provided access to information for students at a rapid rate, it came with new concerns and considerations. With increased technology access comes the increased possibility of students engaging in inappropriate internet behavior such as cyberbullying, photographing, or viewing inappropriate content (Bruder, 2014). By introducing new technology and material from the internet, the teacher takes on an additional responsibility to monitor classroom activities to ensure a safe learning environment. Additionally, students who do not have their own devices, though the number may be small, may feel singled out when asked to participate in BYOD activities.

Fortunately, there are several ways to mitigate these concerns surrounding classroom cellphone use. Teachers must be trained in appropriate classroom use of cell phones. Meyer (2016) suggested school wide training that, among other things, provides resources to support the use of cell phones. One way to eliminate improper usage is to require students to use the school network to filter content. Many schools also require students to sign a code of conduct detailing the responsibility of "digital citizenship" (Meyer, 2016, p.25). Some districts require parents to install classroom management software on their children's devices. These devices allow teachers to remotely monitor and control students' screens (Meyer, 2016). In addition, teachers must remember to physically monitor student activity. Proximity is a great strategy to limit inappropriate internet usage.

Additionally, schools must be prepared to provide devices for students who do not have access. Class sets of Chromebooks and other devices are becoming more common, nationwide (Meyer, 2016). There are also many opportunities for community resources to help fill the need through outreach and mentoring programs (Bruder, 2014). Educating parents on types of appropriate technology is also important. Some districts provide buying guides for parents to purchase devices that are both appropriate for and compatible to school use (Meyer, 2016).

Finally, students must be assured of the security of their devices. Classrooms must provide secured cabinets, and/or rooms when students may be separated from their devices Bruder, 2014). If the teacher decides to collect the devices, he/she may become liable for any damages or loss. Consequently, some effective strategies have been created to combat this potential problem. Some teachers use shoe bags that hang over a door with multiple transparent pockets. Each student is assigned a pocket, and the bag is placed at the front of the room so that all students can see their devices. Other teachers utilize bank deposit bags. The students' phones are placed in the individual, locked bags, and the student keeps the bag while the teacher keeps the key. This way, the students still have the phones in their possession, but they cannot access it without teacher permission.

Integrating Instruction and Mobile Technology

No one is more aware of the impact that cellphones have on instruction than teachers. As the wave of technology surges with every new tool and platform, it has become imperative for educators to join this movement by finding ways to incorporate mobile devices into daily instruction. With internet accessibility literally at the fingertips of students, teachers would be remiss to not figure out ways to capitalize on the benefits of cellphones in the classrooms. When the New London Group (Serafina & Gee, 2017) reconceptualized literacy as inclusive of animation, video, music, and websites, it opened the door to new methods of learning and interactivity that may increase learning in students. These technological advances have freed students from their desks, and even from their classrooms, as they are now able to engage with other teachers and learners all over the world (Serafina & Gee, 2017).

Adopting a Multiliteracies Approach

Coinciding with the ease of access to mobile technology is the growing research that supports the adoption of multiliteracies to foster readers and writers who can participate in and impact their worlds and the world around them in nontraditional forms of communication (Alvermann, 2008). No longer can 21st century educators of 21st century students be limited to the traditional definition of literacy. As sociocultural diversity evolves, the understanding of multiple literacies must evolve with it (Kajee, 2018). Teachers cannot rely solely on prescribed curriculum and traditional, standardized assessments to fairly evaluate students' knowledge. Multimodalities, multiliteracies, and particularly digital media literacy, opens doors that were previously closed to many learners. Kajee further proposed, "We communicate and make new meaning through new media texts, which cannot be devalued, marginalised, or ignored in the curriculum" (2018, p. 1). If this is true, teachers have to be willing to not only increase the breadth of what is viewed as literacy, but also expand the use of multiple modalities in instructional practices. Teachers can encourage this transition by providing students with multimedia, multimodal literary resources and offering assessment options in multimedia, multimodal forms that challenge the status quo.

Ivey and Johnston (2013) posited that social connections around the subject of literature, between students, their teachers, and even their families, could increase engagement and subsequently achievement. Digital forums are conducive to the participatory culture that includes easy access to free expression of ideas with supportive social connections (Alvermann, 2008). In reality, this generation of students is already well versed on many of the technological resources and social platforms that can be utilized to create, edit and publish content; however, teachers must allow them the latitude to explore these mediums within a safe and supported environment.

The necessity of allowing students to express themselves through multiple literacies has never been more obvious to me than in my current teaching situation. My high school is a majority-minority, non-traditional, special entity high school in a northern suburb of Atlanta, Georgia. This school was born out of a need to serve students in the district who were at risk for not graduating because of negative life circumstances that were often outside of their control. These students needed greater flexibility in their academic schedules in order to graduate high school. The school offers several features that are unique to the district, including flexible scheduling, small class sizes, self-directed learning options, a blended counseling model, and a fully licensed daycare for the children of students, so that teen parents can finish high school without the added expense of child care.

The majority of my students are on their last chance to earn a high school diploma before they give up because of age, family, or financial issues. Many of my students have been marginalized by society and may have been failed, in some way, by the educational system that was supposed to help them. For many students, my English Language Arts (ELA) class will be one of the last interactions that they ever have with literature, their last experience with writing creatively, expressively, or with any support. Consequently, the necessity of leaving a lasting, positive impact on their impressionable minds is amplified.

I am certain that I am not the only teacher who finds herself in a precarious situation, caught between district-mandated standards and the reality of our students' needs and abilities. Fortunately, many of the standards that are in place support incorporating multiple literacies and mediums into instruction. Among those, the Common Core Standards (CCS) encourages the examination of various mediums and the English Language Arts Georgia Standards of Excellence (ELA GSE) suggests using technology to produce and publish content in innovative and collaborative ways ("Reading: Literature: Grade 9-10, 2020; English Language Arts Georgia Standards of Excellence," 2020). These existing standards invite teachers to interrogate existing views on literacy. This means increasing the exposure to alternative literacies and modalities, and increased exposure may increase the likelihood of incorporating these new ideas into existing instructional practices. Using multimodal narratives and counternarratives allow students to share their stories with multiple audiences using multiple modalities. There is an ongoing interest in getting students to take advantage of the affordances of multimedia capabilities in order to create, copy, edit, and share digital content in what has been deemed a remix of information (Hafner, 2015). Incorporating Digital Multimodal Compositions (DMCs) into curricula creates opportunities for students to produce content that integrates written text, video, music, and other media in ways that are meaningful to them.

DIGITAL MULTIMODAL COMPOSITIONS

Digital Multimodal Compositions (DMCs) are digital texts created through the use of various modes, including written text, audio, visual, and other interactive media (Park, 2015). Alvermann touts the use of multiliteracies to empower our students to advocate for the betterment of not only their lives, but also the lives of others (Hobbs, 2016). Therefore, if it is the mission of English education to help create more democratic and socially just citizens, then resources, namely multiliteracies and technology, must be utilized in a way that ensures that teachers are at least aiming at the mark (Brauer and Clark, 2008).

The ultimate goal of utilizing multiple literacies to activate and incorporate multimodalities is to more fully engage the student in the learning process. Digital literacy provides a forum in which students can create, collaborate, and evaluate content with relative ease. Kajee (2018) argues, "A multimodal understanding of composing in the English classroom widens the lens of composing to include different modal affordances, identities, structures, social interactions and relationships that shape the engagement of multimodality to produce meaning" (p. 4).

My first experience with DMCs was in a graduate studies course in which students were tasked with composing a multimodal text using digital tools to enhance our "social and literary practices" (Class Notes). Additionally, we were to critique the process and final product by keeping a "Parallel Log" that chronicled the operation (Class Notes).

I did not have to look far for a topic for my DMC. As I searched for a topic about which to write, my mind kept returning to what was foremost in the minds of everyone on the planet. I think we can all agree that the year 2020 unfolded in a way that no one could have imagined. In addition to unprecedented physical, emotional, and economic strain on humanity, for many educators, it marked an abrupt and disastrous ending to a school year, a stressful summer, and an uncertain beginning to a new school year. Many people will desire to write this year off, to completely wipe it from the history books, and I might be inclined to agree, but then I read something on Facebook that said that 2020 had a lesson to teach humanity. I started turning this message over in my mind because anyone who knows me, knows that in every difficult situation, I always ask, "What is the lesson here?" My students hate when I ask that, but I believe that if we are not learning, we have wasted a struggle. The problem is that when we are too engulfed in the struggle, we can miss the lesson. And, with so much pain and ***test***ing, there had to be a ***test***imony on the other side. So, I guess that my ultimate intention was to offer hope, to myself, and to others who may be struggling to make sense of the tragedies of this year.

Since I consider myself more of a tech savage than tech savvy, ease of use was key to my technology choices. I explored several options including www.screencast-o-matic.com and www.slideshare.net, which both have laptop and mobile applications. I actually created content in both resources before I settled on www.wevideo.com. I am more familiar with screencast-o-matic, but I was willing to step outside of my comfort zone to learn about a tool that perhaps my students could use. It took me several days to figure out how to trim the video, how to add music, and how to make the music fit each slide. When I finally figured out, on Day 7, that I needed to record the soundtrack, then my narration, and then make the slides fit, it was a major breakthrough for me! Once I figured out how to manipulate the transitions and control the audio, I was able to produce a product with which I was satisfied. My final product can be viewed at https://www.wevideo.com/view/1760434613.

Suggestions for Practice

With the shift towards virtual learning gaining momentum, now is the time for teachers to increase their digital footprints in the classroom, and cell phones are an effective tool to grant access to more students. Going forward, technology will play a much greater role in instruction as schools fluctuate between face-to-face and online learning or adapt more blended or asynchronous instruction. DMCs are a great way to incorporate multiple literacies into a curriculum, in both face-to-face and virtual settings.

For some students, deciding on a topic for the composition is the starting point. I chose my topic because I felt that the confluence of the pandemic and the civil protests during the time of this assignment was too great to be ignored. This feeling may be true for some students as well. Some will be so overwhelmed by some event or some sentiment that the writing comes easy for them. Be sure to encourage them to explore feelings. Heart Maps are a great way to inspire creativity in students and move them beyond superficial compositions into matters of the heart (Heard, 2020). Information on Heart Maps can be found at https://www.georgiaheard.com/heart-maps/.

DMCs do not have to be long or complex to be effective. In fact, some students may need to be encouraged to edit their content so the meaning does not get lost in the sauce. Sometimes less is more. Consider providing students with a list of media they can use: written text, pictures, narration, video, music, sound effects, animation, etc., and limiting them to two or three to start. The choice of media should come early in the process because it may help to determine the best media tool to use.

A myriad of options exist for DMCs, including photo essays, digital essays, soundtracks, digital diaries, digital storyboards, web cartoons, webpages, interactive stories, and playlists. The intent for the composition should inform the assignment. A photo essay might be a great icebreaker assignment. To illustrate a literary character's development, a digital diary or playlist may be more appropriate. Storyboards, cartoons, and webpages are great to demonstrate plot elements, storylines, or character relationships. Interactive stories can be a great way to extend learning for a post-reading activity.

CONCLUSION

My introduction to DMCs was intimidating, just as I suspect it would be for our students. For this reason, comfortability with technology tools is key. My limited experience with media creation overshadowed whatever confidence I might have had about my writing abilities. These apprehensions are issues that teachers must anticipate and be prepared to address with students. Fortunately, many students are comfortable exploring the various applications found on their cell phones, so attacking the non-written aspect first might be the correct approach for them. For other students who may be more comfortable with writing, the written text may be the best starting point.

For some students, the largest learning curve will be around the technology. Because there are many options for creating multimodal content, offer students several options and allow them ample time to explore the affordances and constraints of each resource. Some great resources can be found at https://www.pixpa.com/blog/video-editing-apps. Become familiar with the resources beforehand, but expertise is unnecessary. The students are often far more skilled at certain aspects of technology than teachers are. Also, there will more than likely be some students who are experts at producing visual content, so utilize their expertise and allow them to assist other students.

Whatever the approach to DMCs and mobile technology, teachers should take creative risks. Do not be afraid to let students become co-creators of the curriculum, providing creativity and innovation, while providing a system of foundation and support. Allow them space to use the tools that are familiar to them to demonstrate what they have learned and assess them accordingly. Become an ally of the affordances of mobile technology and multiple literacies. The students will be better for it.

REFERENCES

Alvermann, D. E. (2008). Why bother theorizing adolescents' online literacies for classroom practice and research? *Journal of Adolescent & Adult Literacy*, *52*(1), 8–19. doi:10.1598/JAAL.52.1.2

Anderson, M., & Jiang, J. (2020, May 30). *Teens, social media & Technology 2018*. Retrieved from https://www.pewresearch.org/internet/ 2018/05/31/teens-social-media-technology-2018

Auxier, B., & Anderson, M. (2020, May 31). *As schools close due to the coronavirus, some U.S. students face a Digital 'HOMEWORK GAP'*. Retrieved from https://www.pewresearch.org/fact-tank/2020/03/16/as-schools-close-due-to-the-coronavirus-some-u-s-students-face-a-digital-homework-gap/

Brauer, L., & Clark, T. C. (2008). The trouble is English: Reframing English studies in secondary schools. *English Education*, (4), 293.

Bruder, P. (2014). Gadgets go to school: The benefits and risks of BYOD (Bring Your Own Device). *Education Digest*, *80*(3), 15–18.

Camera, L. (2020). *Disconnected and disadvantaged: Schools race to give students access*. Retrieved from https://www.usnews.com/news/education-news/articles/2020-04-01/schools-rush-to-get-students-internet-access-during-coronavirus-pandemic#:~:text=According%20to%20the%20most%20recent,higher%2C%20at%2012%20million%20children

English Language Arts Georgia Standards of Excellence. (2020). Retrieved from https://www.georgiastandards.org/Georgia-Standards/ Documents/ ELA-Standards – Grades-9-12.pdf

English Language Arts Standards. (2020). *Reading: Literature: Grade 9-10*. Retrieved from http://www.corestandards.org/ELA-Literacy/RL/9-10/

Goldstein, D., Popescu, A., & Hannah-Jones, N. (2020, April 6). *As school moves online, many students stay logged out*. Retrieved from https://www.nytimes.com/2020/ 04/06/us/ coronavirus-schools-attendance-absent.html

Hafner, A. (2015). Remix culture and English language teaching: The expression of learner voice in digital multimodal compositions. *TESOL Quarterly*, *49*(3), 486–509. doi:10.1002/tesq.238

Heard, G. (2020, July 9). *Heart maps*. Retrieved from https://www.georgiaheard.com/heart-maps/

Hobbs, R. (Ed.). (2016). *Exploring the roots of digital and media literacy through personal narrative*. Temple University Press. doi:10.2307/j.ctvrf898z

Ivey, G., & Johnston, P. H. (2013). Engagement with young adult literature: Outcomes and processes. *Reading Research Quarterly*, *48*(3), 255–275. doi:10.1002/rrq.46

Kajee, L. (2018). Teacher education students engaging with digital identity narratives. *South African Journal of Education*, *38*(2), 1–9.

McGrail, E. (2005). Teachers, technology, and change: English teachers' perspectives. *Journal of Technology and Teacher Education, 13*(1), 5–24.

Meyer, L. (2016). 9 Strategies for managing BYOD in the classroom. *T.H.E. Journal, 43*(6), 24–26.

Park, S. (2015). *Assessing students' digital multimodal compositions.* Retrieved from https://www.literacyworldwide.org/blog/literacy-now/2015/11/27/ assessing-students-digitalmultimodalcompositions#:~:text=Digital%20multimodal%20 compositin%20refers%20to,examples%20of%20digital%20multimodal%20c-omposition

Price, K. M., & Nelson, K. L. (2014). *Planning Effective Instruction: Diversity Responsive Methods and Management, 5th Edition.* Retrieved from https://bookshelf.vitalsource.com/#/books/9781285499918/

Serafini, F., & Gee, E. (Eds.). (2017). *Remixing multiliteracies: Theory and practice from New London and new times.* Teachers College Press.

Simplicio, J. (2015). How to effectively use social media as in-class teaching tools. *Reading Improvement, 52*(4), 142.

Thomas, K., & Munoz, M. A. (2016). Hold the phone! High school students' perceptions of mobile phone integration in the classroom. *American Secondary Education, 44*(3), 19.

APPENDIX: LESSON PLAN FOR DMCS

Recommended Grade Level (s)

- High school, 9-12

Objectives

- Examine a pivotal event in a literary text
- Analyze POV, motivation, and actions based on a character's perspective
- Create a digital journal for the character.

Lesson

After completing the text, students will choose a pivotal scene from the story and retell it from a chosen character's point-of-view, using a journal-style narrative. Students will use a digital platform from their mobile devices to create a journal using at least two different mediums outside of the required written text (pictures, narration, video, music, sound effects, animation, etc.). The journal will consist of three parts: summary, reaction, and resolution. Students will conclude with a brief (one paragraph) reflection that explains their media choices and experiences creating the DMC on their mobile devices.

Resources

- Text
- Cell phones
- Digital Tools

Assessment

Table 1.

Domain	Learning Task Goals	Assessment Criteria
Written Text	The student will produce a written text from the perspective of one of the characters.	The finished product is a well-written, cohesive piece that is written from the perspective of one of the characters without errors that impede understanding. The content of the composition is reflective of the text, demonstrates understanding of the text and extends the meaning of the text. **40pts**
Artifact	The student will demonstrate effective use of technology to produce a DMC that incorporates at least two additional mediums (pictures, narration, video, music, sound effects, animation, etc.) to accompany the written text using their mobile devices.	The DMC is well put together and effectively uses at least two mediums that are appropriate for the context. The technology used to produce the DMC is appropriate and effective for the context of the DMC. **40pts**
Reflection	The student will write a one paragraph reflection that explains the technology choices for the DMC.	The reflection effectively explains the student's thought process, technology choices, and experience using their mobile devices to create the DMC. **20pts**

________100pts

Section 2

Mobile Phones and the COVID-19 Pandemic

Chapter 4
The Role of Cell Phones in Online Learning, Connectivity, and COVID

Katie Rybakova
Thomas College, USA

Cameron Bigelow
Thomas College, USA

ABSTRACT

In this chapter, the authors used the lens of COVID-19 to explore how mobile phones and general technological connectivity can be both a positive learning experience and contribute to connectivity fatigue and burnout for both teachers and students. The authors will reflect upon their own experiences and conversations as well as expand on the research regarding 24/7 accessibility in an online environment. The second author provides a particularly powerful voice in this chapter as a current pre-service teacher. His vignettes were used throughout the chapter to add a student perspective that is often omitted from the scholarship.

INTRODUCTION

The technological, pedagogical, content knowledge framework, also known as TPACK (Koehler & Mishra, 2005), is a well-documented conceptual framework that is now often used in teacher preparation programs (Chai, Ling Koh, & Tsai, 2010; Lehtinen, Neiminen, & Viiri, 2016). What it means to develop TPACK skills goes well beyond technological fluency, and speaks to the complexity of 21st century literacy

DOI: 10.4018/978-1-7998-5805-8.ch004

skills. According to the National Council of Teachers of English (NCTE) Beliefs for Integrating Technology into the English Language Arts classroom statement (2018), educational stakeholders like teachers and teacher educators should view 21st century literacy skills as the ability to view technology itself as a literacy rather than an add-on to the curriculum. [blinded for review] wrote of "digital literacies as a means for ELA 'doing' as opposed to supporting ELA doing," (p. 592) a notion they underline as "deceptively complex" (p. 592). This complexity lies in the redefinition of what it means to be literate in a society where modes of communication occur in multiple streams through an individual personal learning network that varies from individual to individual (Oddone, Hughes, & Lupton, 2019), and which often promotes a gap in access between the 'haves' and the 'have-nots' (Darling-Hammond, Zielezinski, & Goldman, 2014). NCTE's Beliefs for Integrating Technology into the English Language Arts classroom statement (2018) explored this notion through the lens of a belief called 'technologies and associated literacies are not neutral,' which suggested perpetuation or even acceleration of discrimination of various forms. The additional two beliefs of NCTE's Beliefs for Integrating Technology into the English Language Arts classroom include considering literacies prior to technologies as well as technologies as a way to consume and produce texts.

The belief statement referenced above is a clean document that neatly shelves and unravels these complexities in a way that provides a blueprint for teachers and teacher educators. However, in complex times, issues of access, neutrality, and practice of technology as a literacy and as a mode of communication conflate. As we write this chapter, the undergraduates at our college just finished their semester (May 2020), of which eight weeks were unintentionally online due to COVID 19. Across the nation, K-12 and higher education institutions shut down in March, sometimes within only a few days notice. K-12 educators and college instructors alike had to pivot to emergency remote instruction-- intentionally not called online learning-- and do so within two weeks or less. Teachers rose to the extraordinary challenge. Administrators of K-12 schools figured out ways of getting food out to those who qualified for free-and-reduced lunch. Colleges managed to vacate their entire campuses, sometimes in only a few days. The stories of adminstration and teachers stepping up to make sure education was still accessible to students were vast. The platforms of use for that access, however, were not necessarily discussed. Cell phones became primary sources for accessing work, both at the K-12 and higher education level. The cell phone as a means for educational purposes during the pandemic shed light on how the mobile device had already played a part in access to education.

The pandemic shift meant teachers had to navigate TPACK skills that they may have never had to use before. They had to shift a face-to-face paradigm of teaching to an online paradigm of teaching, which differs enormously (Hodges, Moore, Lockee,

Trust, & Bond, 2020). They had to use the pedagogical skill set of trauma-informed education more often as some students went home to volatile and abusive environments and social emotional skill-building as they hosted virtual office hours; they had to use content-knowledge skill set that transferred information virtually, combining both content knowledge and technological knowledge. Even in K-12 and college environments where the learning was initially virtual, teachers had to make shifts to accommodate stress, anxiety, and uncertainty-- the very essence of what Prensky (2012) called VUCA-- a future truncated into volatility, uncertainty, complexity, and ambiguity. As capacity for building out curriculum and check-ins moved away from technicalities and logistics-- in other words, technological fluency-- teachers then had to navigate what Lankshear and Knobel (2007) called "new ethos stuff." "New ethos stuff," part of their New Literacies framework, suggested shifting notions of connectivity and communication with the advent of new technologies. The need to accept and effectively utilize "new ethos stuff" has been rapidly accelerated. "New ethos stuff" also required a shift in the platform with which we access technology. The pandemic again brought to light the connectivity that teachers have with students, and vice versa, when the mobile phone is used to access learning management systems (LMS), emails, and other forms of communication 24/7.

Connectivity in an online classroom is not the same relationship that occurs in a face-to-face classroom (Glazier & Harris, 2020; Martin, 2019). However, that does not mean a positive and powerful relationship between an instruction and a student online cannot exist (Martin, 2019). Online teaching practices further combine "new ethos stuff" and TPACK knowledge. It also creates a differentiated environment where students can work on their own time to complete learning tasks-- the very reason why online education in general is on the rise (Scott, Temple, & Marshall, 2015) and why those who seek out online learning do so because of the flexibility it provides, among a variety of other reasons (Jaggars, 2014). However, the dark side of online education is vast as well, if only in regards to the heavy load it requires of the instructor. The stigma that online classes are 'easy' or less rigorous compared to face-to-face (F2F) classes is unfounded (Columbaro & Monaghan, 2009). In fact, online instruction often takes more time to plan than F2F classes (Scheg, 2014). As instructors continue to work in their virtual worlds, we are beginning to see another effect seldom discussed in online teaching-- connectivity fatigue. In a world where emails can be sent at 2 in the morning and received immediately due to the mobile device, teachers feel an incredible burden, especially considering their knowledge of the need for prompt feedback and how this feedback plays a role in student relationship building (Glazier & Harris, 2020), to stay connected to their students beyond the school day. What used to be somewhat-protected time outside of the classroom walls has been eradicated. The virtual environment means being connected 24/7-- to be "on" 24/7. It is impossible to work virtually without platforms that maintain that connectivity, and the easiest and most accessible of those is the mobile phone.

The objectives of this chapter are to explore how mobile phones contribute to general technological connectivity, and how this form of learning can be both a positive experience and contribute to connectivity fatigue and burnout for both teachers and students. Virtual learning environment connectivity can be detrimental to both teacher and student in myriad ways, but can be leveraged to enhance relationships and provide redefined learning experiences through a device that fits in the palm of our hands. The authors will reflect upon their own experiences and conversations as well as expand on the research regarding 24/7 accessibility in an online environment. The second author provides a particularly powerful voice in this chapter as a current pre-service teacher. His vignettes were used throughout the chapter to add a student perspective that is often omitted from the scholarship.

BACKGROUND

This chapter will address what is essentially the intersection of the online course paradigm, virtual communication between students and teachers, and connectivity fatigue-- the term used to illustrate the combination of feeling "always on" and burnout. In order to do so effectively, the background information shared includes the theoretical frameworks of TPACK and New Literacies, the shift in paradigm between online and F2F coursework, and connectivity fatigue. Within these broader headers there are spatterings of research cited related to trauma-informed education, student-teacher relationships, and the use of mobile phones as a platform for education, as these are closely related to the major topics.

TPACK

In 2006, Mishra and Koehler published the seminal article that would inform educational stakeholders for years to come through the unpacking of a new paradigm of thinking about teaching and theoretical framework called TPCK, or TPACK. They built off of Shulman's (1986) initial work, in that Shulman (1986) conceptualized the convergence of content knowledge and pedagogical knowledge. Mishra and Koehler (2006) accentuated the need to focus on *how* we use technology, not *what* we use, and that the teaching profession ultimately is dependent on "flexible access to highly organized systems of knowledge" (p. 1020). The complexity of the initial convergence of what content and pedagogy combine to look like became more complex with the addition of technology. The authors were quick to point out that technological knowledge did not operate in a vacuum. "Teachers will have to do more than simply learn to use currently available tools; they will also have to learn new technologies and skills as current technologies become obsolete" (Mishra & Koehler, 2006, p. 1023). Technologies do not simply replace traditional tools, like the movement from a written essay to a typed one. They have the ability to transform and redefine content and pedagogy. Mishra and Koehler (2006) called this the "ripple effect" of "defining" and sometimes "constraining" both content and pedagogical decisions (p. 1025). Ultimately, the TPACK framework can be defined as follows:

TPCK is the basis of good teaching with technology and requires an understanding of the represen- tation of concepts using technologies; pedagogical techniques that use technologies in constructive ways to teach content; knowledge of what makes concepts difficult or easy to learn and how technology can help redress some of the problems that students face; knowledge of students' prior knowledge and theories of epistemology; and knowledge of how technologies can be used to build on existing knowledge and to develop new epistemologies or strengthen old ones. (p. 1029)

TPACK and its use for teacher preparation programs at the higher education level has been well researched. While not within the scope of this chapter to explore the variety of scholarship on this topic, it serves to note that scholars believe that TPACK can be used as a reflective tool for preservice teachers (Valtonen, Sointu, Kukkonen, Kontkanen, Lambert, & Makitalo-Siegl, 2017). Tondeur, Scherer, Siddiq, and Baran (2017) found that high ratings of TPACK knowledge and high scores of self-efficacy correlated with perception of a high amount of institutional support. Tondeur, Scherer, Siddiq, and Baran (2019) later studied the impacts of specific strategies in teacher preparation programs on TPACK development in preservice teachers; they found that more exemplary TPACK lessons and experiences were needed to help preservice teachers develop TPACK knowledge and understand the connections between the three factors.

Both the theoretical framework of TPACK and New Literacies informed this chapter. The TPACK framework is the guiding theoretical framework for the course that the authors will use as an example in the main focus of the chapter. Based on the scholarship, the TPACK framework is often used as a guiding principle in teacher preparation programs to develop the cross-section of technological, pedagogical, content knowledge.

The New Literacies framework informs this work in a different way. It allows for the authors to situate more holistically the needs and skills of 21st century citizenship and how these needs and skills inform instructors across K-16. The New Literacies framework also provides the underpinning guidelines of what it means to transition to a digital platform in that it emphasizes the unique communicative skills needed to navigate an online environment and virtual relationship building. The underlying emphasis of the New Literacies framework and how it informs this work is that it connects directly with the *mode* of communication, which is often the mobile phone. Because students and teachers typically have access to a cell phone, this becomes one of the ways in which New Literacies actualizes in practice.

New Literacies

The New Literacies framework, initially published in 2006 by Lankshear and Knobel, situated reading and writing as a sociocultural practice. What this means is that reading and writing is not mechanical-- it goes beyond decoding and comprehension, and is inherently biased based on various factors, some of which include social, cultural, political, and economic situations and experiences (Lankshear & Knobel, 2007). Lankshear and Knobel (2007) borrowed from Gee (1996) to view literacy through various discourses, where communication occurs in a socially meaningful group, and that language and communication shifts when discourses, and thus, rules, differ. This theoretical framework positions literacy as a give and take-- what Lankshear and Knobel (2007) call articulation and interpretation. The "new" in New Literacies speaks to the shifts in this articulation and interpretation with the advent of advancing technologies.

Lankshear and Knobel (2007) split New Literacies into two forms of fluency-- "technical stuff" and "new ethos stuff" (p. 7). Technical stuff is the digital fluency needed to navigate new technologies. Mishra and Koeler (2006) suggested the technological knowledge in TPACK requires the teacher to not only know how to navigate a technology but also learn how to navigate *new* technologies as they are produced. Similarly, Lankshear and Knobel's (2007) "technical stuff" included these kinds of digital tasks-- the logistical movement and use of technology. "New ethos stuff," on the other hand, means that the skills involved in interpreting resources online and new technologies change significantly. Lankshear and Knobel (2007) wrote: "it is possible to use new technologies...to simply replicate longstanding literacy practices-- as we see ad infinitum in contemporary classrooms as well as in many workplaces" (p. 7). Teachers can take two approaches to the use of technology-- what Lankshear and Knobel (2007) called "mindsets" (p. 10). These mindsets include doing familiar work with new technologies, in essence continuing the model of expertise as located within institutional and individual knowledge, and a second mindset, which breaks down the paradigm of what it means to be an expert, and is more fluid, hybrid, and collaborative in nature.

New ethos stuff in online course development and instruction means teachers are encouraged to take on the second mindset, but as Lankshear and Knobel (2007) already noted, this is a hard paradigm to shift to. What the new ethos stuff represents is a shift in dynamic within student and teacher relationships towards collaboration and shared expertise, and ultimately, this simply takes time and practice to incorporate well. The fluidity of this shift makes clarifying specific roles or "rules" difficult. As Schrage (2001) wrote, the significance of technology is not only about the access to information-- it is about a shift in relationships with both those who interpret that information and the information itself.

The need to integrate student-teacher relationships has been underscored as particularly important. As schools prepare for the unknown future, whether virtual or not, organizations like The Great School Partnership (2020) outlined the heavy lifting teachers will need to do to provide space and resources for their students to process trauma and loss due to the isolation of quarantine among other factors, as well as affirm those who have suffered increased racial, gender, and socioeconomic tensions due to coronavirus and subsequent consequences of quarantine, such as loss of employment. Aside from reorientating students to school and whatever that might look like, teachers are also tasked with the need to learn and use trauma-informed education techniques, culturally sustaining pedagogy, and social-emotional learning to combat the complexities of this time. Positioned within the construct of new ethos in New Literacies, this means that teachers are navigating a new way of communication along with new pedagogical practices considered best practice.

Although outside the scope of this work, defining three best practices that function to help develop student teacher relationships and a more equitable classroom include the following, among others:

- In response to high instances of adverse childhood experiences (ACEs), trauma-informed education means that teachers help "repair regulatory abilities and relational capacities" as well as "increase psychological resources" (Brunzell, Stokes, & Waters, 2016, p. 71). These tasks hinge on teacher-student relationships where teachers assume that students have had many experiences with broken attachments and where teachers assume a non judgemental, empathetic, and non-directive role.
- Culturally sustaining pedagogy is the newest conceptualization of best practice in regards to encouraging a diverse and equitable classroom where minority voices are not just relevant but sustained. Working off of Ladson-Billings (1995) initial framework of culturally relevant pedagogy, culturally sustaining pedagogy specifies the need for teachers to provide "explicit resistances that embrace cultural plurality and cultural equity" (Paris, 2012, p. 95-96).
- Social emotional learning is a broad-umbrella term that has multiple definitions, but ultimately is situated within a pedagogical approach that encourages social-emotional competence through explicit instruction (Domitrovick, Staley, Durlak, & Weissberg, 2017). Students learn to apply

knowledge, attitude, and skills that help them manage emotions and make responsible decisions; they include social problem solving, interpersonal skills, self-control, positive mindset, and empathetic responses Domitrovick, Staley, Durlak, & Weissberg, 2017.

The complexity of moving the above best-practices in pedagogy and student-relationship building online is vast. Because "new ethos stuff" is fluid, that means pedagogical lenses like social emotional learning remain fluid in a digital environment as well.

Online vs. In Person Pedagogy

The shift in paradigm towards online learning has been slowly encroaching on traditional face-to-face (F2F) or in person paradigms for years. Online learning continues to grow. The most recent numbers from 2019 show another 4% increase in students attending exclusively online courses for their college degree (Best College, 2020). Many high schools now have online course requirements as well. In regards to online learning success, there is evidence that drop out rates from online courses are higher than F2F classes (Bawa, 2016). However, academic outcomes in various studies vary greatly, from lower achievement to inconclusive to higher passing rates (Bambara, Harbour, Davis, & Athey, 2009; Scott, Temple, & Marshal, 2015). Student satisfaction tends to be higher in F2F classes (Whillier & Lystad, 2012), but a review of literature on course evaluations for both online and F2F courses show parallels across both platforms. For example, Glazier and Harris (2020) found that students rated classes "the worst" based on almost the same factors for both online and F2F classes: instructor unavailability, perception of useless information, unfair grading, and content lack of alignment with assessment. In F2F classes, "worst" classes rated the professor as belittling, while in online courses the workload was too demanding. Aside from those two differences, the parallels are more frequent. "Best" classes in Glazier and Harris' (2020) study also had several parallels across modalities, including relevancy, clear expectations, and interactive material.

Most of the evidence comparing F2F and online classes and pedagogy show students:

- prefer F2F classes for subjects that they perceive important and take perceived easy classes online (Jaggars, 2014);
- compare F2F lectures and online lectures-- their initial impression of F2F lectures matter, and if they enjoy the F2F lectures, they are less open to alternatives (Day, 2015).

- believe that online coursework is not as rigorous as F2F instruction (Scott, Temple, & Marshall, 2015)
- feel disconnected and lack of teacher interaction (Korkut, Dornberger, Diwanji, Simon, & Maerki, 2015)

For teachers, online instruction requires more prep time compared to F2F classes (Lee, Dickerson, & Winslow, 2012). There are best practices associated with online classes that differ from F2F and which attend to the perceived gaps of interaction that students feel. These best practices include participation, reflection, and frequent interaction (He, 2013) as well as instructor-created videos, explicit course expectations, assignment tutorials, video feedback (see also: [blinded for review]), video conferences, and additional tech tools for engagement (Martin, 2019). In short, online classes, while growing in popularity, carry a stigma among students, and those who have yet to teach in this paradigm that have had to switch to it abruptly have found themselves overwhelmed not only with the shift in paradigm but by the extensive and time-consuming nature to "catch up" with student relationships online, which occur, at least according to student perspectives, more naturally F2F.

In addition to the focus of online instruction and the various complexities that it entails, this chapter also has a focus on modality of online instruction. In other words, not only are teachers having to shift classes online and consider various ways to integrate student-teacher relationships, but the access to those online courses differ. It would be remiss, then, to omit the various platforms and modalities that online instruction and new ethos stuff involve, including the mobile phone. The smartphone has become a means for communication, socializing, and entertainment, and has become social currency at a small cost compared to larger devices like laptops (Herrington & Herrington, 2007). Herrington and Herrington (2007) also note that mobile learning, or m-learning, is mediated through a mobile device. Students can watch videos, download podcasts, upload pictures to forums, respond to Flipgrids or voicethreads-- all on their smartphone. In Japan, 99% of 333 polled participants used their phones to send emails (Thorton & Houser, 2004). In the US, two-thirds of the US population own a smartphone, 19% rely on their phone for access to all information, and 7% have a phone but no access to broadband or a reliable platform for internet access (Smith, 2015). 30% of those surveyed for the Pew Research Group study relied on their phones to take a class or for educational content-- this is in comparison to 62% who used phones to look up a health condition and 57% that used online banking (Smith, 2015). The notion of access is particularly important to accentuate here, as the context of this work in particular focused on how to help K-12 students with lack of access or a disparity of access through the use of mobile learning. It is also important to underscore that mobile learning occurs in both F2F and online settings, although the pressure to continually connect via the mobile phone, particularly for teachers, is heightned in virtual learning environments because of the stigma that online courses are impersonal.

Connectivity Fatigue

Hwang and Yang (2009) categorized distance learning as an approach that can be conducted anytime, anywhere. Their focus was on student fatigue--what it meant for teachers when students are far away and teachers cannot effectively supervise students who lack self-discipline. Student fatigue in regards to technological connectivity and emotional fatigue navigating online learning while balancing stress of an emergency event is sparse in the current scholarship. This is not surprising-- while populations all over the world have grappled with educational continuity in the event of a crisis many times (e.g. Hurricane Katrina, the wars in Lebanon), most action plans or contingencies that involve online learning beyond a few weeks are rarely delivered (Day, 2015). During the COVID-19 crisis, which at the time of this publication is ongoing, online instruction has past the 8-week mark in the K-12 sector and meant that almost all colleges finished their courses online for the Spring 2020 semester between March and May, with major institutions like the California University system moving to all-online coursework for, at minimum, the Fall 2020 semester.

A new phrase has entered the lexicon amid the COVID-19 crisis: "Zoomed out" (Supiano, 2020, para. 4). Zoom is one of the most popular platforms that professors and teachers have used in their transition to emergency online learning; at first glance, it offered many of the characteristics that both students and teachers value in F2F instruction, like collaboration and dialogue. However, synchronous teaching is "not the best way to teach online," (Joosten, as cited in Supiano, 2020, para. 12) according to Joosten, the senior scientist and director of digital learning research and development at the University of Wisconsin. Consistent synchronous meetings that replace typical teaching blocks in a F2F schedule mean that students and teachers use a lot of the cognitive energy it takes to partake in F2F dialogue with little to no rewards of those F2F conversations--hence the 'Zoomed out' feeling (Supiano, 2020).

This cognitive exhaustion is coupled with emotional exhaustion that online teachers often feel (Hogan & McKnight, 2007). In Hogan and McKnight's (2007) exploration of online teachers and burnout, they found that online teachers in higher education had average emotional exhaustion scores, high degrees of depersonalization, and low degrees of personal accomplishment-- together, these form to produce high levels of teacher burnout. Factors in teacher burnout, as illustrated in Chang's (2009) research, include individual, organizational, and transactional factors. Individual factors include factors such as age, gender, marriage status, resilience, coping mechanisms, and personality, organizational factors include school cultural, salary, work demands, and role ambiguity, and transactional factors include "teachers' judgements of student behavior, perceived support, and norms of student-teacher interactions" (Chang, 2009, p. 199). Others who study burnout found that job satisfaction acts as a protective factor in burnout prevention, but the more teachers experienced distress, the higher the risk for burnout (Buonomo, Fatigante, & Fiorilli). Praxis shock-- the weighing of expectations vs. reality, caused burnout and subsequent attrition particularly in beginning teachers and in end-of-career teachers (Ballantyne & Retell, 2020).

Couple general higher rates of online teacher burnout with shifting norms in Chang's (2009) organizational and transactional factors in teacher burnout, particularly student-teacher interactions, role ambiguity, and work demands, and it is no wonder that teachers are facing burnout at higher rates during the pandemic. Anecdotally, this is expressed through the feeling of being 'Zoomed out' or 'Always on.' Those who have previously written about academic continuity during unexpected interruptions have noted the complexity of "multitasking and improvisation in an online environment" (Day, 2015, p. 85) and how this, combined with the stress of emergency situations, challenge teachers to appropriately regulate their emotions and prevent burnout (Regan et al., 2012, as cited in Day, 2015).

It stands to mention that the forced transition to online education is just that-- another change that teachers across grade spans are asked to make. This is particularly interesting to view through the lens of change fatigue. Change fatigue is characterized by frustration, stress, disengagement, and skepticism. When teachers are asked to pivot their instruction constantly, publicly scrutinized by educational stakeholders, and told that their "well-established practices are no longer good enough," (Orlando, 2014, p. 428) change fatigue occurs. Orlando's (2014) research focused on change fatigue and its effects specifically on veteran teachers. Orlando used Windschitls (2002) framework of dilemmas to investigate change fatigue in her research, particularly in the adoption of technologies for veteran teachers. She found that veteran teachers were reluctant to accept and use new technologies in their instruction, but the reasons for doing so were multifaceted. While change fatigue underscores the teacher's choice to move towards digital instruction, the requirement to do so adds a unique nuance to the changes teachers have had to make while also facing the burden of having to make changes to their instructional paradigm.

Windschitls' (2002) framework is particularly appropriate in viewing the challenges that teachers, veterans and novices alike, have had to navigate in shifting their courses to use a different paradigm and pedagogical approach. Not only did they have to make pedagogical adjustments, such as fashioning learning experiences that can be downloaded on a mobile phone, called a pedagogical dilemma in Windschitls' (2002) framework, but they have also had to:

- navigate what the scholar called cultural dilemmas (changing ethics and communication norms between teachers and students)

- Adjust to political dilemmas (witnessing DeVos' push to defund public schools and accentuate online learning charters as well as more local organizational factors, such as distance learning pivots and contingency plans that are often communicated as the CDC guidelines shift)
- And rationalize conceptual dilemmas (attempting to understand epistemological differences and approaches in making the transition from F2F to online instruction)

While most evidence in inconclusive regarding online and F2F instruction academic differences (Bambara, Harbour, Davis, & Athey, 2009; Scott, Temple, & Marshal, 2015), Whillier and Lystad (2012), as previously noted, have found that student satisfaction is often higher in F2F settings as compared to online settings-- this adds another facet and challenge to teachers transitioning to remote learning to provide a satisfying experience for the learner. In Day's (2015) autoethnography where he was forced to conduct his instruction remotely for one week, he found that students were missing F2F lectures because they could not see his body language; he found that "body movement...convey[ed] enthusiasm" (p. 80). Ultimately, successful online teaching takes time, planning, and knowledge (Day, 2015; Hodges, Moore, Lockee, Trust, & Bond, 2020). Between translating courses online and all of the complexities involved in that transition and ensuring that students are satisfied and feel in-touch with their instructors, there is evidence of what I term connectivity fatigue that resembles change fatigue as teachers and students adjust to online platforms for learning. This goes beyond feeling 'Zoomed out.' This has serious implications for the well-being and emotional health of teachers during this time as they suffer burnout.

BRIDGING THEORY TO PRACTICE

The Mobile Phone in a Digital Literacies Course

The adoption of distance learning for 2021 and beyond are unknown but likely higher than pre-COVID-19 (Flaherty, 2020). The literature review revealed the complexities of teaching using a digital platform, and how mobile phones play a role in carrying out the various complexities of virtual learning. The objective of this section was to illustrate a positive learning experience completed by preservice teachers in a course required of their teacher preparation program, as well as discuss the challenges of digital coursework, both through the lens of the instructor (the author) and a student (Cameron Bigelow) who successfully completed the course. Cameron's preservice teacher voice is particularly powerful-- there is a gap in the research in promoting and including student and preservice teacher voices. His voice, situated in vignettes throughout this section, are italicized.

Context

The Computers Across the Curriculum course at a small, private higher education institution in the Northeast was a required sophomore-level class for preservice teachers. The teacher preparation program certified early childhood, elementary, and four different content areas of secondary education at the time of this publication. The college itself serves a student body of about 1,000 students, of which over 60% are first-generation college students.

The course was taught online in an asynchronous format. Despite its name, the course content focused on the integration of technology in various forms and modalities for K-12 classrooms. The emphasis was on bridging theory to practice--namely, honing in on and practicing TPACK skills. Every week, preservice teachers engaged in either reflection about technology integration or digital literacy theory or an opportunity to "tinker" with various forms of technology utilizing those theories.

The course utlized mobile phones in both explicit and implicit ways. First, the expectation was that preservice teachers in this course checked their email (regardless of whether on a laptop or phone) every 48 hours at minimum. Second, there were structured opportunities to use the mobile phone for app "play" and discussion. Third, both the instructor and the students sometimes assessed and responses to prompts on the discussion board via the learning management system Moodle via cell phone, although this was not required or expected. Finally, almost every week preservice teachers had materials in various modalities, including podcasts and videos they could watch and listen to on their phones.

The course objectives were as follows:

- Use basic educational software and online web tools for integration into the classroom environment
- Identify and design developmentally appropriate learning opportunities that apply technology-enhanced instructional strategies to support the diverse needs of learners.
- Use technology that will support learner-centered strategies that address the diverse needs of students

The Spring 2020 course, which is the focus of this chapter, included 28 preservice teachers of varying majors. One student was a psychology major but interested in teaching. Otherwise, the rest of the 28 made up a mixture of early childhood, elementary, and secondary education majors. Of the secondary education majors, there was a mixture of those who were seeking certification in Social Studies, Math, English, and Life Science. Below are Cameron's thoughts about the beginnings of the course.

The Preservice Teacher Perspective, Part 1

During the second semester of my 2020 school year at [college], I was introduced to my first true online courses. One of these courses, designed by [blinded for review], specifically focused on Computers Across the Curriculum; touching upon effective technology use inside of the common classroom. Initially, I was unconfident in my own abilities to adapt to such a classroom framework. Time management, workload management, and my own personal attention span were standing in the way of my own visualization of my success. These are challenges I have battled my entire school career, and many students would probably share similar concerns, and these concerns would only be amplified with an online course, where face to face accountability for turning in assignments and personal improvement is missing. Fortunately, being from one of the first generations who had state funded access to laptops through the Maine Learning Technology Initiative (MLTI), the technology aspects of the class were the least of my worries. However, the confrontation of personal pitfalls is what I view to be one of the strongest advantages to distanced learning.

My experience with tech prior to the online course was above average. I had been equipped with a laptop and a proper internet connection inside of school since 7th grade. At first the class was almost not engaging, as most of the program, app, and website basics that were covered were simply rehashing information I had taught myself. However, as we moved towards topics such as the proper integration of technology in the classroom, I found myself exploring more in-depth pedagogical studies, teaching methods, and practical experiences, all of which was complemented by the successes of the MLTI program. Unfortunately, I recognize that my access to technology is not as widespread as it should be.

Throughout the course my perspective on the future of technological advancement has shifted dramatically. Initially my views considered technology as a means of producing work, writing essays, researching, and using creative programs. Upon reflection, I consider technology as more of a literacy skill and as a means to facilitate content specific teaching goals.

Focusing more on the pedagogical properties of technology use in the classroom, one of the main goals of the class was to cover the TPACK model. [Blinded for review] covered the TPACK model as a lense in which to view technology integration into the everyday classroom. The most interesting aspect was the relationship between content knowledge and technological knowledge, as ultimately this furthers pedagogical knowledge. According to Mishra, Koelher, & Cain (2013), "Technology and content knowledge have a deep historical relationship. Progress in fields as diverse as medicine, history, archeology, and physics have coincided with the development of new technologies that afford the representation and manipulation of data in new and fruitful ways" (p. 15-16). To me this is the most impactful connection the TPACK model makes, laying out the argument that because the world is progressing in technological advancement, it becomes imperative to supplement this with the addition of technology and technological literacy as a focus inside the classroom, and the TPACK model is a method of achieving such a lofty goal.

Then Came COVID-19

By the second half of the semester things had changed drastically. The large majority of the country's students were at home, a large portion of the workforce was at home, and the nation entered a semi-lockdown state that would extend through the end of the semester. In the context of the Computers Across the Curriculum course, at first glance it might seem as if we were spared the dramatic 2-week turnaround from a fully face-to-face course to a fully online one. However, it became clear that the course needed to be shifted to accommodate the stress and anxiety that the pandemic caused students. Students who were outstanding and punctual preservice teachers prior to COVID-19 lost motivation and struggled to complete work. Some students went home to abusive and emotionally distressing environments. Some students lacked steady Internet access. Many students felt that the workload from the courses that were F2F originally dramatically increased, and put them under the extra burden of completing all of their work in a timely fashion in a format that they did not choose.

An important observation regarding the shift to emergency remote instruction from our traditional online teaching at the beginning of the semester was that more students were using their phones to connect to their instructors and complete work. Several students mentioned to me that they had techological difficulties with their laptops so they used their phones, or that their rural location meant they had to use their cell phone data to complete work because they had no Internet. Students who never emailed me at the beginning of the semester opted in for "weekly email check-ins," which were conducted on both ends via mobile device (this was clear due to the sign off on the email, which indicated that the email was sent via mobile).

In light of these developments, and to protect the mental health of the preservice teachers in the course, this meant adjustments had to be made to streamline the course. For example, several assignments, including a grant-writing project, were omitted.

Initially, we had planned to have a F2F meeting during the semester with 40 6-8th graders from a local middle school to help them prepare for an annual writing contest, in which our preservice teachers in this course act as judges. While we continued with the contest, this F2F meeting was cancelled. A 3D printing collaboration with a local community college was also cancelled. Every week, I added short mindfulness activities to the weekly prompts for extra credit--many students took advantage of these. Again, below is Cameron's reflection on the experience.

The Preservice Teacher Perspective, Part 2

During the COVID-19 pandemic, the class shifted ever so slightly. Certain assignments were omitted, deadlines changed, and assignments altered. One thing I am thankful for is my close proximity to my sister's experience as a high-schooler going through the crisis. I've done my best to observe her classroom interactions and reactions, paying attention to what specifically seems the most effective and most engaging teaching methods, and by far the most important aspect of technological uses for students is simply the connectivity. By use of the internet and certain apps like Zoom, Facetime, and Microsoft Teams, educators have been able to keep in touch with their students during such a pressing time, and subsequently the health and wellbeing of students can still be checked, albeit not as effectively.

Augmented Reality as a Philanthropic Activity

Upon return from the extended spring break that was granted to us so that faculty could prepare for the shift online, I knew that the "mini-project" for that week had to be particularly engaging, authentic, and motivating, especially because it would take the place of our VR/AR experience that we were meant to have on campus. I also desperately wanted to help those in the K-12 system, many of whom had an even shorter amount of time to pivot their paradigm. "Mini-projects" were the weeks in which preservice teachers had the opportunity to tinker with new technologies and create something authentic that they could then use in their own classroom--in essence, the application of TPACK skills. As I began thinking about our local K-12 schools, I remembered an observation I made when I moved to this state from Florida-- that *every single school* within a 40-mile radius of the college qualified for Title I funds through free-and-reduced lunch percentages. The poverty in the area was an important consideration-- what could our preservice teachers at the college make or do that K-12 students could access? What did K-12 students often have access to? The answer was clear-- while not all K-12 students had broadband Internet, many of them did have access to a smartphone. The project that the preservice teachers would engage in (creation of a short assignment and assessment using either Hyperdocs or the augmented reality app Expeditions; see below for details) had to be accessible via smartphone.

When the preservice teachers logged into our learning management system, they saw the following directions and project goals:

AR/VR and Distance Learning

Well, my ideas to use our VR headsets for a lesson study unfortunately are no longer going to happen. But, we have a really neat philanthropic (and learning!) opportunity here, and we'll make the most of it! I've reached out to several networks of mine to see what teachers are covering right now and what they need in terms of distance learning. Several teachers replied with requests.

So, we're going to be making distance-learning activities using augmented reality or HyperDocs that we will then donate to various schools and teachers so that they can use them with their students. You can use whatever augmented reality you'd like, but I'd suggest Expeditions (it is a free app). The HyperDocs information is linked in the materials below.

Here are the requested topics [hyperlink removed for privacy]. Please sign up for one. Please choose one, or reach out to your own networks to find a relevant topic that you can then create an activity for and donate. Some of you also are in a school—you can use your own classrooms for this activity. Please realize that not all of these are within the grade span that you want to teach, but you are getting certified to teach within these grade spans, so the more practice you get with a variety of grade levels the better! I would like to have at least one item completed for each teacher who requested specific items.

What you will create is a one to two page activity guide that students can complete on their own with either assistance from a parent/guardian or independently. Here is what it should include:

- It should be written FOR THE STUDENT.
- It should have a brief and clear explanation as to how to download the necessary apps/technology. These should be free.
- It should identify the "I can" or "student will be able to" statements. So, it can say, for example: "After this activity, you will be able to identify the five stages of the water cycle."
- It should clearly explain the steps of the activity and the product.
- It should clearly explain the goals of the project.

- This project should not take more than one to two hours to complete. It should not require too many "extras" or materials that would be expensive or possibly handy. Many of the teachers I am in touch with work at schools with high poverty rates. The assignment should be able to be completed only via smartphone.

Logistically, you will:

- Create an aesthetic document using a template of your choice using the "Word templates" available on Word. To open these, open a Word document, then click on file, and then "new from template."
- The aesthetics should fit with the activity. If you are covering the solar system, there should be pictures of the solar system or other applicable images.
- Once you are done with your one to two-page document, save it as a PDF. Don't forget to give yourself credit somewhere! This will be shared via Facebook, social networks, and email to specific schools and teachers.
- Please, please, please revise and make sure your grammar is correct! I do not want to share documents with teachers and students that are not professional.
- Make sure we abide by effective tech practices. We don't want to use AR just for it to look cool. It should have an educational purpose.

The project generated positive comments and excitement among the preservice teachers. It was even highlighted in the local news (Shelly, 2020). I spoke with a colleague of mine, who was a 7th/8th grade science teacher in a high-poverty district at the time of this writing, and he made a powerful statement-- that the AR and Hyperdoc experiences that he received from our preservice teachers were engaging, and that because they were engaging, his students were more likely to do them. He highlighted his major takeaway from the products he received: "If they [his students] do the work and I see it, I know they are okay." This was not just a way to engage K-12 students in learning using an augmented reality app on their phone-- *it was a way of connecting to students to make sure they were okay.* Below are Cameron's thoughts on the project.

The Preservice Teacher Perspective, Part 3

During the recent pandemic many negatives, specifically regarding education have reared their ugly heads, contrasted by very few positives. One of these positives, albeit a personal positive, was the opportunity to get to work within practical real world experiences, specifically an augmented reality hyperdoc assignment that would be used in a local high school. At first the project seemed simple and relatively easy, however the more invested I became with the project, the more I realized just how challenging it can be to create effective, challenging, and engaging assignments through technology.

After I had completed the project two things became very clear to me: The first being, that technologically speaking, creating a hyperdoc is not inherently difficult, at least on a personal level. Secondly, I realized that it is difficult creating a meaningful hyperdoc that students will not just view as more "busy work". To me my interpretation of the assignment lacked, something. I felt that it was a relatively uninterested take on what could have been a carefully curated and creative assignment, instead it turned into the busy work that I so desperately tried not to emulate. However, through this experience I have gained new ideas for such assignments. What if assignments like this were more interactive? What if the students had more say in what they explore through these assignments? What if the students took charge of their own education and learning? These are all incredibly interesting thoughts, as we have hit the crossroads in which education can truly be redefined for years to come.

Throughout this practical exercise, I also learned a lot more about K-12 schooling. Specifically, I think the most important piece of information that I learned was learning how truly broad the scope of intelligence can be from student to student. Because of this, the biggest learning curve was taking all of my knowledge, interests, and love for the specific content knowledge, and translating that to students who perhaps were not as keen about the specific subject material. I think that this, in the future, could become a lot easier as well. The introduction of certain technologies as perhaps pedagogical vehicles, like mobile phones, video game consoles, and even virtual-reality headsets, can go a long way in creating a hybrid of student engagement/interest and proven pedagogical methods that can increase effectiveness in classrooms all across the country.

Notice that in Cameron's perspective, he shared briefly that he believed how the use of the mobile phone can be useful to engage students, but he did not fully recognize that cell phones may be used not only for engagement but also simply for access. This product was meant to be accessed via cell phone simply because it was the platform that students were the most likely to possess. It showed me that I have to emphasize the benefits (and drawbacks) of the use of cell phones as a platform for learning, whether it be for augmented reality, access to Hyperdocs, or F2F activities like Kahoot.

The preservice teachers also valued the products they made. Many of them shared their products with teachers they knew or with their own family, who were teachers as well. One student's mother contacted me and thanked me for the project, because she had used it with her middle school students and it was a great success. The projects "traveled" from within the 40 mile radius of our college to the tips of the state across several county lines. Several of the preservice teachers recognized for the first time the true educational power of the smartphone-- the opportunity to truly bring learning to life.

Project Reflections--The Risk of Connectivity Fatigue

Overall, the project was deemed a success. Preservice teachers used technological, pedagogical, and content knowledge skills to build out informative, engaging, and accessible projects, which were donated successfully to a variety of schools and grade levels. They navigated new ethos stuff in building these projects out, because they had to communicate through various platforms not only to figure out what their project would be on, but also to communicate what they expected in a new format for students they did not know. They authored their own projects, created their own intellectual property, and essentially dispersed it under an unofficial Creative Commons license--here, this is my work, and I want you to remix it the way that you wish that is appropriate for your students.

The course evaluations highlighted the authenticity of the projects, their opportunity to discuss "real" teacher topics, and the connectedness they felt to the instructor and the course participants. Many voiced their initial impressions of online courses being negative, and that this course showed them that online courses really can provide good conversation, academic rigor, and positive student-to-student and student-teacher relationships.

However, I came away with a gut feeling that teachers both at the higher education level and the K-12 level were quickly becoming overburdened with not only the amount of technology they had to navigate, but also the amount of connection they had to maintain make sure their students were transitioning out of school successfully. This project landed in an inbox full of suggestions, district communications and new directions, professional learning opportunities, and free platforms. The comment about making sure students were okay from my colleague haunted me. This was not about learning-- this was about general mental and physical health for some students, and teachers had to prepare not only academic exercises for their students but also continue to build and provide the positive student-teacher relationships they had built up prior to COVID-19.

I shared my colleagues' concerns about students at the K-12 level, because I too had experienced the worry and anxiety of making sure our preservice teachers were okay. I pushed myself to answer emails within an hour, provide feedback even quicker, and send weekly email-check-ins to students who were struggling. I offered virtual office hours, met virtually with professors who were struggling, and talked to colleagues both in and out of state, both in and outside of higher education, about how they were doing the same exact thing. We compared notes, adjusted our courses, and tried to help everyone "over the finish line." Ethical conundrums surfaced. Should a student who was earning an A pre-pandemic earn the C- she ultimately got at the end of the semester because COVID-19 left her stressed and unable to work? Since many of our students worked off of their phones, what was an instructor to do when the LMS, which did not function well on the phone, malfunctioned and erased their post? Were extensions to be granted generously even if they broke syllabus policy? The semester ended and left everyone bone-tired.

I have been teaching online for over five years now; what was different, aside from the stress of the pandemic, that left us all not only "Zoomed out" but burned out? The conflation of needing to use several educational paradigms, from social emotional learning to trauma-informed education to online learning, was one of the factors. Secondly, I recognized in myself and others a compulsive need to connect with our students. At first glance this is normal. All effective teachers know the value of the student-teacher relationship. However, online, academics shift, and so do these student-teacher relationships. They are no longer protected by four walls-- they are accessible everywhere and all the time-- at least this is the expectation. The mobile phone exacerbates this obsessive need to always be connected. We are connected through social media, email that pings to our phones, and our LMS systems that blink with waiting assessments.

The idea of connectivity through the lens of new ethos stuff is particularly interesting, because there is no mention of *how much* in this theory. The fact that communication styles, platforms, and modalities shift when online or when using different tools, such as a smartphone, is clear. What does this mean, though, for relationships? How are we able to do the social emotional learning, the culturally sustaining pedagogy, the trauma-informed education within the online paradigm and when students have access to us through their cell phones 24/7? More importantly, how do we do this successfully without burning ourselves out in the process? As I read the scholarship on change fatigue, it became clear that this exhaustion that seemingly all teachers felt was a culmination of change fatigue or burnout in trying to use new ethos stuff-- a new form of communication-- to continue the traditional student-teacher relationship on a technological platform with a device that gave *too much access* for communication. Accessibility is a good thing. It is a characteristic highlighted as best practice for educators. However, accessibility to the detriment of the teacher's mindset and mental health is connectivity fatigue. It is necessary to be accessible, but it is also necessary to create and hold to boundaries. Below, Cameron talks about this fatigue.

The Preservice Teacher Perspective, Part 4

With the late semester being clearly a dramatic shift in how things were being done, it was only natural to assume that, to some degree, there would be some negative side effects. One such side effect can be dubbed 'Connectivity Fatigue' and is truly a real problem. Students and educators, who previously had not relied upon ample amounts of screen time to get through their day, were now being obligated to spend up to 8 or more hours a day on their technological devices. They were glued to their phones and laptops. The age-old adage of too much screen time being unhealthy is one that is true, both mental and physical side effects can begin to manifest. However, personally I never really struggled with the adaptations. Being in an age range where I have grown up with technology, I think that all the hours spent playing video games, scrolling through social media, and watching my favorite streaming services have more or less conditioned me for such circumstances. But it's important to remember that this is not a universal experience.

This is all compounded on top of the fact that educators have had to work overtime during these unprecedented times. Creating an entire 3 months of online curriculum in a few weeks is a monumental undertaking, and it was compounded with the efforts to stay connected and engaged with students through such a turbulent time in their young lives. These educators should be applauded, and slack should be cut for those who perhaps got tripped up and maybe made a few mistakes.

Distanced connectivity learning and face to face learning, although drastically different, both ideally wind up at the same end goal, which is to meet a set of learning objectives based upon the existing curriculum. While some may think that online education may be inadequate and rife with problems and pitfalls, according to Glazier and Harris' (2020) study of over 1000 graduate students at a large institution, over a quarter selected online courses as those that they not only preferred but learned more from. This goes to show that although currently the idea of online education may be unrefined and is perhaps very rough around the edges, there are some aspects that are proving to be effective, and perhaps these should be what is focused on. This can go a long way in creating a framework of distance learning that is not only engaging, but also effective and maybe even preferred.

As I read the perspective above, it struck me that they did not mention cell phones because the use of cell phones as a way to connect is inherent in their life. It is not something that needs to be said—it is simply a method to connect, rather than a new device or technology to be considered. This is an important reminder for us as instructors. Students will use their cell phones for both in and out of school literacies and academics at some point whether we agree or directly engage them with cell phones or not. For me in particular, since I teach future teachers how to use technology effectively in their future classrooms, explicit instruction as to not only the 'what' but also the 'how' and 'why' of mobile learning is essential.

Moving Forward

I will continue to teach TPACK skills, and I will continue to embrace new ethos skills as a new way of communication in education. I will continue to seek out authentic projects for preservice teachers to engage with, and will continue to highlight the accessibility of the smartphone. I will continue to advocate for online coursework. It has given us the opportunity to maintain the student-teacher relationships when we are barred from attending school because of a pandemic. The experience in shifting courses online showed that F2F and online classes are just not the same, and so should not be compared as if they are. Cameron discusses his thoughts below.

The Preservice Teacher Perspective, Part 5

I will continue to explore the true benefits of technological advances inside of educational settings as well as continue to use what technological literacies I have obtained over my brief lifetime to push forward the conversation of digital literacies and the landscapes of newer and better education. I will continue to push myself, and pursue those crazy ideas of things like video-games and virtual reality in the classroom, not because they will work, but because it is my duty to use my due diligence to explore every possible avenue for student success. I will continue to adapt my own personal knowledge, experiences, and goals into what I want the educational system to look like, and will not stop until every student I have leaves their schooling experience feeling more engaged and more knowledgeable about the world that lies ahead of them.

Continuing to discuss plans for the future in higher education are rife with unpredictability. Some organizations and leaders have taken the major shift in educational institutional structures as an opportunity to dream and hope of a new educational paradigm that will dramatically improve education once our return to normalcy. I caution this optimism--not because I do not want the many complexities of education to change, but because it, once again, places the burden to do the heavy lifting on the shoulders of teachers. I do see the opportunity for change-- a positive change where student-teacher relationships can be further built AND teachers can use the new paradigm shift to carve out a space for themselves to recover and safe-keep their own mental spaces. The smartphone has power-- but only the amount of power and attention we give to it while setting boundaries, both student and teacher alike, to pause.

SUGGESTIONS FOR PRACTICE

As we reflected on our journey through both the use of the mobile phone to create and disperse augmented reality for K-12 students as the online course as a whole through the lens of the pandemic, we recognized several issues that lead to connectivity fatigue, both for teachers and students. These are not listed in any particular order, but rather serve as general reflections as we all reflect upon what COVID-19 has done to disrupt education as a whole, and how technology played a major part in building the metaphorical dam.

It is also important to note that while the COVID-19 crisis is very much a reality now in 2020, it may not be in the future as you read this chapter. However, what the crisis brought to light is that mobile phones already have been used for access to education—it is whether or not as teachers we are willing to and able to navigate the new ethos stuff that the device requires to make the shift to educational platform effective.

Issue 1: Teachers Are Trying to Tackle Too Much

Shifting online does not mean taking all of the materials from a F2F class and simply digitizing them. To shift online means to shift paradigm. Online learning requires that materials are differentiated even more so than F2F classes (Martin, 2019). Instructors should embrace the various platforms that students use to complete their assignments, often involving the smartphone, and plan accordingly. Asking students to read an article is good practice. Including annotations can help. Podcasting or using audio notes that students can download onto their smart phones and listen to as they drive home from work can help as well. There is this assumption that an online teacher has to be incredibly tech-savvy-- while technological fluency helps, it is truly the need for new ethos stuff that is essential (Lankshear & Knobel, 2007). Knowing how to use communication channels appropriately and knowing what students have access to, both in terms of device and information, can greatly impact course success. Using various strategies to provide authentic feedback, such as through video feedback (Martin, 2019; Rybakova, 2020), can help build student-teacher relationships. Attempting to do ALL of these the first time teaching online can lead to the feeling of being overwhelmed with not only the amount of new learning but the amount of new forms of communication, especially when that means that the teacher acts more as a facilitator towards that learning rather than the sole expert.

Online courses require heavy amounts of front-loaded work, so much of the workload for teachers is in preparing and prepping the class, then making adjustments as needed. This was the major key difference between emergency remote learning and true online instruction--lack of time to not only prepare but also wrap our minds around a new worldview and educational philosophy. As we prepare for an uncertain future, it is clear that teachers need to be able to take a step back from all of the professional development opportunities, all of the new technologies, and all of the materials prepared for online instruction. Taking a step back, and then making an informed decision on which of the many options to pursue, is one way of tackling just a little bit of the complex world of online teaching without becoming overwhelmed. Too much shifting can lead to lack of routine and too much uncertainty, and is a huge time commitment for teachers at the same time.

Issue 2: Burnout, Connectivity Fatigue, and Availability

We tout availability as a characteristic of an effective teacher. However, there is a fine line between being available and being available to the point of declining mental health due to burnout and stress. Simply put, teachers who are burnout and emotionally distressed are *not* effective teachers (Buonomo, Fatigante, & Fiorilli, 2017). Teachers who overburden themselves to reply to all of their students 24/7 as fast and as detailed as possible will eventually burn out. The solution here is two-fold. First, communicating with students about boundaries is essential. The teacher should be available, but also should have moments and segments of the day where she/he/they are not available. Teachers need to carve out space for their own selves, and work hard to make sure these spaces are not filled with thoughts of emails, assignments, and students, which they often become. The "two-fold" part of this solution is that in doing so, the teacher sets an example of how to disconnect from technology for students, which is often an issue in and of itself for students. An additional solution for quick feedback, which is an online teaching best practice, is to communicate with students a realistic turnaround time for their assignments. This communication helps students in that they recognize their assignments are not simply lost in cyberspace. What is essential to highlight as part of connectivity fatigue is the role smart phones play in this connection between teachers and students. The phone is an incredibly powerful actualization of new ethos stuff, and we are still working as instructors as to how to navigate the boundaries of the phone, particulalry because the phone functions as both a work space and a play space for both teachers and students. How do we shelve the two when they are accessible on the same device?

Issue 3: Returning to School Outside of the Box

Teachers are innovators--no doubt about it. Innovation takes time and effort. Although this comes from the right mindset, the idea of shifting educational paradigms and returning to school outside of the box overburdens teachers to do the heavy lifting once again. Vasquez (2020) and Smith (2020) both reflect upon the silving lining of the pandemic-- how this opportunity can lead us to consider what education could look like in the future now that the institution has been disturbed. In fact, Vasquez (2020) wrote of a willingness to be disturbed and disrupted, and in doing so, come up with more equitable plans for education. While these are all optimistic and hopeful views for our students' futures, I worry about the extra burden on teachers to carry this load. Now, not only do teachers need to plan knowing that they may or may not be in and out of school due to the virus, figure out a way to build student-teacher relationships amid a pandemic either virtually or F2F, but also dream and put into practice a new paradigm of education that softens inequities that really have more to do with poverty than with anything a teacher has control over (Ravitch, 2014). Additionally, organizations warn that as teachers begin the new school year, they will have to navigate these inequities and new traumas, possibly using new ethos communication in a new way using a modality that is new as well.

This is a great time to re-envision education. The sky did not fall when we did not test students in March, for example. But, we need to temper our calls for re-envisioning our fall and spring semesters with the space to do so, both at the K-12 and college level. We also need to make the space for social emotional learning for teachers, for boundaries, and for better work-life balance, so that we can promote this beloved profession in a positive way. Remember that this profession has siphoned off thousands of teachers due to burnout (Ballantyne & Retell, 2020; NCES, 2014). Protecting ourselves, sometimes from our own smart phones and the connectivity that it provides, is essential as we shift into a new digital age of learning.

FUTURE RESEARCH DIRECTIONS

This chapter serves as a call to unpack further the concept of connectivity and new ethos stuff within the theoretical framework of New Literacies. This is also a call to address how the mobile phone functions as a platform for online learning and online communication, and how this tool can be leveraged. This chapter gave one positive anecdotal experience of such a model, but more empirical work and information is needed. For example, how many college students use their cells to complete their coursework? Does this change when surveying K-12 students? Does this change when SES is factored in? The notions presented in this chapter speak to the complexity and uncertainty of the current educational landscape. We are in uncharted territory and adding more to the research on best practices during the time of crisis whilst online will be imperative for future generations who may encounter another paradigm shift forced by nature.

REFERENCES

Ballantyne, J., & Retell, J. (2020). Teaching careers: Exploring links between well-being, burnout, self-efficacy, and Praxis shock. *Frontiers in Psychology*, *10*, 2255. doi:10.3389/fpsyg.2019.02255 PMID:32132940

Bambara, C. S., Harbour, C. P., Davies, T. G., & Athey, S. (2009). Delicate engagement: The lived experience of community college students enrolled in high-risk online courses. *Community College Review*, *36*(3), 219–238. doi:10.1177/0091552108327187

Bawa, P. (2016). Retention in online courses: Exploring issues and solutions— a literature review. *SAGE Open*, *6*(1), 1–11. doi:10.1177/2158244015621777

Best Colleges. (2020). *Online education trends report*. Retrieved from https://res.cloudinary.com/highereducation/image/upload/v1584979511/BestColleges.com/edutrends/2020-Online-Trends-in-Education-Report-BestColleges.pdf

Brunzell, T., Stokes, H., & Waters, L. (2016). Trauma-informed positive education: Using positive psychology to strengthen vulnerable students. *Contemporary School Psychology*, *20*(1), 63–83. doi:10.100740688-015-0070-x

Buonomo, I., Fatigante, M., & Fiorelli, C. (2017). Teacher burnout profiles: Risk and protective factors. *The Open Psychology Journal*, *10*(1), 190–201. doi:10.2174/1874350101710010190

Chai, C. S., Ling Koh, J. H., & Tsai, C. (2010). Facilitating preservice teachers' development of technological, pedagogical and content knowledge (TPACK). *Journal of Educational Technology & Society*, *13*(4), 63–73.

Chang, M. L. (2009). An approasial perspective of teacher burnout: Examining the emotional work of teachers. *Educational Psychology Review*, *21*(3), 193–218. doi:10.100710648-009-9106-y

Columbaro, C. H., & Monaghan, N. L. (2009). Employer perceptions of online degrees: A literature review. *Online Journal of Distance Learning Administration*, *12*(1). https://www.westga.edu/~distance/ojdla/spring121/columbaro121.html

Darling-Hammond, L., Zielezinski, M. B., & Goldman, S. (2014). Using technology to support at-risk students' learning. *Stanford Center for Opportunity Policy in Education. Alliance for Excellent Education*. Retrieved from https://edpolicy.stanford.edu/sites/default/files/scope-pub-using-technology-report.pdf

Day, J. (2015). Academic continuity: Staying true to teaching values and objectives in the face of course interruptions. *Teaching & Learning Inquiry: The ISSOTL Journal*, *3*(1), 75–89. doi:10.20343/teachlearninqu.3.1.75

Domitrovich, C., Staley, K. C., Durlak, J. A., & Weissberg, R. P. (2017). Social-emotional competence: An essential factor for promoting positive adjustment and reducing risk in school children. *Child Development*, *88*(2), 1–9. doi:10.1111/cdev.12739 PMID:28213889

Flaherty, C. (2020). Zoom boom. *Inside Higher Ed*. Retrieved from https://www.insidehighered.com/news/2020/04/29/synchronous-instruction-hot-right-now-it-sustainable

Gee, J. P. (1996). *Social linguistics and literacies: Ideology in discourses* (2nd ed.). Falmer.

Glazier, R. A., & Harris, H. S. (2020). *Common traits of the best online and face-to-face classes: Evidence from student surveys*. Retrieved from https://preprints.apsanet.org/engage/api-gateway/apsa/assets/orp/resource/item/5e2f9610cd361a001afed294/original/common-traits-of-the-best-online-and-face-to-face-classes-evidence-from-student-surveys.pdf

He, W. (2013). Examining students' online interaction in a live video streaming environment using data mining and text mining. *Computers in Human Behavior*, *29*(1), 90–102. doi:10.1016/j.chb.2012.07.020

Herrington, A., & Herrington, J. (2007) Authentic mobile learning in higher education. *AARE 2007 International Educational Research Conference*.

Hodges, C., Moore, S., Lockee, B., Trust, T., & Bond, A. (2020). The difference between emergency remote teaching and online learning. *Educause Review*. Retrieved from https://er.educause.edu/articles/2020/3/the-difference-between-emergency-remote-teaching-and-online-learning

Hogan, R. L., & McKnight, M. (2007). Exploring burnout among university online instructors: An initial investigation. *The Internet and Higher Education*, *10*(2), 117–124. doi:10.1016/j.iheduc.2007.03.001

Hwang, K. A., & Yang, C. H. (2009). Automated inattention and fatigue detection system in distance education for elementary school students. *Journal of Educational Technology & Society*, *12*(2), 22–35.

Jaggars, S. S. (2014). Choosing between online and face-to-face courses: Community college student voices. *American Journal of Distance Education*, *28*(1), 27–38. doi:10.1080/08923647.2014.867697

Koehler, M. J., & Mishra, P. (2005). What happens when teachers design educational technology? The development of technological pedagogical content knowledge. *Journal of Educational Computing Research*, *32*(2), 131–152. doi:10.2190/0EW7-01WB-BKHL-QDYV

Koehler, M. J., Mishra, P., & Cain, W. (2013). What is technological pedagogical content knowledge (TPACK)? *Journal of Education*, *193*(3), 13–19. doi:10.1177/002205741319300303

Korkut, S., Dornberger, R., Diwanji, P., Simon, P., & Maerki, M. (2015). Success factors of online learning videos. *International Journal of Interactive Technologies*, *10*(1), 116–182. doi:10.3991/ijim.v9i4.4460

Ladson-Billings, G. (1995). Toward a theory of culturally relevant pedagogy. *American Educational Research Journal*, *32*(3), 465–491. doi:10.3102/00028312032003465

Lankshear, C., & Knobel, M. (2007). Sampling "the New" in new literacies. In M. Knobel & C. Lankshear (Eds.), *A New Literacies Sampler* (pp. 1–24). Peter Lang.

Lee, C. Y., Dickerson, J., & Winslow, J. (2012). An analysis of organizational approaches to online course structures. *Online Journal of Distance Learning Administration*, *15*(1).

Lehtinen, A., Nieminen, P., & Viiri, J. (2016). Preservice teachers' TPACK beliefs and attitudes toward simulations. *Contemporary Issues in Technology & Teacher Education*, *16*(2). https://citejournal.org/volume-16/issue-2-16/science/preservice-teachers-tpack-beliefs-and-attitudes-toward-simulations

Martin, J. (2019). Building relationships and increasing engagement in the virtual classroom: Practical tools for the online instructor. *Journal of Educators Online*, *16*(1). Advance online publication. doi:10.9743/jeo.2019.16.1.9

Mishra, P., & Koehler, M. J. (2006). Technological pedagogical content knowledge: A framework for teacher knowledge. *Teachers College Record*, *108*(6), 1017–1054. doi:10.1111/j.1467-9620.2006.00684.x

National Center for Education Statistics. (2014). *Teacher attrition and mobility: Results from the 2012–13 teacher follow-up survey* (NCES 2014-077). Author.

National Council of Teachers of English. (2018). *Beliefs for integrating technology into the English Language Arts classroom.* Retrieved from https://ncte.org/statement/beliefs-technology-preparation-english-teachers/

Oddone, K., Hughes, H., & Lupton, M. (2019). Teachers as connected professionals: A model to support professional learning through personal learning networks. *International Review of Research in Open and Distributed Learning, 20*(3). Advance online publication. doi:10.19173/irrodl.v20i4.4082

Orlando, J. (2014). Veteran teachers and technology: Change fatigue and knowledge insecurity practice. *Teachers and Teaching, 20*(4), 437–439. doi:10.1080/13540602.2014.881644

Paris, D. (2012). Culturally sustaining pedagogy: A needed change in stance, terminology, and practice. *Educational Researcher, 41*(3), 93–97. doi:10.3102/0013189X12441244

Philip, R. T. (2006). *Engaging 'tweens and teens: A brain compatible approach to reading middle and high school students.* Corwin.

Prensky, M. (2012). *From digital natives to digital wisdom: Hopeful essays for 21st century education.* Corwin. doi:10.4135/9781483387765

Ravitch, D. (2014). *Reign of error: The hoax of the privatization movement and the danger to America's public school.* Vintage Books.

Regan, K., Ermenova, A., Baker, P., Jerome, M. K., Spencer, V., Lawson, H., & Werner, T. (2012). Experiences of instructors in online environments: Identity and regulating emotions. *Internet and Higher Education, 15*(3), 204–212. doi:10.1016/j.iheduc.2011.12.001

Rybakova, K. (2020). Humanizing online assessment: Using screencasting as a multimedia feedback tool for first generation college students. In J. Lantz (Ed.), *Handbook of research on integrating digital technology with literacy pedagogies.* doi:10.4018/978-1-7998-0246-4.ch022

Rybakova, K., Rice, M., Moran, C., Zucker, L., McGrail, E., Mcdermott, M., Loomis, S., Gerber, H., Piotrowski, A., Garcia, M., Gibbons, T., & Marlatt, R. (2019). A long arc bending towards equity: Tracing almost 20 years of ELA teaching trends inCITE. *Contemporary Issues in Technology & Teacher Education, 19*(4).

Scheg, A. G. (2014). *Reforming teacher education for online pedagogy development.* IGI Global. doi:10.4018/978-1-4666-5055-8

Schrage, M. (2001). *The relationship revolution*. Retrieved from seedwiki.com/wiki/YiTan/TheRelationshipRevolution.html

Scott, L. A., Temple, P., & Marshall, D. (2015). UDL in online college coursework: Insights of infusion and educator preparedness. *Online Learning*, *19*(5), 99–119. doi:10.24059/olj.v19i5.623

Shulman, L. S. (1986). Those who understand: Knowledge growth in teaching. *Educational Researcher*, *15*(2), 4–14. doi:10.3102/0013189X015002004

Smith, A. (2015). US Smartphone use in 2015. *Pew Research Group*. Retrieved from https://www.pewresearch.org/internet/2015/04/01/us-smartphone-use-in-2015/

Smith, T. (2020). *The invisible blizzard and the importance of e-learning*. Retrieved from https://thehill.com/blogs/congress-blog/education/489752-the-invisible-blizzard-and-the-importance-of-e-learning

Supiano, B. (2020). 'Zoomed out:' Why live teaching isn't always the best. *The Chronicle*. Retrieved from https://www.chronicle.com/article/Zoomed-Out-Why/248401

Thorton, P., & Houser, C. (2004). *Using mobile phones in education*. Retrieved from https://www.it.iitb.ac.in/~vijaya/ticet/dokuwiki/media/01281326.pdf

Tondeur, J., Scherer, R., Siddiq, F., & Baran, E. (2017). A comprehensive investigation of TPACK within preservice teachers' ICT profiles: Mind the gap! *Australasian Journal of Educational Technology*, *33*(3), 46–60. doi:10.14742/ajet.3504

Tondeur, J., Scherer, R., Siddiq, F., & Baran, E. (2019). Strategies to prepare pre-service teachers for Technological Pedagogical Content Knowledge (TPACK): A mixed-method study. *Educational Technology Research and Development*. Advance online publication. doi:10.100711423-019-09692-1

Valtonen, T., Sointu, E., Kukkonen, J., Kontkanen, S., Lambert, M. C., & Makitalo-Seigl, K. (2017). TPACK updated to measure pre-service teachers' twenty-first century skills. *Australasian Journal of Educational Technology*, *33*(3), 15–31. doi:10.14742/ajet.3518

Vasquez, H. (2020). What if we...don't return to school as usual. *National Equity Project*. Retrieved from https://medium.com/national-equity-project/what-if-we-dont-return-to-school-as-usual-4aceb5227df5

Whillier, S., & Lystad, R. P. (2012). The effect of face-to-face teaching on student knowledge and satisfaction in an undergraduate neuroanatomy course. *Anatomical Sciences Education*, *6*(4), 239–245. doi:10.1002/ase.1338 PMID:23225606

Windschitl, M. (2002). Framing constructivism as the negotiation of dilemmas: An analysis of the conceptual, pedagogical, cultural, and political challenges facing teachers. *Review of Educational Research*, *72*(2), 131–175. doi:10.3102/00346543072002131

Chapter 5
Decriminalizing Cell Phones: Before and After the Pandemic

Glenn Henry Rhoades
Gwinnett County Public Schools, USA

ABSTRACT

The purpose of this chapter is to discuss cell phones in the classroom before and after the pandemic. The author discusses the problematic history of cell phones in the classroom, and how teachers have struggled and fought against them, many times outright banning cell phones. Instead of this approach, the case is made for the need for students to learn how to use them, and why they are so useful in the classroom for both formative assessment and feedback. Next, this chapter discusses how the author leveraged cell phones during the period of crisis instruction at the end of the 2019-2020 school year. The author was able to launch and successfully complete a unit that combined social justice themes, graphic novels, and podcasting – all of which utilizing cell phones. Finally, specific tools, resources, and strategies are shared and discussed that were used during this time, with recommendations for the future of education no matter how it may look.

INTRODUCTION

A Problematic History

There is a connection between the way teachers conceptualize their role in managing student behavior and their perspective on the purpose and function of cellular phones in the classroom. From the first cell phone that crossed the threshold into the classroom, safely stowed in a pocket, teachers have been asking the question of

DOI: 10.4018/978-1-7998-5805-8.ch005

what to do with these devices. Teachers are creative creatures by nature: this has produced some unique contraptions to help remove them from the idle hands (or hands wishing to be idle) of their students.

One of these contraptions was an outlet rental scheme. They were popularized in about 2014. There was be a power-strip or three plugged into outlets around the room where students could plug in, leaving their phones on the wall, and twenty-five cents in a jar. When this was done for charity, I thought it was a great idea, though a few of my colleagues charged students for outright profit. Teachers had discovered that giving students a charging station would help students keep their phones off their desks and out of reach. This gave students a "choice" about what to do with their phones – but the message was clear: they were unwanted.

In schools where cell phones have become illegal in classrooms, students are positioned as offenders and law breakers. Mupinga (2017) found that many schools are switching to Bring Your Own Device (BYOD) or Bring Your Own Technology (BYOT). This is a system that lessens the technology gap but does not hold the school systems accountable for one-to-one devices. Even with these initiatives, high schools still have policies to deter their use in the classroom. While many schools had these listed on their websites, Mupinga (2017) surmised that the schools that were silent on their policies might be so out of fear of seeming unprogressive in an age where cell phones are normalized in society (p.71). In their study, a small sampling of 27 high schools, 66% had policies that no cell phones were to be seen during school hours and students must always keep them in their lockers. My own school district in Georgia, despite being BYOD, has policies restricting cell phones in individual classrooms.

My district is one of the largest public-school systems in the country and serves over one-hundred-and-fifty-thousand students across twenty clusters. Every school's front door proudly displays the BYOD sticker, while most classrooms in my county use restrictive systems of management to keep them sometimes literally locked away under lock and key. In classrooms like these, cell phones are only thought of in terms of behavior management and policies on the syllabus. I have worked in two different high schools in our district over the last five years, but the rhetoric involving cell phones in the classroom has remained the same – "lock them up."

Like most Americans, when teachers see a rule being broken, they institutionalize and incarcerate. According to Wendy and Sawyer (2018), the United States incarcerates six-hundred-and-ninety-eight Americans for every one-hundred-thousand citizens. This is the highest rate in the world. If twenty-three states were countries, they would have higher incarceration rates than any other country on the planet. America solves problems by putting them behind bars. This is no different for children. Fabelo et al. (2011) found that sixty percent of students between grades seven and twelve were suspended or expelled at least once with significant increases in repeating grades, dropout rates, and gang activity – all of which leads to higher rates of incarceration. Teachers, seeing cell phones as problems, do the same to cell devices creating *phone jails*. These are not always hinged boxes (I have seen some that actually have bars). Using Amazon.com to cheaply order closet organizers and bolt them to the brickwork, teachers can number these pockets for corresponding students to drop their devices into, and possibly retrieve them if the lesson requires technology. Cheong et al. (2012) found that "…[educators] ambivalent reactions to digital media management might be rooted in the same complex practices they enact to maintain their authority, leading to tensions in digital media use and evaluation" (pp. 1-20). Phone jails, as they are lovingly called, are lauded throughout faculty meetings and development sessions all over the country. The proponents of this incarcerate state would attempt to kill me with their eyes whenever I would bring up how much I love cell phones in the classroom.

At best, cell phones get used in my classroom daily, at least once. They are an integral part of creation, assessment, and the learning we do collaboratively. At worst, students work on the new skill of learning how to manage their technology themselves. We had a graduate, some years back, who went off to work for a major corporation out of college: a six-figure job. This young man was let go in the first month of employment for his blatant, laissez faire attitude with his cell phone during a board meeting. Unfortunately, self-management is essential, in all things, and cannot be taught without experimentation, failure, strategies, and coping mechanisms. Both Cheong et al. (2016) and Langford et al. (2016) make the case for educators to train students rather than banning technology. Students need the opportunity, especially with technology, and these experiential teachers for success in self-management. Despite this, some schools in the county like, Mateo High School, are moving towards systems like mechanized pouches to "lock up" student cell phone use for the entire day (Woo, 2019). Compliance has never been my goal or dream for learners in our classroom. Besides, students would find something else to distract themselves with instead of doing their work. Perhaps this is exactly why more work gets done, despite the phones, than in many classes I have observed with a no-phone-policy. Over time, we practice giving ourselves breaks throughout our class period to check our phones, change the songs on our playlists, and to check ourselves and decide that we should finish the current paragraph before picking up our devices. It is a process, but something I would rather they struggle with in our classes than deny the opportunity for growth. There are also the obvious benefits for how they enhance our lessons and allow for collaboration.

This chapter will discuss how cell phones can be used with formative assessment and feedback. Next, I will examine how things changed with cell phones as we shifted into pandemic and crisis instruction. I will discuss the challenges students had and ways that we used cell phones to navigate through the challenging times in the fourth quarter of the 2019 academic year where we (as a class) tackled podcasting, social justice, and graphic novels. Finally, I will examine specific tools that helped us to achieve the best end to the school year as possible. Cell phones can help create magic.

BACKGROUND

Cell Phone Magic in Formative Assessment

With cell phones, I like to think of myself as a (mad?) scientist: always experimenting with what might work to help students learn. We have been experimenting in our classroom with both policies and applications. When I started teaching, Kahoot (http://www.kahoot.com) was the rage, and still, in my darkest moments, I can still hear the theme song playing. Many other games have since sprung up; my favorite being Quizizz (http://www.quizizz.com). Using gaming platforms for formative assessment has been a real win for my teaching, regardless of the platform. If teaching can be thought of as a cycle, one step that is often missed is the formative assessment. *If* the formative step is taken, what are teachers doing with this data? How is assessment driving future instruction? These are two questions I often ask in my own professional learning community (PLC). Technology can help with the answer to these questions. While technology is just a tool, and not the result, lesson, or goal, one of the biggest reasons I have failed to do formative assessment is time. Grading takes time. Quiz style tools on cell phones can give teachers feedback on standards-based questioning – no laptop cart required. Another way teachers can reclaim time on formative assessments is through feedback.

When considering what helps students grow in their writing and development, feedback matters more than grades. Grades represent the terminal and inevitable result of work completed. The longer teachers can abstain from grading something, the longer a student will continue to work and develop it. I started out in the classroom giving students temporary grades on their writing, expressing to them that they could revise the writing for full credit. An amazing thing happened: none of them every resubmitted their papers. Or, if there were one or two, they were from students who already earned an A on my carefully crafted grading rubric (you know, the one designed to have as little subjectivity as possible). Students equate grades with finality for more reasons than there is time to unpack here. What matters is that teachers do not grade less frequently, but we offer feedback with greater fidelity and frequency. Kim (2018) found that with audio-visual feedback (AVF) students not only performed better on writing assignments throughout the semester, but also had more motivation. Her research also supported a stronger bond between learners and their teacher (p. 47). Teachers (using cell phones) can leave students audio and/

or visual feedback embedded or recorded for students. Throughout the COVID-19 pandemic, I have left hours of AVF feedback for students that was recorded while chasing my toddler around the house and neighborhood. Students were able to listen to my voice or even see me while I commented directly on their writing; most of my recordings were made with my cell phone. While cell phones can seem like a panacea, they only offer us tools. In a conversation with a young adult author and friend, Jackson Pierce, she explained that "If our result with feedback is to only make a writer realize that they are a terrible writer, we have failed them." There are tools to help offer continuous feedback, collaboration, and growth. Like all teacher-tech, teachers must learn how to do the moves before moving to digital. Understand your goals for your students first, and then you can select a tool to meet those targets.

When I want my students to grow as writers, I need a tool that will help them work as a writer, in a community of writers, and receive feedback on their writing frequently. Ultimately, this has become how I assess their learning: I examine their work. Using Google Drive, teachers can have students work in shared folders to form their "groups" and work collaboratively on documents together or give feedback on each other's writing when working independently. A key tip for teachers is to set up a writing folder with shared permissions for everyone in the group so everyone has access, especially the teacher. While the Google Suite can be difficult to use on cell devices, phones are getting bigger. Students can use voice-to-text to type, and then go in and edit their writing with a critical eye later. As a teacher, I give students access to my writing as well, as I write alongside them and solicit their feedback as well as part of my own writing process.

The ability for technology to help build writing communities moves the cell phone far beyond simple quiz apps and gameshows. When I work with technology, I first think about what I want to accomplish with the tool, then I think about how the tool can support the teaching and learning. If the tool does not fit, then I use something else. In this way, I attempt to make technology adapt to the needs of our classroom. Jones and Hafner (2012) published *Understanding Digital Literacies*, a fantastic book on the way that technology becomes a way to mediate information, but it is not always used as it was intended.

Pandemic Technology

Despite recent pandemics and acts of terror, teachers and school systems were not prepared for long-term school closures. Hodges et al. (2020) argues that what we experienced in this shift was not actually on-line learning, but "emergency remote teaching" (para. 1). This is significant because many educators are mislabelling what occurred out of necessity for what online instruction is: "careful instructional design and planning, using a systematic model for design and development" (Hodges et al.,

2020, para. 8). Migrating classrooms to online spaces was rapid, unplanned, and constantly evolving. This caused for the crisis response to be vastly different from true online learning, with many additional constraints beyond an online environment existing during normal conditions. My own school system pivoted multiple times with parents and the community on what the expectations would be for student learners. Keep in mind, this involved over 10,000 teachers and support staff and nearly 180,000 students. I was teaching high school – tenth grade specifically. Initially, we were told to grade normally. Several weeks in, we were told that students should not fail any assignment they attempt. Finally, we were told that at the end of the semester we would input whichever grade was higher: either their final average, or their average before the quarantine started.

During the pandemic, we did something ambitious: we launched a podcasting unit focused on social justice topics with graphic novels as mentor texts. We did not rely on Zoom meetings, scheduled class times, or being tethered to computers. We used our cell phones for nearly everything. The catch? None of my students had ever made podcasts, and many had never read graphic novels. I wanted to do something that would be challenging but students would feel supported. Teaching engaging content in engaging ways has always been the secret to my classroom and keeping students plugged in, and I knew with the pandemic and the instantaneous shift to online (crisis) education I would need these superpowers more than ever. In the first week, I taught them how to use the podcasting app on their cell phones and got them started with their graphic novels. I told them to go outside; we were not stuck in a classroom anymore, so work in the fresh air! We built book groups, started doing discussion posts, and picking the topic we would like to focus on in our podcasts. Students chose everything from racism to equal access to education.

A Lofty Goal: Podcasting in a Pandemic

When we were told on March 13, 2020, that schools would close for two weeks while our local government and county could evaluate next steps, I knew that things had to immediately change. Luckily, we were wrapping up a unit of study, and about to begin with something fresh after spring break, which thankfully followed the two weeks of round-one of closing school in my district. I made a snap decision to start a unit that was a huge success the previous year. It was centered on the students' lived experiences with social justice and utilized graphic novels (also following social justice themes), student sourced news articles, and podcasting. I knew this would work in the classroom, but I was not sure about during this crisis. There would be challenges, but of course, there already were so many. I knew that technology, specifically cell phones, could be a part of this solution as long I focused on solutions from the beginning. Cell phones allowed students to work where they wanted when they wanted. At a time when we were isolated, I wanted them to feel connected.

FINDINGS

Reactions to Challenges

Unpopular opinion: many students do not like using technology in the classroom just because it is an opportunity to do assignments or tasks digitally. While this opinion is supported by Phillip and Garcia (2015), I have had countless conversations with my own students who have anecdotally reminded me of this hard-won truth. All students, at times, struggle with technology. One of the most important steps to helping students to overcome their challenges is to identify what misconceptions we hold as educators before we even begin. We assume, wrongly, that all kids are technology wizards. The International Association for the Evaluation of Educational Achievement (IAE) released *The International Computer and Information Literacy Study* (2018) that examined twelve different countries educational systems and learners' skills with technology. The results suggest students will not naturally develop high-end skills and competencies. In a statement released by the IAE (2018) regarding the results of the report, Dirk Hastedt, the executive director of the IAE, stated, "It is essential that young people are taught these skills at schools, and that their teachers are well supported in delivering this bedrock of modern education." The older we get and the newer the technology is, the more we seem to make this assumption. The latest social media craze seems so inaccessible to me, and when I see students executing flawlessly on a new platform it is easy to think that they must have inherit gifts with technology.

We also (wrongly) assume that since students enjoy using technology to make Tik Toks, Instagram posts, and other forms of capturing themselves creatively through their cell phones that they will enjoy doing it for an educational purpose. Phillip and Garcia (2015) found that "youth interest is not tied to the device" but rather the "activities that the device facilitates" (p. 681). Even if an academic task is similar to an activity that students enjoy outside of the classroom, it does not mean that they will find enjoyment or easy success in performing the academic task. Teachers must not assume that students will be attracted to a task simply because they are able to use their phones or technology. The researchers add, "...adult assumptions about youth interests in new technologies and their neglect of the situated social meanings of these devices often occlude meaningful learning in schools despite enormous investments of time and money" (Phillip & Garcia, 2015, p. 686). All our adult excitement does not transfer to student interest, engagement, or success. Students, especially during a pandemic, are going to have challenges with all three.

Just because activities or tasks were to be performed on technology, it does not mean that students will stay engaged. Students in Phillip and Garcia's (2015) study reported that the devices they were required to use did not cause students to focus or engage – that these were naive assumptions (p. 693). When I designed my podcasting unit, I tried to first understand my misconceptions and anticipate challenges. I knew that no single aspect of our project (especially during quarantine) would ensure focus or engagement. Student choice in reading and the direction of their podcasts, real world tools and tasks, and the opportunity to engage with their peers was a blend I was trying to create to overcome the quagmire of our crisis instructional period. For many students, we were successful, but there were still challenges.

SUGGESTIONS FOR PRACTICE

Tricks of the Trade – Asynchronous Communication

One of the ways that I overcame challenges was creating a chart that students could comment on. We called it the "muddiest point chart" – something stolen from English Studies in the Schools, an online graduate level course I took with Dr. Jennifer Dail, a professor of English Education at Kennesaw State University in Georgia. The chart, created on a Google Doc, enables students to ask questions, but also for other students to respond. I tell my students upfront that they often have better solutions to problems than I do. The teacher can also respond, but I let them know it might take me some time to see their questions, so if they notice a student question they should go ahead and try to help. This empowers students to take ownership of the classroom and decenters myself from the being with all the answers. This chart became a place for a lot more than just questions during our podcasting adventure.

While many students engaged with the unit, especially the graphic novels, there were some students who continuously struggled with technology. One student decided to lash out against the unit and myself instead of using the chart to ask questions. The question they did ask was why they could not simply be assigned worksheets. They stated that they hated podcasting, did not understand how to do it, and felt that it was, in summary, doing too much. I knew that my response was crucial, and if I responded with anger then I would risk losing them further. I also knew that they had chosen a very public forum to express their frustration – I did not think this was a coincidence. I could have just deleted their response, but I left it up instead. I made a series of help videos that were stripped down versions of the longer tutorials I had been posting. I tried to keep the time down to just a couple minutes and tried to have as few steps as possible. Privately I reached out to the student via email and tried to make myself available via videoconferencing. I was able to help many students overcome their challenges.

Overcoming Obstacles

Modeling, and doing the work I asked my students to do alongside them helped the most. I completed every assignment or step of the process to better understand what I was asking my students to do. This allowed me to scaffold accordingly based on student need as I had to unpack my own steps. I was also able to record myself doing each step and provide a final product. Many students struggled with the tools as well as the task. I leaned heavily on student voices, and even asked several students to become leaders in their groups to help others when they became stuck by a technological hurdle. Some students found it easier to work in groups and share the load, but others requested to work individually. I had to be flexible if I wanted to help students overcome their challenges.

There were many obstacles for students to navigate. Some families had only one device but four siblings who needed to get schoolwork completed. Some students did not have high-speed internet. When parents became unemployed, some students became the breadwinners of their family. I had a student who wrote me to let me know that they would be taking my final, but was worried about timing because they would have to complete the multiple choice exam on their cellphone during their lunchbreak at their second job. During this crisis, some students were lost, but some students chose to respond to this adversity by finding their way back.

Lost and Found

Before Covid-19, James would come into my classroom every day and put his head down on the desk. He demonstrated just how much he didn't want to be in my room with body language, and his too-loud headphones that he knew would be a conversation. Every day we'd do the same dance - I'd ask him to take his headphones out, and he'd protest and slump, and sigh. Some days, his behaviors would be more social, attempting to recruit others in his group to buy in to how I was being unreasonable or ridiculous. I tried hallway conversations, after-class conversations, before class conversations, and anything I could think of to try to build a relationship. Reflecting back, it was really more about managing his behavior.

After moving to learning on a cell device, James participated in the first week of class. He completed the two or three introductory assignments, and everything appeared like he would be participating in digital learning. By week two, I stopped hearing from him completely. Nothing: cold turkey, he was gone. I did what I had always done before in class, I reached out to him to talk. Our hallway conversation looked a little different, as it was now over email. I emailed him my concerns and attempted to address his behaviors - but I still wasn't listening. I wasn't taking the time to try to get to know him, his situation, or his motivations for why he was resistant and disconnected.

This all changed one night when he sent me an email. It was nearly one in the morning, and I was playing Animal Crossing in bed on my Nintendo Switch. The only light came from my small screen, with my perfect island villagers. This game, it was my safe spot and my escape during quarantine. The email from James brought me back to reality and asked me into his reality. At first, I did not read it that way. I did not read his words as the cry for help they were.

His email was filled with sentences about how he hated the work I was asking him to do, and how unfair it was that it was so hard. He wanted to know why we could not just read some articles and write about them. Podcasting would be hard, and he was not interested in trying. Couldn't he just pass without having to work hard? These sentiments stung, in some ways, and in others, they made me laugh. I wanted to brush them off without thinking deeply, feeling, or caring. That would take much more work. I took a breath, and I thought.

In that dark room, I had a small epiphany. I realized that it must have been hard for James to write that email. In fact, it was two paragraphs, and even though he was doing so aggressively, he had to admit that he was struggling. He felt overwhelmed. Things felt impossible, and he did not see any other way out of the hole he was in other than writing an email like this. As adults, we can choose how we communicate. In my experience, young people often communicate with the first and most clear mode available. They do not stop to think about their message and if it can be said another way. Knowing this, it should be clear how desperate his email was - and not something I interpreted as a personal attack. I could feel my gears shifting.

I chose to, for perhaps the first time, listen to his words. I reread the email. Then I read it a third time. Each time, I tried to imagine how he was feeling when he wrote it. I was reminding myself of what I already knew: different students have varying degrees of emotional maturity. If this was the only way he knew how to communicate and engage, this is where I had to meet him. I asked him what I could to help.

We spent the rest of the semester emailing back and forth via cell devices. We kept the dialogue open. There were times he would get frustrated - but he would tell me. He almost gave up a few times. There were some goals that he was not able to meet, like collaborating and making a podcast as part of a team. However, he did make several small episodes himself, conduct an interview, and make a full-length episode on his own. He thanked me, many times, for not giving up on him. He called me a great teacher, even thanking me on his podcast. The truth is, I wasn't a great teacher when I started with James. I learned so much because of our relationship: he helped me to become a better teacher when I listened to what he needed.

Without cell phones, could this have happened in the classroom where our routine was so ingrained and established? With thirty-five other students in his class, could I have ever given him the attention that he needed or stopped long enough to care about him? The answer is that yes, it should have. I am hopeful that this will be the answer when we return to school in the fall because this is the teacher that other students like James will need. I want to always be that teacher - the one who listens, but I honestly think that our digital environment helped to disrupt our norms and create space for this work to be done between the two of us. It continued to facilitate this differentiated instruction by allowing the time for me to create videos for him personally every day. We spoke more virtually than we ever did in the classroom. James taught me just as much last year as I taught him. Our lessons could not start until we were quarantined.

Digital Tools for Online Instruction

Teachers are discovering many new tools for cell phones (most of them are not actually new at all) that they can use to build community in the classroom, give students multiple opportunities for success, and demonstrate knowledge and growth. It is best not to introduce too many tools too quickly; teachers need to select a few tools for consistent student use and then teach their class how to use them. Miller et al. (2020), in an article for middle grades students, raises awareness about three such tools: Padlet (http://www.padlet.com); Libby (https://www.overdrive.com/apps/libby); and Anchor (http://www.anchor.fm). In crisis instruction, restoring access to identity, resources, and community are essential.

Table 1. Three Digital Tools for Online Instruction

Padlet	Libby	Anchor.FM
Creates a board where students can make posts, much like an electronic corkboard. With one click, students create a post-it note style text box that they can type in and post on the board or even integrate images, memes, and .gifs. Students can comment, "like" and "heart" responses.	An app that works on cell devices to allow students to check out books through library systems. Sorted multiple ways, students can explore books before committing. Vast selection available of new releases as well!	The best podcasting app and platform available for students in the classroom. This app has incredible functionality on cell phones – more features than using it through the web. Students can record in groups on the same podcast, integrate music and effects, and edit all in one app.
Web Application http://www.padlet.com	Free- Android and Apple App https://www.overdrive.com/apps/libby Registration with a library card	Free – Android and Apple App http://www.anchor.fm

Padlet allows for the curation of resources and sharing of information from both students and teachers. Miller et al. (2020) describes how the entire school and community can come together to discuss book recommendations (p. 60). In my classroom we used Padlet on our phones to help build our new classroom guidelines where students reported their needs from their teacher, their classmates, and themselves. One weakness, not discussed in the article, is that this tool does not always work well on cell phones and can cause inequity if students do not have access to a computer. It does allow for multiple modes of response, as students can use images and text to mediate their responses. While Padlet is a great tool for book reviews, if students do not have access to books in the first place it becomes a moot point. We also used this tool when podcasting to help organize our thinking, post links to our podcasts, and respond and give feedback to each other. We engaged in a writing community, and a podcasting community: we gave each other glows and grows throughout the remainder of the year. Through Padlet, students were creating for each other more than they were creating for the teacher.

Libby is a tool that students can use to check out eBooks from home. Getting a library card, or even accessing a library can be impossible for some students. Many libraries require an adult with identification to set up an account for a minor. Libby allows students to quickly create accounts and access books which teachers can use to create book groups or implement independent reading. In my classroom last Spring, students were unable to access books on their own, and Libby changed the outcome in my classroom. Currently, most local libraries allow students to create temporary accounts with their school identification in lieu of physically accessing a library and attempting to set up an account. It takes some experimentation, and sometimes collaboration with local libraries, but the end result is access to thousands of high-quality young adult literature titles. Teachers can use this resource with cell phones to help create book groups or thematic lists, which can help groups form literature circles or even create a podcast that is tied to the themes in the student reading.

Podcasting was a major component in the last quarter during the pandemic. This is not something that I had previously done with my students, and it would have been impossible if not for a tool like Anchor. Anchor is a podcasting application that can be accessed on the web or through a cell phone. Students' voices gain access to the world while they learn how to engage with a global audience on the issues that are important to them. During the pandemic, I had students do an audio journal and daily reflection that allowed classmates to share in their experiences and feel less isolated. Through the app, they were able to form groups and create a shared podcast to respond to the novels they were reading. Miller et al. (2020) explained, "Anchor takes the complexity and anxiety out of podcasting and allows kids to do what they want to do: make an awesome show" (p. 61). My students were able to engage with the whole world across all major podcasting platforms with Anchor.

We started small, with micro-projects and goals that were obtainable. I slowly added in new skills and direction, and eventually they produced a full episode that integrated a chosen social justice theme found in their graphic novels, local current events involving that theme, and their own lived experiences. Most students used little more than their own cell phones.

CONCLUSION

Cell phones have a problematic history, as many teachers see them as distractions or another annoyance or disruption that must be controlled or policed. School systems create rules and policies that create a battleground over handheld technology that pits teachers against their classes. The way that educators conceptualize their role in the classroom can affect the outcome, and possibly prevent a war in the first place. At the very least, cell phones are just a tool, like all technology. The practices that a teacher has based on their self-conceptualizations and pedagogical philosophy will determine how cell phones will be used and the success that will hopefully be found. Situating cell phones as problematic or as a panacea misses the fundamental truth of what matters in education: the needs of your students. Ultimately, with distance learning or crisis education - what your students need is you.

As we move back into classrooms this year, mandatory Zoom classes with synchronous learning, and bell schedules, what bothers me the most is that we might be moving farther away from the magic of cell phones. This idea of space: social distancing, school spaces, classrooms, can become limited by the technology we impose and enforce on our students. Instead of being liberating, it becomes another mechanism for control and compliance. The freedom that cell phones offer is asynchronous and roaming. Students can work in any space they would like and collaborate on their terms with their own devices. A Zoom window is more like something from Phillip K. Dick's *A Scanner Darkly* (1977); it is a way for teachers to bring the classroom and all of the rules aforementioned into the homes of our learners. I have heard of teachers policing cell phones through their Zoom meetings while children are at their dining room tables.

Cell phones, more than ever, are a pathway to student expression, freedom, and engagement. As students return to schools, they will bring cell phones. The pandemic has disrupted so much in our educational systems and policies. We learned to depend on cell phones during the period of crisis instruction with the COVID-19 pandemic. With the need to keep students separated, but still collaborating, the potential for these devices to continue to play a strong role in the classroom is evident. What remains to be seen is how school systems and teachers will choose to position digital technology in the classroom.

REFERENCES

Cheong, P. H., Martin, J. N., & Macfadyen, L. (2012). Mediated intercultural communication matters: Understanding new media, dialectics and social change. In P. H. Cheong, J. N. Martin, & L. Macfadyen (Eds.), *New media and intercultural communication: Identity, community and politics* (pp. 1–20). Peter Lang.

Cheong, P. H., Shuter, R., & Suwinyattichaiporn, T. (2016). Managing student digital distractions and hyperconnectivity: Communication strategies and challenges for professorial authority. *Communication Education*, *65*(3), 272–289. doi:10.1080/03634523.2016.1159317

Fabelo, T., Thompson, M. D., Plotkin, M., Carmichael, D., Marchbanks, M. P., III, & Booth, E. A. (2011, July). *Breaking Schools' Rules: A Statewide Study of How School Discipline Relates to Students' Success and Juvenile Justice Involvement*. The Justice Center. https://knowledgecenter.csg.org/kc/system/files/Breaking_School_Rules.pdf

Hodges, C., Moore, S., Lockee, B., Trust, T., & Bond, A. (2020, March 27). The difference between emergency remote teaching and online learning. *EDUCAUSEreview*. https://er.educause.edu/articles/2020/3/the-difference-between-emergency-remote-teaching-and-online-learning

International Association for the Evaluation of Educational Achievement. (2018). *Preparing For Life In A Digital World IEA International Computer and Information Literacy Study 2018 International Report*. Springer Publishing. https://www.iea.nl/sites/default/files/2020-04/IEA%20International%20Computer%20and%20Information%20Literacy%20Study%202018%20International%20Report.pdf

International Association for the Evaluation of Educational Achievement. (2018). *ICILS 2018 Results | IEA*. IEA. https://www.iea.nl/news-events/news/icils-2018-results

Jones, R. (2012). *Understanding Digital Literacies: A Practical Introduction* (1st ed.). Routledge. doi:10.4324/9780203095317

Kim, V. (2018). Technology-Enhanced Feedback on Student Writing in the English-Medium Instruction Classroom. *English Teaching*, *73*(4), 29–53. doi:10.15858/engtea.73.4.201812.29

Langford, S., Narayan, A., & Von Glahn, N. (2016). Revisiting the Technology and Student Learning Debates: Critical Issues and Multiple Perspectives. *Transformative Dialogues: Teaching & Learning Journal*, *9*(2), 1–15.

Miller, D., Sharp, C., Minnich, C., & Sokolowski, K. (2018). Digital tools you need to know. *Voices from the Middle*, *25*(4), 60–62. https://secure.ncte.org/library/NCTEFiles/Resources/Journals/VM/0254-may2018/VM0254Notes.pdf?_ga=2.235130433.1521800320.1594835033-855434546.1587059887

Mupinga, D. M. (2017). School-wide and Classroom Policies on the Use of Mobile Technologies: An Exploratory Study. *The Journal of Technology Studies*, *43*(2), 70–79. doi:10.21061/jots.v43i2.a.2

Philip, T. M., & Garcia, A. (2015). Schooling Mobile Phones: Assumptions About Proximal Benefits, the Challenges of Shifting Meanings, and the Politics of Teaching. *Educational Policy*, *29*(4), 676–707. doi:10.1177/0895904813518105

Wagner, P., & Sawyer, W. (2018, June). *States of Incarceration: The Global Context 2018*. Prison Policy Initiative. https://www.prisonpolicy.org/global/2018.html

Woo, E. (2019, August 19). *Sick of distracted students? Some schools have started locking up their phones*. The Mercury News. https://www.mercurynews.com/2019/08/19/sick-of-distracted-students-some-schools-have-started-locking-up-their-phones/

Chapter 6
Early Childhood Teachers' Usage of Mobile Phones in English Language Arts Classrooms in Nigeria:
Challenges and Prospects

Hannah O. Ajayi
Obafemi Awolowo University, Nigeria

Johnson O. Okewole
Obafemi Awolowo University, Nigeria

Joshua O. Salami
Obafemi Awolowo University, Nigeria

ABSTRACT

The study explored the use of mobile phones by the early childhood teachers of English language arts (ELA) in Nigeria. Descriptive survey design was used using an online survey to assess early childhood teachers' use of the mobile phone in their classrooms. Ninety-eight teachers who responded to the instrument online formed the sample for the study. The instrument entitled Mobile Phones in ELA Classrooms' Questionnaire (MP-ELA-CQ) was used to collect data for the study. Data were analyzed using percentage and Pearson Moment Correlation Coefficients. Results indicated that teachers—both preservice and in-service—need regular training in technology and education to help them effectively utilize mobile phones in their classrooms.

DOI: 10.4018/978-1-7998-5805-8.ch006

INTRODUCTION

English Language Arts (ELA) occupy a prominent place in the academic success of learners. There is no school subject that is not connected to ELA. Learners must listen to the teacher in every subject, employ speaking skills to express their understanding of the content areas, read the subject and write certain information about the subject before gaining mastery. Besides, the mastery of ELA skills is vital for lifelong learning and the determinants of a quality education being advocated in the global agenda of Sustainable development Goals (SDGs), especially Goal 4. It is, therefore, imperative that all students—and especially those in Nigeria--be proficient in ELA, not only for academic performance or lifelong learning but also for the attainment of SDGs in the country by 2030.

ELA skills comprise listening, speaking, reading and writing. In the Nigerian system, ELA is incorporated into the English language or English language studies at the elementary and junior high school. Considering the importance of the skills to other school subjects and to life, (and more importantly that English in Nigeria is the official language of governance, politics, religion, business transactions, religion and education), it makes it more imperative to give attention to teachers' instructional procedures in the teaching of these skills to enhance proficiency among the pupils. This is because the strategies or methods of teaching can either positively or negatively influence learners' performance. Several studies have posited that the methods or techniques employed by teachers have a great impact on the performance of the learners (Asikhia 2010, Guloba, Wokadala, & Bategeka, 2010; Ganyaupfu, 2013; Njoroge et al., 2014). In light of this, teachers' methods that incorporate instructional devices is a germane issue that must not be glossed over--especially in the ELA classrooms. This chapter reports on the results of a survey of mobile phone use among early childhood teachers in Nigeria.

BACKGROUND

To date, it has been pointed out that many pupils are deficient in language skills, both in their first and second languages. This deficiency might be connected with the teachers' instructional strategies, as some studies have discovered (Ajayi, 2006; Okewole, Odejobi, & Ajayi, 2018; Okewole, 2016; Saheed, 2019; Salami, 2019). Critical attention is expected to be given to the instructional process to guide against what Stanovich (1986) refers to as the "Matthew effect," not only in reading but also other aspects of ELA. Studies indicate that various strategies have been employed to enhance language skills; however, there is no clear-cut study to show that the most common technological device, which is the mobile phone, has been employed in classrooms by teachers in Nigeria.

In this technological age in which the learners are well-versed in the use of technology to the extent that they are referred to as digital natives (Prensky, 2001), the teaching of ELA also needs to be technologically inclined as well. Applying the technological device that is common to every learner in the ELA classroom may enhance the learning of language skills, especially English. Using mobile phones in ELA classes has advantages that are too numerous to overlook. Mobile phone use connects teachers and students around the globe. It means that both the teachers and the students can interact with other teachers and students all around the world by sending and receiving instructional messages through text, voice or even images as stated by Kim, Rueckert, Kim, and Seo, (2013), hence they would be able to compete favorably with their counterparts around the globe. Technology skills are ensured when mobile phones are put into use in ELA classrooms in Nigeria. Besides, listening and speaking skills, which are skills of oracy, would be given a prime place in the classroom when mobile phones are used. Mobile phones can be used to replay a lesson, and reading and writing can be enhanced through the adoption of keyboarding, notepads, messaging or even the use of Google to explore reading resources. But these uses have not been explored in the classrooms of Nigeria. After exploring the literature, the few studies we found focused on the use of mobile phones among university and secondary school students (Mojaye, 2015) or on Nigerians generally (Omeruo, 2009). No studies were found that examined the usage of mobile phones in Nigerian ELA classrooms. For the learners to be able to explore this medium successfully, teachers have to be able to employ and apply the device themselves. Young and Bush (2004) stated that for learners to cultivate the technology literacy, the teachers should also simultaneously cultivate it.

Hence, the following objectives guided this study, to: 1) examine teachers' usage and their extent of usage of mobile phones in ELA classrooms; 2) assess the relationship among teachers' demographic variables of qualifications, gender, experience and the usage of mobile phones in ELA classrooms; 3) investigate the challenges of mobile phone usage in ELA classrooms; and 4) assess the prospects of using mobile phones in ELA classrooms. Ward (2016) also stressed that when dealing with digital natives, educators must consider how they could integrate technology into learning and more importantly, into ELA classrooms where language skills are the crux of everyday lessons.

From the objectives raised, the following research questions were asked to guide the research:

1. Do teachers make use of mobile phones as a teaching tool in English Language Arts classrooms?

2. Is there any relationship among teachers' demographic variables (qualifications, gender, experience) and the usage of mobile phones in ELA classrooms?
3. Are there challenges to the use of mobile phones in ELA classrooms?
4. Are there prospects to the use of mobile phones in ELA classrooms?

The study is based on the mobile learning theories of behaviorism, constructivism and experientialism. In behavorism, Pavlov, Thondike, Watson and Skinner explains that learning can be observed and measured in learners; learning materials can be sequenced, and feedback can be provided with learners monitoring their progress (International Association of Mobile Learning, nd.). The constructivism theory of Vygotsky, Dewey and Piaget emphasizes that learning takes place when learners are able to construct learning on their own, which they are able to do when mobile devices are incorporated into the classrooms. Craigs and Van Lom (nd.) stress that constructivism encourages independent learning, since the learners place value on the technology rather than it imposing values on them. With mobile phones, the learners are able to achieve independence if the device is allowed and used in the teaching-learning process. In experientialism, Dewey, Kolb and Lewin state that experience is the foundation of learning and leads the learner to acquire the knowledge, skills, attitudes, emotions, and values necessary for life. They further opined that through the cycle of concrete experience, reflection, observation, abstract conceptualization of learning and active experimentation, knowledge is created (International Association of Mobile Learning, nd). When mobile phones are used in the classroom--especially in the ELA classroom--learners are more actively involved in language processes that enhance proficiency.

METHODOLOGY

This study adopted a descriptive survey design with early childhood teachers in Nigeria. An online survey was carried out with early childhood teachers to examine the use of mobile phones in ELA classrooms. An online survey was chosen as a result of the coronavirus pandemic that hit the global society. However, the information on the use of mobile phones in ELA classrooms focused on the teachers' usage of the device in their regular class before and during the pandemic (if there was any online class organized). The survey instrument, titled Mobile Phones in ELA Classrooms' Questionnaire (MP-ELA-CQ), was sent to respondents through emails and WhatsApp modes. Results were collected for not less than three weeks. Reminders were sent to respondents at one-week intervals. The data collected was analyzed using percentage, mean and Pearson Product – Moment Correlation Coefficient. Findings are presented, and recommendations are provided.

RESULTS

Results from the study are presented below in graph form, then explained after each graph.

Fig 1. shows that 98 respondents attended to the questionnaire with 80 (81.6%) female teachers and 18 (17.4%) male teachers.

Figure 1. Pie chart showing the percentage of respondents by sex

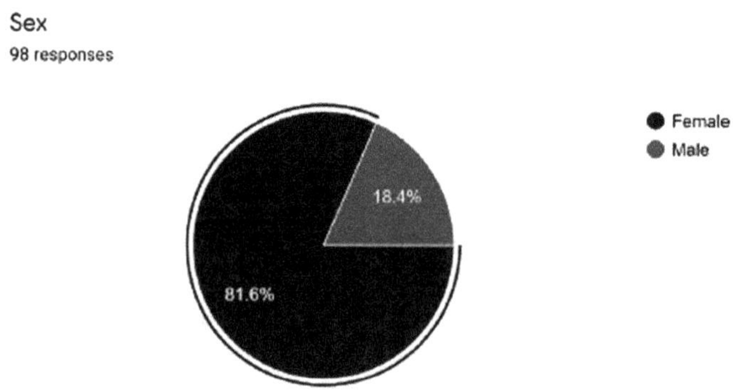

Fig. 2 shows that 97 indicated the type of school where they work, and 93(95.9%) of the respondents work in the private schools, while just 4(4.1%) of them work in the public schools.

Figure 2. Percentage distribution of respondents by school type

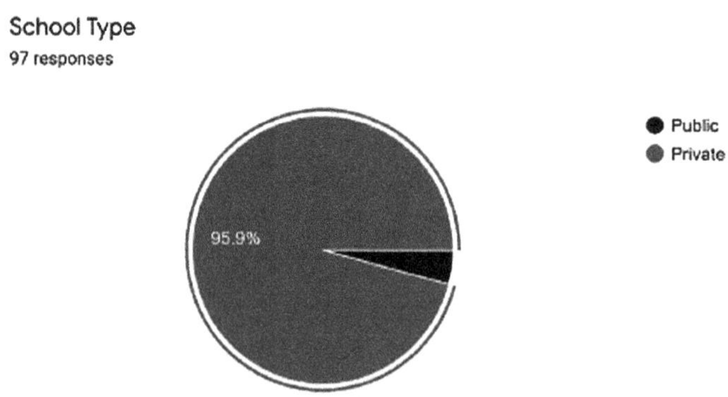

Fig. 3 shows that 97 respondents indicated their school location. While 76(79.4%) of the respondents have their schools in the urban area, 12(12.4%) are in the rural area and 8(8.2%) are in the peri-urban area.

Figure 3. Percentage distribution of respondents by school location

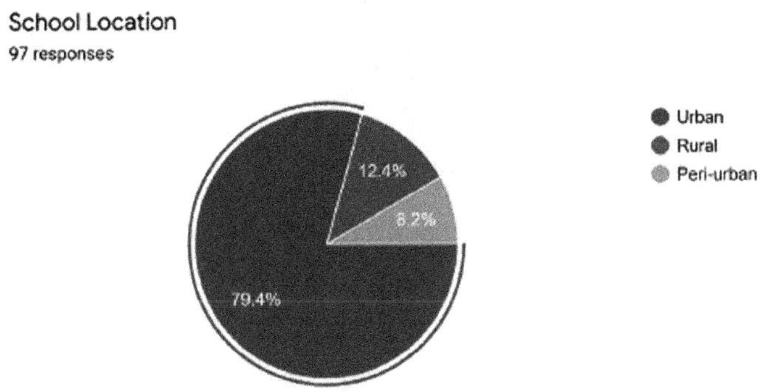

Fig. 4 shows that 50(51%) of the respondents possess first degree, 24(24.5%) have a Nigerian Certificate in Education (NCE) while the remaining percentage was shared among other qualifications.

Figure 4. Percentage distribution of respondents' qualifications

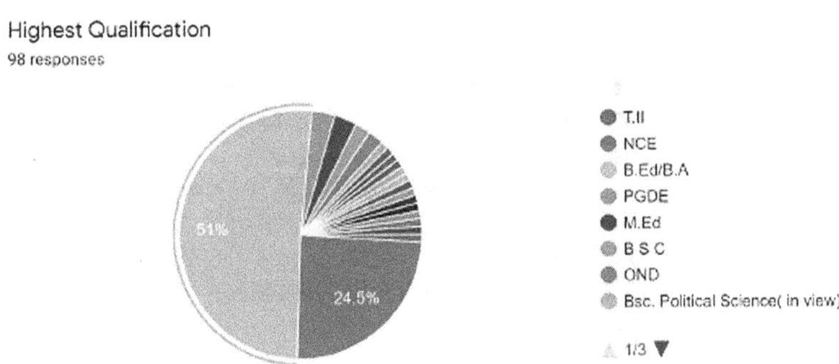

Fig. 5 shows the experience of the respondents with 59(60.2%) of them having spent between one to ten years in teaching, 31(31.6%) have been teaching for eleven to twenty years while 8(8.2%) have spent twenty-one and more in teaching.

Figure 5. Percentage distribution of respondents' year of experience

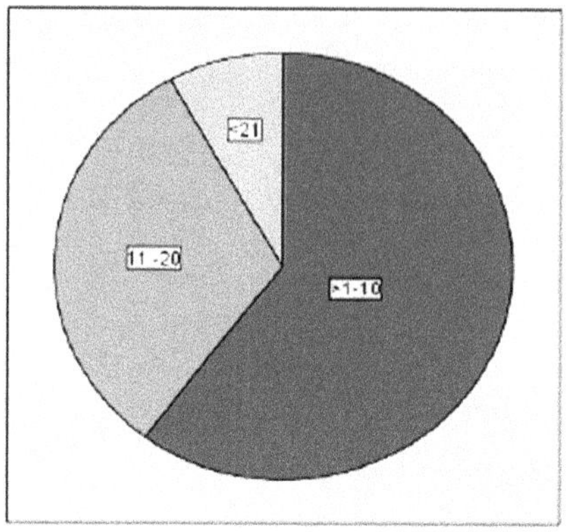

Key: >1 – 10 – 59(60.2%), 11 – 20 – 31(31.6%), <21 – 8(8.2%)

Fig 6 shows the skills of ELA being taught by the respondents in their schools. 82.5% teach reading skills, 78.4% teach writing skill, 66% teach speaking skill, 59.8% teach listening, 53.6% with literature, 34% with viewing, 70.1% teach English while 2.1% do not teach any.

Figure 6. Percentage distribution of respondents' teaching of ELA in class

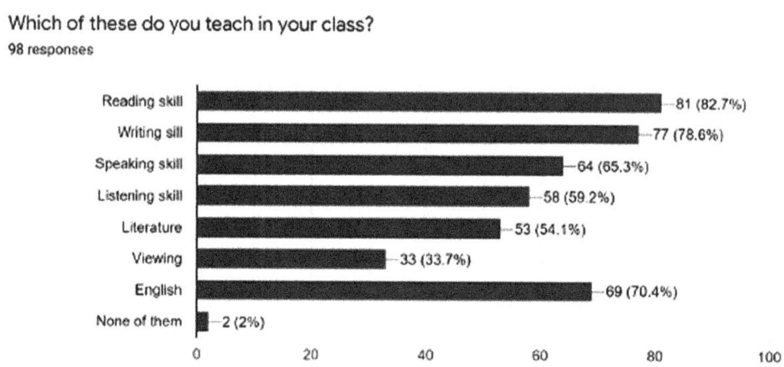

Fig. 7 shows that 54.1% of the respondents teach ELA skills as part of the English language subjects, indicating that there is no time allotted to the teaching of the skills on the school time-table.

Figure 7. Percentage distribution of respondents' mode of teaching ELA

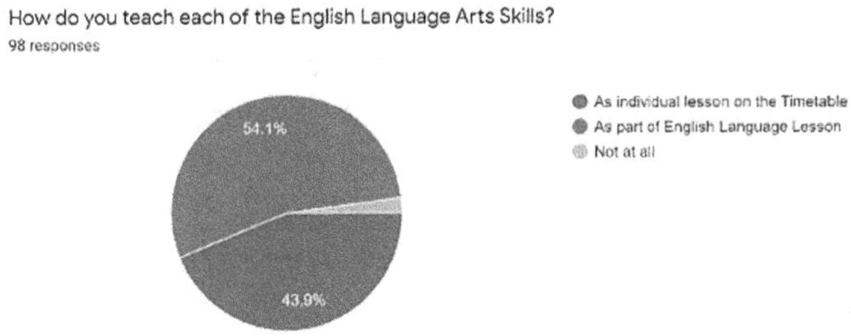

Research Question 1: Do teachers make use of mobile phones as a teaching tool in English Language Arts classrooms?

Fig. 8 shows that 73.5% of teachers do not use mobile phones as a teaching tool in the ELA classroom. Only 26.5% of the respondents use mobile phones in their ELA classrooms. There could be many reasons that may account for this non-usage. Many studies that have been carried out on the use of mobile phones as a learning device still emphasize the negative impact of the device on learning. It is seen as a class disruption or distraction device because of ringing or students' distraction from WhatsApp, texting or messaging in the classroom (Porter, 2016; Tindell & Bohlander 2011; Thomas, & Muñoz, 2016). In countries like France, New South Wales, and Australia, there was even a move for or a total ban on the usage of mobile phones in schools as a result of misuse (Russell, 2018). Although teachers in Nigeria might not be as concerned about misuse per se, it might be that many of the teachers could not afford the device. To make the matter worse, private school teachers are more poorly remunerated than public school teachers, and the majority of the respondents in this study work in the private schools (MySalaryScale, 2017;

Figure 8. Percentage distribution of teachers' use of mobile phones in ELA

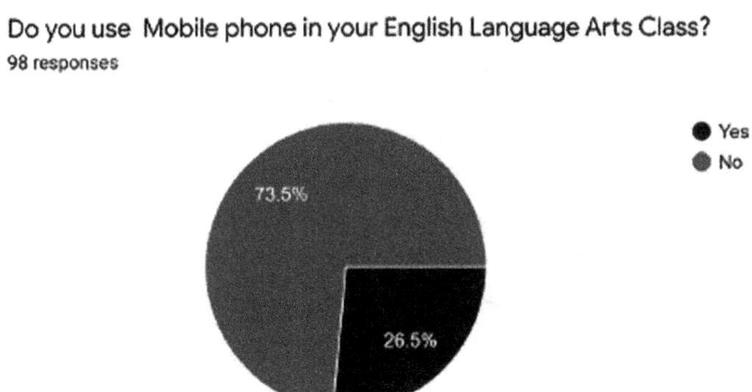

Agu, 2019). Another possibility for the non-usage might be the issue of maintenance of the device in terms of purchase of airtime, poor network system or electricity problems (Forenbacher, Husnjak, Cvitić, Jovović, 2019).

Fig 9 shows the percentage distribution of the features used by the respondents in ELA Classrooms. Out of the 97 respondents, only 26(26.8%) indicated that they use mobile phones in the ELA classroom, while the remaining 71 (73.2%) do not use it. Most-used features by the respondents are video with 19(73.1%), WhatsApp, 12 (46.2%), sound recorder, 11(42.3%). Keyboarding and internet exploration had the same number of teachers 10(38.5%) using the features. Only 9(34.6%) saw making phone calls with the mobile phone as relevant to the teaching of ELA. YouTube and music features were used by 8(30.8%) teachers, followed by games 6(23.1%), radio, calendar and email, which were used by 5(19.2%) of the respondents. Other features such as messaging, cameras, Zoom, files, Google maps, and Notebook were used by just 4 (15.4%), Contact and sketchbook were used by 3(11.5%) respondents, while Google Drive and Facebook were used by 2(7.7%) respondents. Although the usage of the features is very low, it can still be assumed that some teachers could figure out the relevance of the mobile phones' features in the ELA classrooms. This study is corroborating Leyden's (2018) view of the different ways of using mobile phone features in classrooms.

Figure 9. Percentage distribution of mobile phones' features used in ELA classrooms

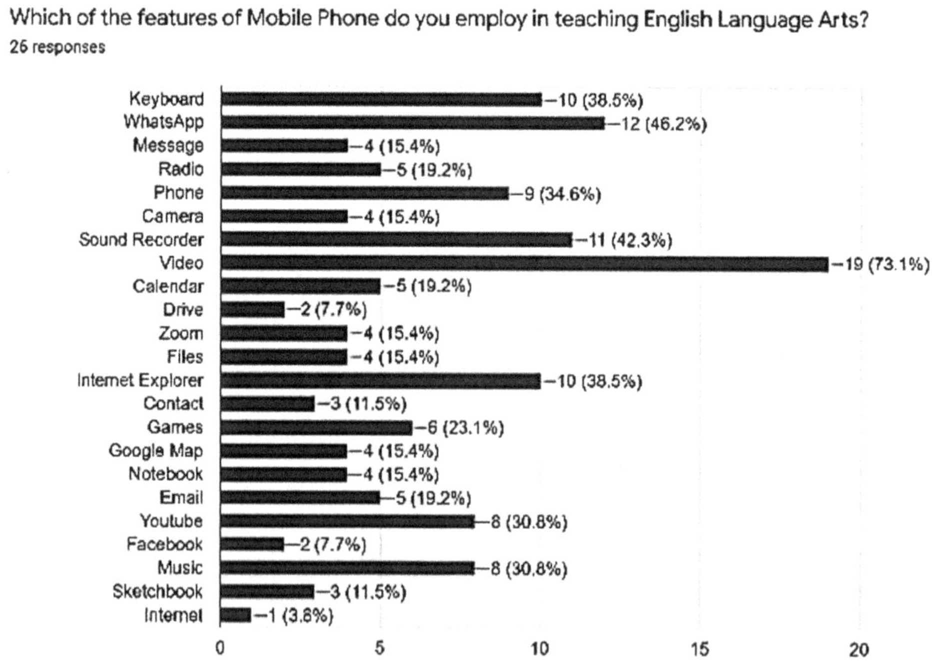

Research Question 2: Is there any relationship among teachers' demographic variables (qualifications, gender, experience) and the usage of mobile phones in ELA Classrooms?

Table 1 shows the correlation matrix of the respondents' demographic variables of the school type, school location, respondents' experience, qualifications and sex with the usage and how the teachers used mobile phones. School type, in terms of

Table 1. Correlation Matrix of the Demographic Variable of Respondents with The Usage of Mobile Phones in ELA Classrooms

		Type	Experience	Location	Sex	Qualification	How	USAGE
Type	Pearson Correlation	1	.549**	-.225*	-.489**	.421**	.182	.386**
	Sig. (2-tailed)		.000	.026	.000	.000	.073	.000
	N	98	98	98	98	98	98	98
Experience	Pearson Correlation	.549**	1	-.584**	-.712**	.284**	.586**	.774**
	Sig. (2-tailed)	.000		.000	.000	.005	.000	.000
	N	98	98	98	98	98	98	98
Location	Pearson Correlation	-.225*	-.584**	1	.806**	-.446**	-.386**	-.819**
	Sig. (2-tailed)	.026	.000		.000	.000	.000	.000
	N	98	98	98	98	98	98	98
Sex	Pearson Correlation	-.489**	-.712**	.806**	1	-.690**	-.372**	-.789**
	Sig. (2-tailed)	.000	.000	.000		.000	.000	.000
	N	98	98	98	98	98	98	98
Qualification	Pearson Correlation	.421**	.284**	-.446**	-.690**	1	-.018	.402**
	Sig. (2-tailed)	.000	.005	.000	.000		.861	.000
	N	98	98	98	98	98	98	98
How	Pearson Correlation	.182	.586**	-.386**	-.372**	-.018	1	.472**
	Sig. (2-tailed)	.073	.000	.000	.000	.861		.000
	N	98	98	98	98	98	98	98
USAGE	Pearson Correlation	.386**	.774**	-.819**	-.789**	.402**	.472**	1
	Sig. (2-tailed)	.000	.000	.000	.000	.000	.000	
	N	98	98	98	98	98	98	98

**. Correlation is significant at the 0.01 level (2-tailed).
*. Correlation is significant at the 0.05 level (2-tailed).

public and private has a significant relationship with the usage of mobile phones (r=.000) while there is no significant relationship with how (r= .073). Teachers' years of experience, location of their school, and the sex of the teacher have a significant relationship with the usage and how (r= .000), while the qualification is significantly related to the usage (r=.000). The implication of this result is that teachers' demographic variables correlate with the usage and how mobile phones may be applied to teaching in the ELA classrooms.

Research Question 3: What are the challenges for mobile phone usage in ELA classrooms?

Fig. 10 shows the various challenges (C) that the respondents encounter in the use of mobile phones in ELA classrooms. 26(26.5%) of the respondents indicate that the device is not available for them to use. This may be because the teachers do not have a mobile phone or they expect schools to provide them. 22 (22.4%) indicate lack of funds as a challenge, which is a reflection of the earlier challenge stated as well as the poor remuneration of private school teachers in the country. Going by this, it justifies the claim that Nigeria is mobile phone underpenetrated among other sub-Saharan countries (Gillwald, Odufuwa & Mothobi, 2018; GSMA, 2018; GSMA, 2017). Out of 98 respondents, 39(39.8%) of them indicate that the use of mobile phones is against the school policy and this might be another reason for the non-availability of the device as stated by some respondents. It implies that some schools have established a policy against the use of mobile phones in schools

Figure 10. Percentage distribution of the challenges of mobile phone use in ELA

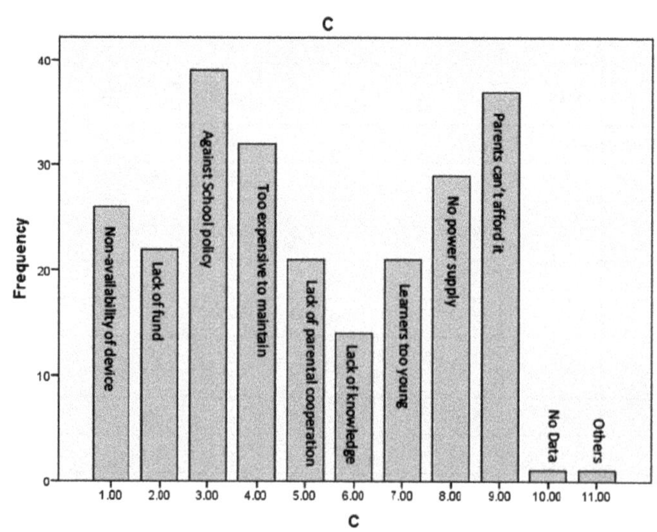

but this has not received attention in research the reason(s) for taking such a step. Another challenge identified by the respondents 32(32.7%) is that mobile phones are too expensive to maintain. This is in line with the findings of Forenbacher, Husnjak, Cvitić, Jovović, (2019) who highlighted high tariffs on data and irregularity in electricity supply as part of challenges mobile phone users face in Nigeria. Chukwuedo and Nwachukwu (2014) indicated that hardware, software or setting faults such as battery, keypads faults, no network, and slow phone operation are some of the maintenance challenges experienced by mobile phone users in Nigeria. All these can discourage the usage of the device in all classrooms--not only in ELA classrooms. The respondents 37(37.8%) identify another challenge as parents' inability to afford the device for children, which may not be unconnected with the socio-economic status of parents or beliefs of mobile phones usage by children that it is harmful to their developmental growth (Mehta, 2017;). Some respondents 21(21.4%) express lack of cooperation from parents which may still be linked to the earlier challenge. Furthermore, 21(21.4%) see children at the early childhood period being too young to be exposed to the use of mobile phones.

Research Question 4: What are the prospects of mobile phones?

Fig. 11 shows the prospects (P) of using mobile phones in ELA classrooms as identified by the respondents. Fifty-eight (59.2%) of the respondents are of the view that the use of mobile phones is very relevant to the learning of ELA. 63(64.3%) indicate that it will help learners' vocabulary development, 55(56.1%) show that it will help to improve conversational skills of learners. Out of 98, 37(37.8%) express that mobile phones help learners to keep record of their works, and 53(54.1%) of the respondents state that learners will be able to access additional materials for their studies using mobile phone 6(6.1%) do not see any prospect of mobile phones for teaching ELA skills, 43(43.9%) of the respondents explain that learners learn about the global environment early through the use of mobile phones, 7(7.1) do not have the ideas of using mobile phones to teach in the ELA classrooms. The implication is that teachers' knowledge of whether pedagogy or content has an impact on quality of instruction and learners' achievement. So, if teachers do not know or have an idea of how to adapt mobile phones to teaching in ELA classroom, then the learners cannot gain such knowledge from the teacher. Brown (2016) emphasized that teachers' pedagogical belief is one of the factors that may influence teachers' adoption and use of online tools. However, a larger percentage of teachers attested to the prospects embedded in the use of mobile phones in ELA classrooms. This corroborates Russell's (2018) assertion that both teachers and students are favorably disposed to the use of mobile phones in the classroom--hence the popular trend of Bring Your Own Device program in the United Kingdom. Kennedy (2014) also

Figure 11. The prospect of mobile phone use in ELA

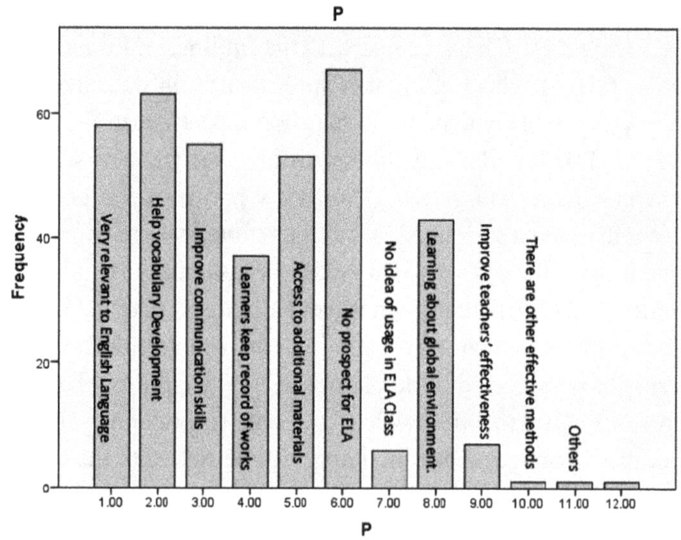

revealed that teachers have positive attitude to the use of mobile devices in the classroom to enhance learners' performance. This finding, like Mahdi's (2017) and Kayaoğlu, Sağlamel and Kobul's (2017) study, indicated that the use of mobile phones in ELA classrooms would enhance vocabulary.

CONCLUSION

English language arts as a subject is relevant to day-to-day life apart from academic activities. Hence, learners need to be proficient in the ELA skills, especially in Nigeria where English is a second language and is required subject. Teacher, then, need to be innovative in the technological age in their integration of the most common technology device into the classroom. Teachers need pedagogical training in the use of mobile phone technology. This would give them the tools available to work with and provide them with skills to enhance their performance. However, as this study demonstrates, many ELA teachers have not been adopting the use of mobile phones into their classrooms, thereby limiting the learning opportunities of the learners. It is therefore recommended that teacher pedagogical training should be looked into so that preservice teachers are technologically prepared. In addition, in-service teachers also need regular professional development in technology and education.

REFERENCES

Agu, Z. (2019). *Teachers salary structure in Nigeria in 2019*. https://www.legit.ng/1215762-teachers-salary-structure-nigeria-2019.html

Ajayi, H. O. (2006). Correlates of primary school pupils reading proficiency. *International Journal of Applied Psychology and Human Performance*, *1*, 207–215.

Asikhia, O. A. (2010). Students and teachers' perception of the causes of poor academic performance in Ogun state secondary schools in Nigeria: Implications for counseling for national development. *European Journal of Soil Science*, *13*(2), 229–242.

Brown, M. G. (2016). Blended instructional practice: A review of the empirical literature on instructors' adoption and use of online tools in face-to-face teaching. *Internet and Higher Education*, *31*, 1–10. doi:10.1016/j.iheduc.2016.05.001

Chukwuedo, S. O., & Nwachukwu, C. E. (2014). Maintenance practices in mobile phones for training prospective electronic technologists. *JORIND, 12*(1). www.transcampus.org/journals; www.ajol.info/journals/jorind

Craig, T., & Van Lom, M. (n.d.). Impact constructivist learning theory and mobile technology integration. In *Theories of Educational Technology*. EDTECH, Boise State University. https://sites.google.com/a/boisestate.edu/edtechtheories/craig_and_vanlom

Forenbacher, I., Husnjak, S., Cvitić, I., & Jovović, I. (2019). Determinants of mobile phone ownership in Nigeria. *Telecommunications Policy*, *43*(7), 101812. doi:10.1016/j.telpol.2019.03.001

Ganyaupfu, E. M. (2013). Teaching methods and students' academic performance. *International Journal of Humanities and Social Science Invention*, *2*(9), 29–35. http://www.ijhssi.org/papers/v2(9)/Version-2/E0292029035.pdf

Gillwald, A., Odufuwa, F., & Mothobi, O. (2018). *The state of ICT in Nigeria. Policy paper series (5): After access of ICT in Nigeria*. Retrieved from: http://extensia-ltd.com/wp-content/uploads/2018/11/After-Access-Nigeria-State-of-ICT-2017.pdf

GSM Association. (2017). *The mobile economy – Sub-Sahara Africa 2017*. Retrieved from: https://www.gsma.com/subsaharaafrica/wp-content/uploads2018/11/2017-07-11-7bf3592e6d750144e58dcfac6adfab.pdf

GSM Association. (2018). *The mobile economy – West Africa 2018*. Retrieved from: https://www.gsmaintelligence.com/research/?file=e568fe9e710ec776d82c04e9f6760adb&download

Guloba, M. M., Wokadala, J., & Bategeka, L. (2010). *Does teaching methods and availability of teaching resources influence pupils' performance: Evidence from four districts in Uganda.* Research series No. 77, Economic Policy Research Centre. http://citeseerx.ist.psu.edu/viewdoc/download;jsessionid=C3A254921E07B00628 2B85561A749D92?doi=10.1.1.670.7103&rep=rep1&type=pdf

International Association for Mobile Learning. (n.d.). *Six learning theories for mobile learning*. https://iamlearning.pressbooks.com/chapter/six-learning-theories/

Kayaoğlu, M. N., Sağlamel, H., & Kobul, K. (2017). Learner perspectives on mobile phone integration for vocabulary development in translation classes. *Lublin Studies in Modern Languages and Literature, 41*(1), 191 – 214. http://www.lsmll.Umcs. Lublin.Pl

Kennedy, D. M. (2014). M-learning to support English in a Hong Kong university. *Journal of Online Learning and Teaching*, *10*(4), 640–653.

Kim, D., Rueckert, D., Kim, D. J., & Seo, D. (2013). Student perceptions and experiences of mobile learning. *Language Learning & Technology*, *17*(3), 52–73. http://llt.msu.edu/issues/october2013/kimetal.pdf

Leyden, A. (2018). *40 uses of smartphones in school*. https://www.goconqr.com/en/examtime/blog/40-uses-for-smartphones-in-school/

Mahdi, H. S. (2017). Effectiveness of mobile devices on vocabulary learning: A meta-analysis. *Journal of Educational Computing Research*, *56*(1), 134–154. doi:10.1177/0735633117698826

Mehta, D. (2017). *Excessive use of mobile phones in children*. https://www.lybrate.com/topic/excessive-use-of-mobile-phones-in children/cf8aa2d927af556f4a2f0b3741769eca

Mojaye, E. M. (2015). Mobile phone usage among Nigerian university students and its impact on teaching and learning. *Global Journal of Arts Humanities and Social Sciences, 3*(1), 29-38, http://www.eajournals.org/wp-content/uploads/Mobile-Phone-Usage-among-Nigerian-University-Students-and-Its-Impact-On-Teaching-And-Learning.pdf

MySalaryScale. (2017). *Salaries of Nigerian teachers and their perceived lack of competence*. https://www.mysalaryscale.com/blog/salaries-nigerian-teachers-perceived-lack-competence/

Njoroge, G. N., Changeiywo, J. M., & Ndirangu, M. (2014). Effects of inquiry-based teaching approach on secondary school students' achievement and motivation in physics in Nyeri County, Kenya. *International Journal of Academic Research in Education and Review.*, *2*(1), 1–16. doi:10.14662/IJARER2013.010

Okewole, J. O. (2016). *Comparative effects of literature circle, dialogic reading and self-selection vocabulary on lower primary school pupils' reading skills in South Western Nigeria* (Unpublished Ph.D. Thesis). Obafemi Awolowo University, Ile-Ife, Nigeria.

Okewole, J. O., Odejobi, C. O., & Ajayi, H. O. (2018). Effects of literature circles, dialogic reading and vocabulary self selection strategies on the reading comprehension skill of lower primary school in Osun State. *Journal of Education and Practice, IISTE*, *9*(5), 29–36.

Omeruo, K. (2009). *The impact of GSM mobile phones on Nigerians*. Retrieved from: http://techtrendsng.com/the-impact-of-gsm-mobile-phones-on-nigerians/

Porter, G. (2016). How mobile phones are disrupting teaching and learning in Africa. *The Conversation*. https://theconversation.com/how-mobile-phones-are-disrupting-teaching-and-learning-in-africa-59549

Russell, D. (2018). Controlling smartphone use in schools. *Teacher Bulletin*. https://www.teachermagazine.com.au/articles/controlling-smartphone-use-in-schools

Russell, D. (2018). Mobile phones in the classroom – what does the research say? *Teacher Bulletin*. https://www.teachermagazine.com.au/articles/mobile-phones-in-the-classroom-what-does-the-research-say

Saheed, U. (2018). Factors affecting the teaching and learning of English language in primary school Nigeria. *Myschooltrick*. https://www.myschooltrick.com/2018/07/factor-affecting-the-teaching-and-learning-of-english-language-in-primary-school-nigeria.html

Salami, J. O. (2019). Effects of two instructional strategies on the acquisition of English basic phonology and morphology by lower primary school pupils in Ile – Ife, Osun State (Unpublished Master of Arts in Education). Obafemi Awolowo University, Ile-Ife, Nigeria.

Stanovich, K. E. (1986). Matthew effects in reading: Some consequences of individual differences in the acquisition of literacy. *Reading Research Quarterly*, *21*(4), 360–406. doi:10.1598/RRQ.21.4.1

Thomas, K., & Muñoz, M. A. (2016). Hold the phone! High school students' perceptions of mobile phone integration in the classroom. *American Secondary Education*, *44*(3), 19–37. https://www.ashland.edu/coe/about-college/american-secondary-education-journal

Tindell, D., & Bohlander, R. (2011). The use and abuse of cell phones and text messaging in the classroom: A survey of college students. *College Teaching*, *60*(1), 1–9. doi:10.1080/87567555.2011.604802

Ward, F. (2016). Integrating technology and literacy. *Classroom Technology*. https://www.edutopia.org/blog/integrating-technology-and-literacy-frank-ward

Young, C. A., & Bush, J. (2004). Teaching the English language arts with technology: A critical approach and pedagogical framework. *Contemporary Issues in Technology & Teacher Education*, *4*(1), 1–22.

Section 3

Mobile Phones and the Arts

Chapter 7
Mobile Phones, Arts Integration, and English Language Arts

Stephanie Loomis
https://orcid.org/0000-0002-4067-5091
University of Nevada, Las Vegas, USA

ABSTRACT

This chapter considers the affordances of smartphones as tools for arts integration in English language arts classrooms. It discusses the importance of students as creators of content and how teachers may capture the social tools already within student possession to function as learning tools as well. Arts-based instruction is briefly discussed as an important element for students' full participation in the multiliteracies that make up much of communication in modern society. While literacy in the form of reading and writing must always be the goal of the ELA teacher, it is also important to recognize the role of multiple literacies as legitimate forms of text. The chapter also includes specific ideas for students' smartphone compositions that teachers may consider.

INTRODUCTION

English Language Arts (ELA) classes may be the most important classes students take during their high school careers. Some students excel in Science Technology Engineering and Mathematics (STEM) classes and go on to have successful careers. Other students find their ways to careers in the trades: contractors, electricians, plumbers, and other essential fields that Mike Rowe (2003) called "dirty jobs."

DOI: 10.4018/978-1-7998-5805-8.ch007

Still other students move from high school and college into the service industries of hospitality, law, marketing, or sales. And still other students graduate from high school and colleges to become educators.

As different as the sectors of economy are, and as important it is to have diversity of jobs, services, and careers, every student leaving high school must be able to communicate. The heart of ELA is the foundational skill set around the ability to think critically, communicate information in ways appropriate to a given situation, and to connect to other people in language. Words are the most familiar mode of communication, particularly in ELA, but additional modalities, particularly through arts integration, adds dimension to communication. Access to digital tools makes integration of image, video, and sound easy, and more importantly, is relevant in today's multimodal world. Education is dependent on multiple literacies for understanding each content area and how content areas overlap and merge in the world at large. To be literate in the 21st Century is to understand modes of communication in multiple contexts through multiple media.

This chapter discusses the role of smart phones as tools for arts integration in the ELA classroom, replacing the materials of foam core, construction paper, and markers. The author provides background for students as content creators in online spaces and includes specific ideas for how arts-based smartphone exercises might look in a high school ELA classroom.

BACKGROUND

Regarding ELA educators, Dana Maloney (2017) said, "What we do is not trivial or incidental; it is essential" (ncte.org/blog). What ELA educators do is provide a base for each student's future ability to inquire, question, reason, synthesize, and then discuss information from multiple points of view. ELA teaches people to give good directions, to read instructions, to understand the difference between fact and fiction, and to make informed decisions about everything from voting in a representative democracy to which cereal might work for both breakfast and dessert.

The Common Core State Standards break ELA into five distinct but interwoven skills: reading, writing, speaking, listening, and language (http://www.corestandards.org/). Each of these skills is essential for engaging in all the nuances of communication. Reading and writing are probably the first things people think of when they recall English classes, but speaking is the ELA skill people use the most and listening may be the thing people need the most. Language, the ability to put texts together in ways appropriate to the domain or context, becomes a key element to creating content in virtual spaces because each site has particular requirements for how language is used. The requirements manifest in modes of communication: sound, image, movement, and sometimes, words. Some sites have limits to the number of characters allowed, while others only permit a certain length of posts. Hashtags and @ signs mean different things in different online spaces. Images dominate. Adapting to new language skills is becoming increasingly important for everyone as technology changes.

Arts Integration

It is important to integrate art into courses called English Language *Arts*. Arts integration in learning has been well documented as a best practice for learning for decades. (Dewey, 1932; Eisner,2002; Zoss, 2009). Gee and Hayes (2011) observed, "[L]anguage itself is and has always been a mixture of sound, words, images created in the mind, and gestures used in contexts full of objects, sounds, actions, and interactions. Language has always been 'multimodal'..." (1). Visual art offers a space for students to consider alternate ways to think about texts beyond the printed word. The variety of texts, both linguistic and non-linguistic, reveal multiple ways of thinking, reading and responding with both image and language (Zoss, 2009). These multimodal ways of meaning making and communication through visual texts embody personal, social, and cultural elements because language itself "is always internalized by an individual human being in transaction with a particular environment" (Rosenblatt, 1988, p. 3). That is, whatever the mode of communication, be it words, images, or some combination thereof, meaning- making is inherently personal and is influenced by the culture of the meaning maker.

Literacy includes the visual arts as forms of expression, understanding, and communicating meaning. Creating new texts as transactions with existing texts begins as the mind blends the existing text with prior knowledge, personal experiences, and an understanding of different modes of expression (Rosenblatt, 1978). To read the words of a book and then create an illustration of a particular scene requires the reader to understand the author's intent, but also uses the reader's own knowledge of the world and experiences in it, applying those elements to the visual representation of the scene through a given medium (e.g. charcoal, paint, crayon). The effect of visual literacy is a shift from knowledge acquisition (and regurgitation) to artifact creation (Beach, et al., 2011). Creation of new texts is part and parcel of the human experience, as people interpret what they see, hear, or read visually, linguistically, and interactively (Dewey, 1938/1978; Heath, 2008; Rosenblatt, 1978).

Visual art projects have been part of ELA classrooms for many years (Fond, 2018; McGuire, 1984). Dioramas, posters, sculptures, paintings, altered books, book covers, and collages all play a part in most ELA teachers' repertoire of engaging activities for student participation. More recently, however, the time it takes for students to do physical arts or crafts is unreasonable given how busy they are. Sports, extracurricular school activities, jobs, and family responsibilities mean today's students have limited time in their days for large cumbersome projects. Enter the smart phone. Students no longer need to buy materials from a craft store, wait for glue to dry, or find themselves wearing more paint than is actually on the project. Smart phone apps open the doors to creative expression and content creation without the mess. Like physical artwork, digital creations engage students' creative minds while they simultaneously solving problems, thinking critically, and transacting with texts in new ways. As students transact with online texts, they compose new texts in multiple modes that embrace arts integration.

Students as Creators of Content

One effect of the turn to nearly universal cellphone accessibility is the availability of ways for students to not only consume content, but to create content for an audience outside the ELA classroom. This content includes images, video, sound, and different ways to use language. School based composition continues to dominate formal writing, but there are a multitude of ways for students to expand their ELA skills online. In response to new ways of communicating, ELA instruction can bend to embrace alternative forms of text so that students are fully prepared to communicate in multiple ways. Using both traditional print and newer digital texts, ELA teachers can infuse their praxis with the language and tools of online learning, online composition, and online communication.

Distance learning has been part of education for over a century, but virtual learning online began in earnest in the-mid 1990s (Harasim, 2000). New modes, new principles, and new processes continue to change the look of online learning. The COVID-19 pandemic of 2020 tested the power of online learning and demonstrated the need for digital pedagogy for every subject at every grade level as schools and educators navigated unfamiliar terrain in a matter of days (Horn, 2020; https://www.ed.gov/coronavirus). Teachers who already utilized technology, including mobile phones, were ahead of the curve and able to make the transition to online without having to learn a new skillset. One teacher said, "My team used to tell me I used technology too much, but now they're coming to me for help" (personal correspondence, March 30, 2020). Educators who use their own smart phones for internet access, social media, news updates, and communication may have an advantage over those who do not.

The mobile phone as a handheld computer can be a tool for communication in tumultuous situations but can also be a tool for creating timely and relevant creative texts that can be shared to a large audience quickly. Encouraging students to create content as responses to current events allows them to practice reading, writing, and language skills. Most students use their smartphone to stay updated on friends while they consume information about their interest areas. Students can also keep up with current events, including natural disasters, politics, climate, and the world. Being aware of the news around them may be helpful in making connections to literature. Students can then use their devices to compose responses utilizing the available apps before sharing with the virtual world.

Content Creation

The first thing most people think of when considering mobile devices and teens is social media use and misuse. It is apparent by just watching a group of students that their primary interests are in platforms like Instagram or Snapchat and other socially driven media. Both teens and adults admit to using their smart phones as distractions that lead down rabbit holes of information, both factual and fictional (Elgan, 2017; Kamenetz, 2019; Vedantam, 2019). For content creators, however, the skills required to create and post are similar to the skills required for success in an ELA classroom.

Traditional ELA skills of reading, writing, listening, speaking, and language each translate to online practices. Reading and critical thinking come with combing through information and deciding which things to share with social media networks. Writing comments on threads is still writing, and often with immediate feedback, whether it's a Facebook post or a reaction to a digital news story on National Public Radio (NPR) or on Youth Voices, a site designed for teen voices to be head on culturally relevant topics. YouTube and other video-based sites offer opportunities for both listening and speaking. Language use varies with each site; the language used for responding to a Twitter post is decidedly different than the language used when engaging in online discourse about the economy on a business-based periodical site or in a conversation in a multiplayer game (MPG).

Since many people use their smart phones as their primary access to the internet, the language arts skills people need are dependent on their purpose for going online and the sites they visit (Cakebread, 2017; Handley, 2019; Silver, et al., 2019). Students who know how to engage through multiple skills, including art-based interactions will likely have an advantage in the online world over those who excel only in traditional essay writing. Students who use many social media sites are composing texts through words, images, effects, and remixing, even though many of them consider their time on social media as entertainment and not work (Kamenetz, 2019). Their social media play gives them the skills they need to do the work of composing for arts and technology integration in class.

Mobile Phone Integration in ELA

In 2019, 95% of teens had access to a smartphone (Shaeffer, 2019). Most of the time they report using their phones as a way to pass the time, but they also post images on a regular basis. As students become creators of online content, rather than consuming content in more traditional school forms like printed textbooks, their transactions are influenced by the affordances of digital media, including mobile phones (Beach, et al. 2011). Technology integration, including mobile phones in class, is a reasonable response to the reality of modern culture. (Cercone & Garcia, 2017; Gee & Hayes,2011; Hicks & Turner, 2013; Lessig,2008).

Creating content adds depth to learning and enhances adaptability by engaging creators in meaningful integration of multiple skills (Briggs, 2014; Lippincott, 2007; Robinson, 2013). Creating content allows students to ask questions and then explore possible answers, sharing what they find along the way. Teachers can facilitate meaning-making as students consider what they will create in response to a query or prompt and as they determine how they can do it and for what audience. Online content creation adds a level of authentic learning because students are creating for authentic audiences. Students nearly always have their mobile phones with them, so they have constant opportunities to create and communicate digitally (Briggs, 2014; Dodds, 2017; Fond, 2018; Lalonde, 2019; O'Byrne, 2013; Wormelli, 2015). Even if they are not actively using the devices, they are aware that there is a whole world happening outside the school.

The number of free apps for creating on a smart phone are astounding. Many students already use them for their social media account postings, so it makes sense to apply what they already know to what they're learning in class. Apps like Instagram allow users to create stories and add stickers and music. Snapchat has filters that change the way people look and sound. Tiktok allows users to create short videos. Boomerang lets users choose an action to repeat in a loop. VSCO, an app that originally produced filters for photo editing programs, turned exclusively to creating smartphone filters (xiaomist, 2020). Users may not know educational ramifications (they are composing texts), but they are utilizing the skills that transactions with texts require knowledge, experience, and understanding of the tools included with their mobile devices. Mobile phone app users are also aware of the possibilities that come with remixing images and sounds. Forward thinking teachers can harness those skills and show their students how to capture their ideas about literature or writing prompts with arts-based tools they use every day.

Play and Work

Dewey (2001/1916) wrote, "The desirability of starting from and with the experience and capacities of learners, a lesson enforced from all three quarters, has led to the introduction of forms of activity, in play and work, similar to those in which children and youth engage outside of school" (p. 202). Smart phones are the current tools used for play and work; harnessing that interest may allow teachers to connect the power of the tool to classroom learning in ways that are both relevant and fun. Wormelli (2015) wrote that the best way to learn how to do all this is to do it, meaning that playing with the affordances of mobile phones is the best way to learn how powerful a tool they can be.

There is no argument that writing is an essential part of the ELA classroom, however, the inclusion of digital media in CCSS addresses speaking, listening, and language with reading and writing as parts of literacy (CCSS.ELA-Literacy.SL.9-10.5; CCSS.ELA-Literacy.SL.11-12.5). The rationale for including multimodal representations as options for student response is grounded in the need for students to complete high school able to communicate in the ways common to the culture; increasingly, Western culture relies on digital communication, including images, graphics, and videos (Mills & Ekley, 2014).

Digital Art

Digital visual art as a form of digital literacy offers new ways by which students can represent what they know and learn. The internet is shifting more and more from a place to store and retrieve information to a virtual community of creators and producers. As a result, the ways in which people think about expression and communication continue to shift toward interactive transactions that continue to evolve as the new texts become subject to continual interpretations by new readers (Dewey, 1938/1978; Hookway, 2007; Rosenblatt, 1978).

Digital visual art, produced digitally and shared online, allows people to both archive and exhibit their new texts to an unlimited audience (Wilson, 2018). Teens are aware of the audiences they reach on social media, and often consider who may see their posts as they compose them (Auxier, et al, 2019; Lalonde, 2019). Most teens use mobile phone art as a method for making connections through selfies, recording social events, and documenting their daily lives (Shaeffer, 2019). To extend the use of mobile phone art to making connections with literary characters, recording their visions of social events they read about, or documenting the daily lives of people in a different time and place makes use of skills teens already have. Additionally, artistic representation allow teachers to focus on student thinking and processing without being tempted to correct every mechanical error of their writing.

Artistic Effort as Student-centered Text

Images, music, and videos may also benefit students who are behind their peers in writing. Using the affordances of mobile devices to create digital art in various modes may offer these students the opportunity to share their critical thoughts is alternative and differentiated ways. English language learners (ELL) may be able to use digital art as a mediary between languages, allowing their ideas to develop so they can be shared before the task of writing in a new language. For ELL, the idea that art is a legitimate form of literacy may well keep them committed to persevering in learning the language of their adopted home (Ingraham & Nuttall, 2016).

For students who excel in traditional writing processes, adding digital arts-based compositions encourages the additional measure of considering the most effective modes to communicate their messages (Schoffner, et al., 2010). Digital art produced on smart phones may also change the balance of expertise in the classroom. The students who are already adept at using their phones to create can teach those who are less familiar with transformative apps and how they are used for the greats impact.

Constraints of Mobile Phone Use

Before considering specific ways, teachers can incorporate smart phones into their lesson plans, it is important to recognize the hazards inherent in online spaces. One of the reasons teachers hesitate to consider promoting smart phones as composition tools is the responsibility, they feel for protecting students from online hazards, including cyber-bullying, excessive screen time, and student privacy. (Chen, 2018; Silver, et al., 2019; Zoch, et al., 2016). Additionally, teachers and administrators often see cell phones as distractions to learning. The distraction factor is not limited to the US; in 2018, the French government banned cell phone use in schools (Hess, 2019). Access is also a consideration; even though 95% of students say they have access to smart phones, they may not have reliable access to the internet. Many of the constraints can be addressed by specific mobile phone pedagogies that include specific expectations, teaching students how to self-monitor and also reflect on their smartphone use, and by communicating with parents and guardians the purposes behind digital art projects (Bejba, 2019; Kay & Lauricella, 2011; Graham, n.d.; Kolb, 2019).

SUGGESTIONS FOR PRACTICE

Ideas for Integration of Mobile Devices Into the Classroom

Social media play incorporates a number of elements that might be easily drawn on for school purposes, particularly for responding to literature in ways that are relevant to students' lives. Online, students create content by starting with an idea, analysis, or message to communicate, finding the images they want to use, adding filters or music, and then posting for an audience. The same principles work in responses to literature in a variety of ways. Teachers who ask students to compare literary characters, settings, and conflicts to their own lives in written assignments can use a variety of alternative media accessible via student smart phones as creative ways to assess the same information. Smart phones are not only places where information can be accessed, but also tools for creating content in multiple modes, particularly visual and auditory modes.

Photography

The cameras on today's smart phones rival some of the standalone cameras available. There are manual settings, automatic settings, effects, multiple lenses, and guides to help amateur photographers frame a shot for the best effect. Some mobile phones have built in filters with the cameras, and the newest models can automatically blur the background, create three-dimensional effects, and capture 360 degrees in a single shot. Simply allowing students to add photographs to their work, especially in personal work like journals, expands their notions of what text may include. Adding photos to written work may be the easiest way to incorporate visuals into written work, but the possibilities of composition through photography include photojournalism, stop-motion illustration, lessons in perspective and point-of view, and documentation of daily life.

Photojournalism

Photojournalism uses images to tell the news. Photojournalist Mark Hancock (1996) defined the role of a photojournalist as putting together the best stories and best pictures, locking them into frozen images. He added that the distinction between photographers and photojournalists are verbs. Photographers typically work in planned scenarios to tell a story (e.g. weddings, landscapes), while photojournalists capture images of an unfolding story in action. Using smart phones as the tools of photojournalism gives students the voice to record the world and world events from a distinct, albeit objective point of view.

Photojournalism was first part of the news during the Crimean War of the 1850s but became a major element of telling the world's stories with Matthew Brady's images of the Civil War (Stewart, 2017). Since then, images of natural disasters, wars, nature, exploration, and expeditions have made indelible marks on each generation. Consider Dorothea Lange's images of the Great Depression or the images of the American flag raised at Iwo Jima during World War Two and at the World Trade Center after 9/11.

The pandemic of COVID-19 in 2020 offered a new generation of aspiring photojournalists an opportunity to use their cell phones to capture images of health care workers in masks, teachers and students figuring out how to manage an overnight shift from face-to-face to online learning, and people choosing to ignore pleas for social distancing. The images captured by students during the crisis will one day become the source material for anthropologists and social scientists to understand human behavior during an unprecedented viral outbreak. Teachers who encouraged students to use their cellphones to document the stories around them may contribute to a better understanding of why and how population respond to crises.

Personal Narrative and Documentation of Daily Life

Personal narratives are standard writing expectations for all students, beginning with the earliest years of education. The story of the self is the easiest to approach, since the author knows the subject best. Photo essays of daily life sometimes fall under the genre of photojournalism but creating a personal narrative through photography adds a level of intimacy that sometimes words can't express. Additionally, personal photo narratives may be the beginnings of students telling their stories of home life, culture, and belief systems that can generate conversations. Using pictures as places to begin writing also reduces the "I don't know what to write" problems that keep many students from beginning their narratives. Students can explain the people, setting, and occasion of a photo or a series of photos. They can then tell the emotions that were present. After students verbally say what the pictures are and what they represent, they have the beginnings of the words they might use to write the story down, either immediately, or at some point in the future. Photo narratives bypass some of the obstacles to writing, whether they be language-based (for some language learners), sensory (for some students on the autism spectrum), or fear of failure.

Digitally Altered Images

Photographs can also be changed to tell a different kind of story. There are dozens of free photo editing apps for smart phones available. Filters are the most prevalent, and savvy selfie-taking students will already know how to create a mood by applying one or more filters to an image. They are also likely to know why they choose particular filters over others, giving teachers insight into the image composing process that can then be used to discuss choosing words to create an effect in much the same way students choose filters. Stickers and frames also allow users to embellish their photos to elicit desired reactions.

There are also apps that allow users to alter images beyond basic corrections, giving artists options to create everything from oil-painting looks to comics. Any of the online smartphone stores lists dozens or more apps to create composites, add effects, and play with color. Many apps include options to layer images and change transparency to create a double exposure effect. Some of the apps are free, while others may have ads, in-app purchases, or up-front fees for licensing the product. Most of the free apps offer enough manipulative power to suffice for school-related artistic pursuits.

Some of the more popular computer apps also have mobile versions that can be licensed for educational work for free. Both Adobe and Apple offer multiple mobile versions of their desktop editing and publishing software. Having the smartphone apps available allows classrooms or media centers to free up computers so that all students can participate in art-integrated ELA activities during class. Smartphone apps allow students to photograph a scene, alter it, layer it with textures, original art, and graphics, and then submit the work as a poster, album cover, or marketing tool for a book without ever leaving school property.

Fake Social Media

Social media sites have definite features that set them apart from each other. Teachers have created lesson plans that include fake Facebook, Instagram, and Twitter platforms (LaFave, 2017; Zamarvide, 2019). Students who already use these sites will find them familiar, and they may be a suitable introduction to what kinds of creative academic work is possible on a mobile phone. Students can reimagine famous scenes as they might have played out on Facebook or Snapchat. They might explore how to capture the theme of a sonnet as a tweet, and then compare the structures, limitations, and affordances of each kind of text. Instagram selfies of tragic lovers may help students illustrate the despair and longing of those unfortunate characters' emotions.

Often the fake social media ideas are designed for school computers, but there is no reason students cannot complete these kinds of assignments using their phones. They may find the experience more realistic since that is how most students participate in social media on real life. Merging modern social media language practices with older ways of telling stories may also be an interesting way to trace the evolution of the spoken and written word. If sections of Hurston's (1937) *Their Eyes were Watching God* were told as a fake-Twitter thread, what hashtags might be used? How might the characters' dialects be captured? Conversations like these allow students to not only demonstrate mastery of the story, but also the genre and the power of language in creative ways. Because the conversations, whether part of a class discussion, a writing prompt, or a creative exercise are based in student ideas, the possibility of plagiarism is also limited.

Playlists

Many people, including students create musical playlists for their personal lives, events, and activities. Most streaming services have free options that allow users to create personal compilations of songs from multiple genres (White, 2017). Playlists are often named for the activity for which they are designed (e.g. pool party, workout), genre (e.g. classic country, movie soundtracks), or particular artists (e.g. Post Malone, Yo Yo Ma). Playlists can set or evoke a mood (e.g. romance, excitement) or be used as ambient sounds for studying or meditating (e.g. instrumentals, white noise generators). While playlists can be generated on personal computers, many playlists are created and played through smart phones simply because it is easy to do on the go.

Using smart phones to generate playlists for the classroom can be collaborative efforts wherein students have to defend why a particular song should or should not be included or students may create playlists individually. Depending on the goal of the lesson, student-generated playlists might be an in-class project that could be easily shared with the instructor and then used as background music during class. Studying *The Great Gatsby* (Fitzgerald, 1925)? Ask students to create a playlist of songs from the 1920s and compare it to a possible playlist of songs for a modern star-studded celebrity party designed to impress someone. Alternatively, if the class is reading, *The Things They Carried* (O'Brien, 1990), students could create playlists of protest songs from the Vietnam War era and consider how those songs affected public opinion of the war.

Music as text involves both intellectual and emotional analysis (Agawu, 2001; McGuire, 1984). Students who choose playlists as alternative texts may be expected to justify their choices, compose a musical analysis, or combine the music they select with images that connect others to the literature in both visual and auditory modes. Teachers who offer playlists as alternatives to traditional writing assignments will want to have specific guidelines, clearly connected to a pedagogical rationale of arts-based learning and linked to one of the learning standards of their districts or states.

Video, Audio, and Movies

It wasn't so long ago that creating a video in class required checking out equipment and logging hours in the editing lab, if a school even had one. Filming required multiple days, and reshooting a scene was costly even after reusable tape cartridges were common. Today, however, most mobile devices come with software that allows for shooting and editing in one device. There are no costs for camera equipment or film. Reshoots are a matter of just running the scene again and every take can be saved in the cloud. Slow-motion, stop-motion, and live focus are standard features on smartphone cameras. Built in shake-reduction keeps videos in focus.

Students opting for movie-making can recreate or update scenes from epic poetry or plays. In phone video and editing apps make it possible for *Beowulf* to slay Grendel and convincingly raise the monster's arm. They might also create original infomercials that include the graphics that are part of that form of television. Commercials and infomercials are forms of argumentation and persuasion, both genres of writing expected in CCSS.

Social media apps often include "stories," short videos shared as they are being created. Dozens of apps, both free and paid, make almost anything possible for the creators and composer using smart phones to create videos that were impossible to make even with the heavy equipment of decades past. Mashups and special effects can be automatically or manually generated. Adding voiceover or music takes minutes, not hours. Splicing clips together from multiple angles or points of view does not require the hours of cutting and taping that old school movie making required. Some of the available apps are specifically designed for particular publishing platforms like YouTube.

Additionally, audio only apps allow users to compose and produce music, record original compositions of stories, poetry, or podcasts, and voiceovers for slideshows or static images. Voice recordings remove some of the learning curve that video requires, so students can ease into the technology if they are not already familiar with it. Additionally, student creators may determine that audio without video is the more appropriate and powerful way to communicate their message. Podcasts are particularly popular and might be a long-term project on literary connections to current events with students sharing the roles of host, guest, producer, and editor.

Collaboration is a key feature of both audio and video production. Scripts must be written, actors assigned, editing and production completed, and the final project submitted. Students can play to their strengths and some of the work can be done asynchronously. Collaborations in which students perform the tasks that suit their abilities also mirror real-world collaborations better than some other collaborative projects that require students to simply split the workload.

Remixes

In addition to composing new texts through original photos, videos, and music, students also remix existing multimedia texts. The remixes themselves can take multiple forms, most of which can be done through free mobile device apps. Simply defined, remix is taking existing elements (e.g. images, sounds, or words) and blending them into original compositions. Knobel and Lankshear (2008) called remix "endless hybridization" (p. 25), asserting that merging independent elements, and even genres, opens possibilities for continued change. Rosenblatt (1978) referred to this idea of continual remix when she wrote that once the creator of a new text (or remix) called the work complete, that work was then a text that could be transacted with (or remixed) by someone else.

To transact with a text involves creating a new text which may then be the source of transaction for someone else. Alvermann, (2016) wrote, "Remix involves acting on our human capacity to create new meanings with words, images, and sounds made possible through interacting with others like ourselves and with others whom we've not yet met but have the opportunity for doing so" (p. 92). A recent example comes from the Broadway show *Hamilton.* The most prominent comes in the sampling (borrowing) for the number, "Ten Duel Commandments", with the count sampled from B.I.G.'s "Ten Crack Commandments", which borrowed riffs, vocals, and lyrics from Les McCann (1977), Public Enemy (1991), and Keith Murray (1994) (McCarthy, 2015, whosampled.com). New texts, whether digital or physical, are the result of people making meaning of existing texts through the lenses of their experiences, prior knowledge, and the tools at their disposal.

Digital texts, including remixes, may be created with computers or tablets, but increasingly, smart phones are the most ubiquitous and convenient tools for digital remix and composition. The ability to hold a device in one hand and manipulate images, words, sounds, and videos into something new and then immediately share it with a specific audience for instantaneous feedback is nothing short of remarkable, especially given the speed at which computers have evolved. In the broad scope of human history, it wasn't so long ago that computers took up whole rooms and required specialist to operate. Now people can create and publish content to the world in a matter of a few finger swipes on a smartphone.

CONCLUSION

The first priority for ELA must be literacy, but literacy is not limited to traditional printed texts (NCTE, 2018). Literacy includes being able to communicate in the modes and media of a particular time and space, and includes reading, writing, speaking, listening, and language. If one goal of education is to produce literate individuals, then it follows that educators include the ways in which people both produce and consume texts: creatively, critically, and compositionally (Hicks, 2006). Arts-based composition produced on mobile devices has the potential to offer students ways to demonstrate their literacy skills in multimodal contexts.

The current world is one of multiliteracies, in multiple modes and multiple media. As educators, it seems reasonable to engage all the tools available and teach students how to be content creators and composers, not only for the classroom, but for their own edification and continued self-expression for life.

REFERENCES

Agawu, K. (2001). African Music as Text. *Research in African Literatures, 32*(2), 8–16. doi:10.2979/RAL.2001.32.2.8

Alvermann, D. E., & Harrison, C. (2016). Blowin in the wind. *Journal of Adolescent & Adult Literacy*, *60*(1), 91–93. doi:10.1002/jaal.566

Auxier, B., Anderson, M., & Kumar, M. (2019, December 20). 10 tech-related trends that shaped the decade. *Fact Tank, News in the Numbers.* Pew Research Center. https://www.pewresearch.org/fact-tank/2019/12/20/10-tech-related-trends-that-shaped-the-decade/

Beach, R., Hull, G., & O'Brien, D. (2011). Transforming English Language Arts in a Web 2.0 world. In D. Lapp & D. Fisher (Eds.), *Handbook of research on teaching the English Language Arts* (3rd ed., pp. 161–167). Routledge.

Bejba, S. (2019). The new point and shoot: Photography lessons using phones and scanners. In J. C. Castro (Ed.), *Mobile media in and outside of the art classroom: Attending to identity, spatiality, and materiality* (pp. 165–182). doi:10.1007/978-3-030-25316-5_8

Briggs, S. (2014, September 20). *Students as creators: How to drive your students to be more than just consumers.* https://www.opencolleges.edu.au/informed/features/students-as-creators/

Cakebread, C. (2017, November 15). Without mobile phones, hundreds of millions of people wouldn't have internet access. *Business Insider.* https://www.businessinsider.com/mobile-phones-only-connection-internet-developing-world-chart-2017-11

Chen, G. (2018, August 06). Should public schools ban cell phones? *Public School Review*. https://www.publicschoolreview.com/blog/should-public-schools-ban-cell-phones

Dewey, J. (2001). *Democracy and education*. Penn State Electronic Classics. (Original work published 1916)

Dewey, J. (2005). *Art as experience*. TarcherPerigree. (Original work published 1932)

Dodds, L. (2017, January). Students as social media content creators. *CSLA Journal, 40*(2), 13–16.

Eisner, E. W. (2002). *The arts and the creation of mind*. Yale University Press.

Elgan, M. (2017, August 12). *Smart phones make people distracted and unproductive*. Computerworld. https://www.computerworld.com/article/3215276/smart phones-make-people-distracted-and-unproductive.html

Fond, C. (2018, October 9). *Turning kids from consumers to creators: How to boost student creativity in schools*. Medium. https://medium.com/the-edtech-world/boost-student-creativity-830bc68348c1

Garcia, A. (2017, October 19). *Teens, teachers, and mobile tech*. Confessions of an Aca Fan. http://henryjenkins.org/blog/2017/9/7/an-interview-with-antero-garcia-part-two

Gee, J. P., & Hayes, E. R. (2011). *Language and learning in the digital age*. Routledge. doi:10.4324/9780203830918

Graham, E. (n.d.). *Using smart phones in the classroom*. National Education Association. https://www.nea.org/tools/56274.htm

Hancock, M. (1996, January 1). *What is a photojournalist?* http://markhancock.blogspot.com/1996/01/what-is-photojournalist.html

Handley, L. (2019, January 24). *Nearly three quarters of the world will use just their smart phones to access the internet by 2025*. CNBC. https://www.cnbc.com/2019/01/24/smart phones-72percent-of-people-will-use-only-mobile-for-internet-by-2025.html

Harasim, L. (2000). Shift happens: Online education as a new paradigm in learning. *The Internet and Higher Education, 3*(1-2), 41–61. https://go.aws/341sDn7. doi:10.1016/S1096-7516(00)00032-4

Heath, S. B. (2008). Vision for learning; History, Theory, and Affirmation. In J. Flood, S. B. Heath, & D. Lapp (Eds.), *Handbook of research on teaching literacy through the communicative and visual arts* (Vol. 2, pp. 3–12). Lawrence Erlbaum Associates.

Hess, A. (2019, January 19). *Research continually shows how distracting cell phones are—so some schools want to ban them*. CNBC. https://www.cnbc.com/2019/01/18/research-shows-that-cell-phones-distract-students--so-france-banned-them-in-school--.html

Hicks, T. (2006). Expanding the Conversation: A Commentary Toward Revision of Swenson, Rezema, Young, McGrail, and Whitin. *Contemporary Issues in Technology & Teacher Education*, *6*(1), 46–65.

Hicks, T., & Turner, K. H. (2013). No longer a luxury: Digital literacy can't wait. *English Journal*, *102*(6), 58–65.

Hookway, C. (2007). Short on Peirce's Early Theory of Signs. *Transactions of the Charles S. Peirce Society*, *43*(4), 619–625.

Horn, M. B. (2020). COVID-19s long term impacts on education in 2020 and beyond. *EdSurge*. https://www.edsurge.com/news/2020-03-23-covid-19-s-long-term-impacts-on-education-in-2020-and-beyond

Ingraham, N., & Nuttall, S. (2016). The story of an arts integration school on English-language-learner development: A qualitative study of collaboration, integrity, and confidence. *International Journal of Education & the Arts*, *17*(28). http://www.ijea.org/v17n28/

Kamenetz, A. (2019, October 31). *It's a smartphone life: More than half of U.S. children now have one* [Radio Broadcast]. NPR. https://www.npr.org/2019/10/31/774838891/its-a-smartphone-life-more-than-half-of-u-s-children-now-have-one

Kay, R. H., & Lauricella, S. (2011). Unstructured vs. structured use of laptops in higher education. *Journal of Information Technology Education: Innovations in Practice.*, *10*, 34–42. doi:10.28945/1363

Knobel, M., & Lankshear, C. (2008). Remix: The art and craft of endless hybridization. *Journal of Adolescent & Adult Literacy*, *52*(1), 22–33. doi:10.1598/JAAL.52.1.3

Kolb, L. (2019, February). Smart classroom-tech integration. *The Tech-Savvy School, 76*(5), 20-26. http://www.jite.org/documents/Vol10/JITEv10IIPp033-042Kay840.pdfhttp://www.ascd.org/publications/educational_leadership/feb19/vol76/num05/Smart_Classroom-Tech_Integration.aspx

LaFave, N. (2017, July 25). *Creative lessons with fake texts, tweets, Facebook pages, and more.* https://www.fractuslearning.com/get-creative-fake-texts-tweets-facebook-pages/

Lalonde, M. (2019). The connected image in mobile and social media: The visual instances of adolescents becoming. In J. C. Castro (Ed.), *Mobile media in and outside of the art classroom: Attending to identity, spatiality, and materiality* (pp. 27–46). doi:10.1007/978-3-030-25316-5_2

Lessig, L. (2008). *Remix: Making art and commerce thrive in the hybrid economy.* Bloomsbury Academic. doi:10.5040/9781849662505

Lippincott, J. (2007, November/December). Student content creators: Convergence of literacies. *EDUCAUSE Review, 42*(6), 16–17.

Maloney, D. (2017, March 10). *The essential work of English Language Arts- and our ELA teachers- in our democracy.* NCTE. Https://Ncte.Org/Blog/2017/03/Essential-Work-English-Language-Arts-Ela-Teachers-Democracy/

McCarthy, E. (2015, November 17). *24 Things you might not have known about Hamilton.* Mental Floss. https://www.mentalfloss.com/article/71222/20-things-you-might-not-have-known-about-hamilton

McGuire, G. (1984). How Arts Instruction Affects Reading and Language: Theory and Research. *The Reading Teacher, 37*(9), 835–839.

Michielse, M., & Partti, H. (2015). Producing a meaningful difference: The significance of small creative acts in composing within online participatory remix practices. *International Journal of Community Music, 8*(1), 27–40. doi:10.1386/ijcm.8.1.27_1

Mills, K., & Exley, B. (2014). Research and Policy: Narrative and Multimodality in English Language Arts Curricula: A Tale of Two Nations. *Language Arts, 92*(2), 136–143.

National Council of Teachers of English. (2018). *Beliefs for integrating technology into the English Language Arts classroom.* https://ncte.org/statement/beliefs-technology-preparation-english-teachers/print/

National Governors Association Center for Best Practices and Council of Chief State School Officers. (2010). *Common Core State Standards English Language Arts.* National Governors Association Center for Best Practices, Council of Chief State School Officers. http://www.corestandards.org/ELA-Literacy/

O'Byrne, W. I. (2014). Online content creation: Empowering students as readers and writers of online information. In K. E. Pytash & R. E. Ferdig (Eds.), *Exploring Technology for Writing and Writing Instruction* (pp. 276–297). IGI Global. doi:10.4018/978-1-4666-4341-3.ch016

Pilon, A. (2019). Integrating traditional art making processes and new technology in the high school curriculum. In J. C. Castro (Ed.), *Mobile media in and outside of the art classroom: Attending to identity, spatiality, and materiality* (pp. 151–226). doi:10.1007/978-3-030-25316-5_7

Robinson, K. (2013, April 23). *The dynamics of creativity.* http://sirkenrobinson.com/the-dynamics-of-creativity/

Rosenblatt, L. (1988). *Writing and reading: The transactional theory.* Bolt, Beranek, & Newman, Inc.

Rosenblatt, L. M. (1978). *The reader, the text, the poem: The transactional theory of the literary work.* Southern Illinois University Press.

Schaeffer, K. (2019, August 23). *Most U.S. teens who use cellphones do it to pass time, connect with others, learn new things.* Pew Research Center. https://www.pewresearch.org/fact-tank/2019/08/23/most-u-s-teens-who-use-cellphones-do-it-to-pass-time-connect-with-others-learn-new-things/

Shoffner, M., de Oliveira, L. C., & Angus, R. (2010). Multiliteracies in the secondary English classroom: Becoming literate in the 21st century. *English Teaching, 9*(3), 75–89.

Silver, L., Smith, A., Johnson, C., Jiang, J., Anderson, M., & Raine, L. (2019, March 7). *Use of smart phones and social media is common across most emerging economies.* Pew Research Center. https://www.pewresearch.org/internet/2019/03/07/use-of-smart phones-and-social-media-is-common-across-most-emerging-economies/

Smart phones won. VSCO officially abandons personal computers to focus on the mobile application. (2018, December). https://www.xiaomist.com/2018/12/smart phones-won-vsco-officially.html

Smith, B. E. (2017). Composing across modes: A comparative analysis of adolescents' multimodal composing processes. *Learning, Media and Technology, 42*(3), 259–278. doi:10.1080/17439884.2016.1182924

Stewart, J. (2017, June 20). *The history of photojournalism. How photography changed the way we receive news.* https://mymodernmet.com/photojournalism-history/

Vendantam, S. (2019, September 6). *The distracting draw of smart phones* [Radio Broadcast]. https://www.npr.org/2019/09/06/758199383/the-distracting-draw-of-smartphones

White, M. (2017, April 12). Why everyone needs to make playlists. *The Odyssey Online*. https://www.theodysseyonline.com/everyone-needs-make-playlists

WhoSampled.com. (n.d.). https://www.whosampled.com/The-Notorious-B.I.G./Ten-Crack-Commandments/

Wilson, S. (2018). On digital otherness: Being 'of art' in the age of the internet. *International Journal of Contemporary Humanities*, *3*(1), 1–11. https://www.researchgate.net/publication/329625846_On_Digital_Otherness_Being_%27of_Art%27_in_the_Age_of_the_Internet

Wormell, R. (2015). *Moving students from passive consumers to active creators.* Association for Middle Level Educators. https://www.amle.org/BrowsebyTopic/WhatsNew/WNDet/TabId/270/ArtMID/888/ArticleID/526/Moving-Students-from-Passive-Consumers-to-Active-Creators.aspx

Zamarvide, N. L. (2019, March 29). *Fake social media generators- Ideas for the classroom.* https://natalialzam.wordpress.com/2019/03/29/fake-social-media-generators-ideas-for-the-classroom/

Zoch, M., Myers, J., & Belcher, J. (2016). Teachers' engagement with new literacies: Support for implementing technology in the English/Language Arts classroom. *Contemporary Issues in Technology & Teacher Education*, *17*(1). https://citejournal.org/proofing/teachers-engagement-with-new-literacies-support-for-implementing-technology-in-the-englishlanguage-arts-classroom/

Zoss, M. (2009). Visual arts and literacy. In L. Christenbury, R. Bomer, & P. Smagorinsky (Eds.), *Handbook of Adolescent Literacy Research* (pp. 183–196). The Guilford Press.

Chapter 8
Music and Mobile Phones:
How Students' First Space Mobile Phones Afford Third Space Opportunity

Angela Tudor
Kennesaw State University, USA

ABSTRACT

In a discussion of student behaviors, the author considers the affordances of mobile phones in the English language arts (ELA) classroom. The author believes that mobile phones establish a private, first space where students interact both socially and academically as they appear as audience/observers and agents/creators. In addition to practical affordances, the author discusses social-emotional aspects of mobile phones as they have become part of students' first space, representing both culture and identity. The author believes that music, which exists in students' private first spaces, affords teachers an opportunity to establish and engage students in a neutral third space where meaning and knowing occur without scripts or strategies but rather curiosity, respect, and connection. The author also provides vignettes of practical implementation of digital literacies.

INTRODUCTION

As a secondary English teacher, I am constantly reflecting and questioning; I examine the attitudes and engagement of each class community, and I work to accommodate the needs of the whole as well as the individual. My pedagogical focus is literacy: instruction to encourage critical thought and the cultivation of transferable skills leading to competency of both the written and spoken word as it applies to students'

DOI: 10.4018/978-1-7998-5805-8.ch008

academic, cultural, and individual needs. A few years ago, however, I experienced a crisis of practice. I found that traditional methods were failing to provide the learning experience I wanted for my students. The prevalence of mobile phones, at nearly one hundred percent, became a source of contention; my belief in a physical world of paper, books, and pens was usurped by students' preference for digital efficiency. Too often, my focus shifted from literacy goals to behavior management. But I was determined to hold the line many teachers had drawn in the sand, refusing to be undone by an electronic device. Searches for trends in adolescent literature or cutting-edge authors was replaced by discipline protocols and administrative referrals. As my role changed, so did my relationships with students, and I could not accept that.

It was a slow transition; the need to control the mobile phone was strong, and I was resistant. One day, however, I recognized an olive branch extending from students' mobile phones connecting our love of music; I grabbed on and allowed myself to view the classroom from the other side. I developed empathy in my students' view of the physical world of the classroom, recognizing that the mobile phone had not only evolved technologically, it had also become part of their persona. What follows is a reflection of the way music provided the impetus as well as the ambience to change my perceptions, my classroom environment, and my practice. My students and I share a common appreciation for music, and with music, I have reimagined the classroom, and I have reconsidered space as it applies to the physical, virtual, and ideological world of education. This chapter reflects my understanding of students' first space identity, a governed second space, and a third interventional space where learning occurs through negotiation.

Third Space Theory is attributed to Bhabha (1994) who relates identity to both space and power: an individual resides in the first space of origin, tradition, and culture and then becomes subject to a second space of authority, which becomes a "place of splitting" (p. 44). While Bhabha (1994) refers to the politicization of colonization, Benson (2010) asserts that schools are also political institutions subject to bureaucracies and forms of colonization. Moje et al., (2004) agree, suggesting that second-space schools become colonizers by valuing certain skill sets and knowledge over others, increasing the need of a third space. While Bhabha's (1994) third space emerges as neutral, where meaning is both new and negotiated, Gutiérrez (2008) conceptualized third space in education, identifying it as a space "where teacher and student scripts--the formal and informal, the official and unofficial spaces of the learning environment--intersect" (p. 152). Students' first space represents individual, familial, and cultural identity; the second space classroom represents the formality of both language and tradition; the third space exists in between as indicated in Figure 1.

Figure 1. Interlocking rings showing the relationships between separate spaces of identity and authority.
Adapted from H. Bhabha, The Location of Culture, and K. Gutiérrez "Developing a Sociocritical Literacy in the Third Space".

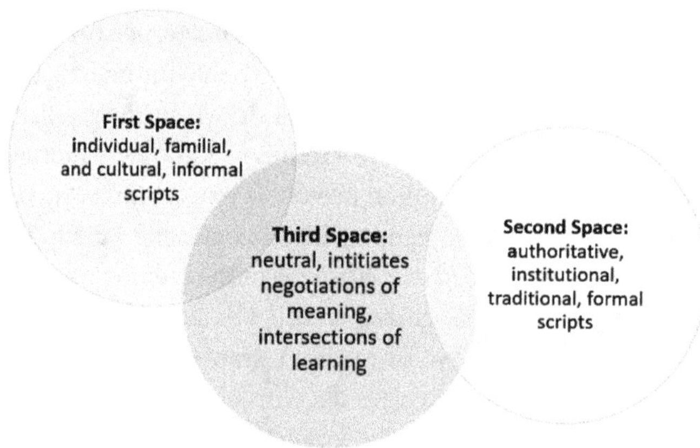

To achieve a third space of negotiation and learning, teachers must first manage the tensions that exist in the institutional tradition which may deny student motility, lived experience, and authentic learning (Ehret & Hollett, 2014; Nixon, 2013). Implementation of new and digital literacies may be difficult for teachers in the second space. Before we attempt to help students find meaning and authenticity, we must also release some traditional methods of practice and interaction. My intention is to emphasize the importance of a third space, an envisioned state of being where, in my experience, negotiation often commences with music. I also discuss the synonymous nature of a third space as an affinity space where student engagement is transformed from obligation to enthusiasm (Gee, 2018; Hillocks & Smith, 1995). I believe that soon the mobile phone will be bigger than my ability to control it, so my best hope is to accept it and perhaps learn to tame it.

BACKGROUND

I was teaching middle school when students started bringing mobile phones into the classroom; there were a few here and there, but they were a novelty. I was unconcerned about the phones, and I regarded them as a gadget, an occasional annoyance, similar to an iPod or Gameboy. But just as I was getting used to texting and primordial game playing, mobile phones evolved. With its name change to *smartphone*, students were given a free ride on the *information superhighway*, and pretty soon they were driving themselves into consumer hubs and exploring back alleys of the Internet. It was around this time that teachers started focusing on constraints associated with mobile phones because students had been afforded instantaneous access to a bright, new world luring them like a pied piper to all sorts of wonderlands far from the learning environment. Ávila and Pandya (2013) describe students' digital freedom as "traveling," surmising that "the human soul is now transported in virtual non-linear worlds" (p. 1). I see the authors' point as I superimpose images of students' facial expressions over this metaphor, their attention fixed to their screens, obviously enchanted by their travels.

As mobile phone use became more pervasive in the classroom, educators' concerns mimicked warnings from research. Yan (2018) explored the phenomena associated with children's development in the age of the mobile phone, identifying dangerous, and fear-filled possibilities such as brain cancer, brain tumors, sexting, and distracted driving. The mobile phone, which had at first appeared benign, became an object of fear and uncertainty. Stoking those fears, Carr (2011) cautioned that an insatiable desire for information was limiting our ability to think deeply and critically; the Internet was literally changing our brains. Did we believe it? Maybe, but with a cache of affordances and a side of codependency featured in every new model, society embraced desensitization, and our relationships with our mobile phones became more important and more complicated. Like it or not, the mobile phone has ingratiated itself to the culture, and its heavy presence in the classroom can no longer be ignored.

As a teacher of young adults and adolescents, I was vexed by the choices before me: to become a disciplinarian--*the mobile phone police*, or to embrace the affordances of the mobile phone while also cultivating respectful relationships with my students. Choosing the latter, I needed a creed to extinguish the critical and disquieting eyes of colleagues and administrators who might pop in only to find my students immersed in their mobile devices with their look conveying the message, "Oh, I see you've given up." But I have not given up; I am giving in to the affordances of an existing digital culture. Ávila and Pandya (2013) contend that educators should be building on the literacy practices students engage in outside classrooms, suggesting that implementation of digital literacy is simply meeting students where they live and are already absorbed in literacy as both authors and creators. These pursuits often involve music, which I have come to recognize as a portal of instructional possibilities.

Music: The Maestro of the Third Space

Lynch (2008) applied the metaphor of the musical fugue, *a subject introduced and repeated throughout a composition*, to classroom practice where students take first space musical interests into a third, evolutionary space. Music, when given life in the third space classroom, "creates newness; when it ends, it begins" (Lynch, 2008, p. 337). Bhabha (1994) refers to the third space as "an encounter with 'newness' that is not part of the continuum" (p. 10). According to Hensley (2019), the value of music in the classroom is immeasurable where critical connections support learning, engagement, and motivation, and these resources are easily accessible through students' ever-present mobile phones.

Students remain connected to the external world through social media aps, and they are masters of ICT (information and communications technology). They are also motivated to interact using social networking services like Instagram, which Magraner and Ramos (2020) found productive when combined with music to accomplish second space tasks. Using Instagram, students applied creative ingenuity followed by critical analysis to discover tensions and socially-driven themes in music (Magraner & Ramos, 2020). Hrebik (2019) examined the commonality of music, suggesting that as teachers allow music to become a *motif* in the second space, students approach tasks from familiar ground. Music establishes harmony between the first and second space when students use mobile phones to access primary resources instead of textbooks which limit their choices. Storvas (2011) asserts that "being able to write about themselves and the music they love gets students energized immediately about the writing process" (p. 27). It isn't just about choice and preference; music offers opportunities to reimagine conceptions of literacy as students learn cross-curricular elements such as setting, theme, and purpose (Storvas, 2011). Incorporating music into the English curriculum encourages the cultivation of close reading strategies including empathy through analysis of characters' motivations (Hensley, 2019; Hrebik, 2019). When students are immersed in music as literacy, it is easier for them to approach writing tasks inspired by the structure music provides. Hrebik (2019) contends that teaching composition through music keeps students in touch with first space identities, and it also teaches them to value their culture as they develop as writers. Examples of practical implementation of music in the English Language Arts classroom are available in Table 1.

Music speaks to the commonality of shared language and the individuality of culture. Edmin (2013) addresses the chasm between students' first space cultures and second space narratives suggesting that there is "space in the classroom for hybridized discourse" (p. 96). Nash-Ditzel and Brown (2012) posit that "popular culture in the classroom can be a means of bridging gaps between students' out-of-school and in-school literacies" (p. 97). Pedagogy that omits culture and identity in the second space occurs in what Bhabha (1994) terms as "splitting" (p.44). Edmin (2013) refers to this as "pedagogy of poverty" where the student, separated from first space culture, exists as "docile recipient" instead of independent agent (p. 95). Edmin (2013) asserts that applying the language of music to classroom discourses provides students with an opportunity to decipher complicated master narratives, promoting

Table 1. Resources for practical implementation of music in ELA

Source / Weblink	Strategy	Practical Implications
Countryman and Rose (2017)	Accessing students' first space music using online gaming with connections to the Hero's Journey to build student efficacy and well being	• Connects to commonly taught plot structure (Hero's Journey) to encourage prediction and inferencing • Encourages creativity • First space familiarity
Edmin (2013) https://hiphoped.com/	Expand student understanding through language -- emphasis on code switching between cultures and discourses including the cultivation and practice of literacy --Science Mindedness to Pillars of Hip Hop	• Forming hypotheses • Making informed decisions • Recognizing dogma • Rhetoric • Acquisition and organization of facts
Hensley (2019)	Practice and projects utilizing musicals - *Hamilton: An American Musical*	• Close Reading • Inquiry Model • Student Discovery & Analysis • Creative Development
Hrebik (2019)	Songwriting to explore literacy, identity, and other elements of literacy and English-Language-Arts	• Song #1: construct a song describing a particular "place" which could be either metaphorical or literal in nature • Song #2: construct a song describing a particular "person" who made a significant impact on you at some point • Song #3: construct a 6-line stanza describing a particular "time" or moment in your life that has left a lasting impression upon you.
Magraner & Ramos (2020) https://www.instagram.com/?hl=en	Using Instagram to create music memes; multimodalities in literacy	• Teaches critical thinking through analysis • Concepts of genre • Author's purpose • Themes • Social Justice
Moje et al., (2004)	Using Music in the science Classroom with practical implications for cross-curricular study	• Synthesizing and cross-referencing skills using music artists, song titles, and CD titles • Classify and identify musical genres to teach comparison skills and to introduce naming and classifying solids, liquids, and gasses

a negotiated third space. Chase (2018) agrees, suggesting that as counter-narratives surface, tensions compel new normative discourses in a third space. Benson (2010) asserts that the third space "shifts the balance of power [to position] students and teachers as co-learners and co-teachers" (p. 561). It is through music and culture that Edmin (2013) believes teachers have an opportunity to respond to students culturally, emotionally, and academically in changing formal scripts to reflect the equality of the third space. Bhabha (1994) contends that to achieve a negotiated third space, we must "think beyond narratives or originary and initial subjectivities and to focus on those moments or processes that are produced in the articulation of cultural differences" (p. 2).

Music creates cultural conversations; students offer suggestions when I stream music or ask about my preferences, and certain artists or lyrics may generate additional, even critical discussion. Music initiates a third space, a respite where negotiation and connection occur. Nash-Ditzel and Brown (2012) agree, suggesting that students' first space interests initiate third space engagement to promote growth in much the same way Vgotsky defines the Zone of Proximal Development. As relationships are strengthened, and students see me as human, music creates a space of cohabitation and negotiation, a space as well as an experience where things get done.

Space: A Novel Frontier

The advent of the mobile phone changed human social interaction, propelling the transmission and acquisition of information into new modes and inquiries, including the field of literacy research. Leander, Phillips, and Taylor (2010) insist that changes in social interactions outside the classroom must also be a consideration within it; the authors identify divergent views of a classroom environment as "a container-like perspective on the one hand and a nexus-like perspective on the other," each view replete with contrasting philosophies of what constitutes learning and where learning may occur (p. 332). When I decided to incorporate mobile phones into my practice, I was searching for a neutral ground between these two perspectives; I was searching for what Mills and Comber (2013) describe as a "shift from reproducing literacies that are disembodied from the materiality of students' lives" (p. 4). I knew that traditional curriculum approaches amounted to *doing* school rather than addressing the immediate and long-term literacy interests and needs of students. So, while researchers encourage teachers to reconsider the viability of traditional tests and worksheets, they also emphasize a fresh view of a living classroom space, subject to the contextual needs of each community grouped there (Mills & Comber, 2013). The classroom lives solely for the purpose of students who embody the space individually and corporately in a socially constructed context, so in pursuit of change, I had to take a step back to take a closer look at students as human beings.

Students physically enter my classroom as the embodiment of sociocultural experiences and ideologies representing multifaceted identities. Among their belongings and symbols of self, their most protected artifact is their mobile phone. The mobile phone connects them to worlds beyond the geography of the classroom to support their social and emotional needs. Walsh, White, and Young (2009) found the need for belonging was a strong predictor of students' attachment to their mobile phones. The mobile phone has become an extension of the student, linked to their identity through a blending of social and cultural practice in much the same way Bhabha (in Rutherford, 1990) describes *hybridity* as the blending of two independent parts to create a new whole. In this way, students, along with their mobile phones, embody a single, symbiotic space, a first space of being.

First Space. The first space refers to the student's individual, physical, and virtual spaces; it is the incarnation of language, experience, and culture. It is both metaphorical and literal; students occupy a physical space as well as a virtual space when they enter classrooms with their mobile phones. Russo (2018) reported that in 2015, seventy-one percent of adolescents aged thirteen to seventeen had access to the Internet through a smartphone. The Pew Research Center (2020) updated those statistics, reporting that ninety-six percent of Americans own a mobile phone and eighty-one percent of those are smartphones. That number is closer to one-hundred percent among students in my classroom who rely heavily on mobile phones to connect to the outside world. It is important for teachers to recognize that students may choose to retreat into virtual worlds depending on circumstances which may relate to a need for social-emotional connection or to avoid negativity (Nikolopoulou & Gialamas, 2018). In this way, the mobile phone arrives with a disclaimer: researchers contend the mobile phone is connected to students' psychological well-being; to demand separation means to defer emotional support and intrinsic, cultural identity (Walsh, White, & Young, 2009). While some teachers say this is akin to addictive behavior, students' need for this connection does not necessarily equate to dependence as asserted by Griffiths (2013).

It is impossible to enter a neutral third space if I remain immovable in the second space, decreeing that mobile phones may not exist in the realm. I have tried this before, and it does not bode well; students turn away from me, mentally and emotionally. I become the enemy. If I accept students' mobile phones as an extension of themselves, I am honoring and respecting their right to a first space.

Second Space. The second space represents the physical space of the classroom; this space exists through levels of control and hierarchies. As a subordinate of the second space, I provide instruction as mandated by curriculum. While I am an agent of the second space, research affirms options for implementing standards-based curriculum where interpretations of literacy are as varied as school populations (Avila & Moore, 2012). Leem and Sung (2019) contend that teachers' attitudes toward curriculum, technology in particular, influence students' digital learning opportunities. My goal in the second space is to create a safe and welcoming environment to promote opportunities for a third space where learning becomes contextual and authentic. I continue to adjust my second space agenda while learning to use the affordances of the mobile phone to my advantage, and I have discovered that a path to third space intervention involves music.

Third Space. The third space represents a space of neutrality where members leave their first and second spaces to enter an unspoken negotiation. In the third space, hierarchies exist, but their power has been displaced in favor of cooperation (Bhabha in Rutherford, 1990). Learning events are guided by authentic collaboration; inquiry is born of curiosity, and meaning is driven and remade as a result of contextual need (Gee, 2018; Hillocks & Smith, 1995). *Third space* may become synonymous with *affinity space*; this occurs when students enter *flow*, where, driven through inquiry, they are fully engaged and fully present; it is a space where obligation gives way to desire (Gee, 2018; Hillocks & Smith, 1995). Lynch (2008), suggests that a third space emerges when students' first space interests are acknowledged as a valued part of the second space process. While my goal is to establish a collective third space, my hope is to advance each student individually. Moran (2018) found that third space experiences go beyond collaboration and skills acquisition to instill confidence while contributing to students' positive self-efficacy.

Affinity Spaces: Gee (2018) introduced *affinity* space which refers to physical, virtual, or mental spaces occupied out of interest, engagement, connection, or desire. When I think about my students' affinity spaces, I recognize a common portal where they engage in myriad activities--their mobile phones. In my classroom almost all students have headphones, wired or wireless, phones in hands. Their activities are as varied as their interests; Gee (2018) refers to these unhindered choices as affinity spaces. Choice is crucial; this is a space where students feel alive, engaged, or valued (Gee, 2018). Affinity spaces certainly exist in the physical world, but students are devoting more of their time to virtual opportunities to express creativity and connect with others (Alvermann, 2008; Gee, 2018). Students' mobile phones are a vehicle, acting nearly prosthetically to support engagement in the affinity or first space. What is interesting, however, is that even as students engage in individual choices on their mobile phones, there is often a background space drawing them together: music. Regardless of their virtual choice, music compliments the setting for affinity and first space activities.

FINDINGS

Vignettes: Third Spaces in the Classroom

When my students feel safe and respected, they are open to learning experiences; learning does not occur in fear, angst, or frustration associated with the loss of mobile phones. Bhabha (in Rutherford, 1990) suggests that the third space may also represent a place of safety, a zone free of agendas and enforcement. Occasionally the third space may be cajoled or manipulated into being, but from my practical experience, the best third spaces rise organically, initiated by students and inspired by music. The following vignettes represent some of my experiences along the way to understanding, negotiating, and embracing third space opportunities in my classroom.

When All Else Fails, Try a Sing-along: Second Space Compromises

My American Literature students were studying the Puritan poet Anne Bradstreet. I had attempted to paint a verbal picture to explain the harsh ocean passage and obstacle-filled life of the New World's first poet, but students' interests were waning before the first poem. A colleague shared guided notes accompanied by a short video found on the Internet with Bradstreet's background set to music, "Don't Stop Believin' by the popular 1980's band Journey (Cain, Perry, & Schon, 1981). Students bought in; it was literacy engagement, and it was an exercise in duality. They sang along while taking notes either with pen and paper or using their mobile phones; through music and technology, students challenged school-based narratives where learning is controlled from a second, controlled space (Curwood & Gibbons, 2010). Students who were caught up in the song (which also generated some dancing) used their mobile phones to access the video and a few others as we shared a Journey revival. It became an intermission from the mundane, rising to accommodate our need for a third space to connect and learn. In the third space they were listening: Bradstreet is proof that your talent will make room for you--even if you are living in a pious, sexist society. We had been worlds apart, but music brought us together.

When my students read Bradstreet's (1598 / 2008) "To My Dear and Loving Husband," I invited them back to this musical third space, asking them to compare the sixteenth-century poem to Peter Gabriel's (1986) song "In Your Eyes." Students used their mobile phones with headphones to access the audio link, and they explored the lyrics and the poem first independently, then in pairs, and finally in whole class discussion, which included student-generated critical analysis and inquiry: *Is Gabriel's first-person narrator a misogynist?* Those discussions changed the way I read Gabriel's lyrics just as the musical third space changed my practice.

Mobile Phones, the New Pad and Quill: From Participatory Cultures to Presentation of Texts

In English courses, class discussions eventually turn into writing tasks, which I prefer to accomplish using Google Docs; students usually download the app on their mobile phones, accessing hotspots to avoid the slow school Internet. While the documents are created by students in their Google Drive, they are also shared in a class folder. The documents become what Mills (2010) references as "transportable texts," because they are created, retrieved, edited, and shared virtually from different physical locations (p. 249). As a method of practice, when students write, I often give real-time feedback, displaying individual work on the big, class screen; this is a second space where students may access academic resources and strategies for growth. As it appears on the screen, the text consumes the front of the room, commanding the second, teacher-centered space, designated for instruction. Highlights I have made, or special fonts or text colors students have used in their writing process appear as opportunities for others to observe or mime the process. In this way, the text is more than words; meaning is made in the image itself as "the textual entity is treated as a visual entity in ways in which the page never was" (Kress, 2003, p. 64). I rotate between individual documents in their class file, displaying various work for all to see. I explain that writers learn by example, that imitation (not plagiarism) is the highest form of flattery, and that we are a community learning from each other. Prior to the efficiency afforded by mobile phones and Google, I used a similar strategy with a document camera. It was cumbersome, and there was too much lag time as I wrote feedback on the paper. Students lost interest while waiting, and third space interactions were rare.

While they write, most students listen to music on headphones, which they remove for our one-to-all feedback session. In this way, students remain in touch with their private first space, but they are also welcomed into the second space of instruction and feedback where music also streams from my computer. Students respond well to this method, and they may stop their work to observe editing and revision in process. Experts in the field explain that adolescents' penchant for online creation and publication relates to their awareness of the audience; they are constantly editing and revising online profiles using adaptive methods to achieve individual goals (Alvermann, 2008). When I provide feedback, it is generally questioning--did you consider *this* or *that*; what if you moved *this* here and added *that* there? And I am not alone. Students also receive commentary and compliments from their classmates. These sessions accomplish what one-to-one writing conferences cannot; they are timely, direct, and reflective as I am typing comments directly onto student work as a visual reference. Students' collaborative efforts represent what Alvermann (2008) believes warrants additional study; they have become a participatory culture where, unbidden, they freely contribute abilities and resources to the class community. Music is a covering here, housing spaces where students move freely and privately in their first space as both audience/observer and agent/creator, and in the second space where they are invited to access resources and strategies for growth, but there is also a third space.

According to Cook (2005), the third space experience requires flexibility; deviating from plans may prove more beneficial when students engage in authentic and contextual learning. A third-space interaction generated by a common love of music often leads to a common awe of literacy. In the third space, hierarchies do not exist as the space emerges through curiosity and respect to exist symbiotically and independent of the first two spaces. The third space is nearly ethereal as it ebbs and flows in our communal search for knowing and authenticity. According to Cook (2005), the third space is purposefully "unscripted" to establish a space where "there is equality of participation," where learning moves beyond "the activity that produces it...showing the contributing influences of both learner and teacher" (p 86). When I ask a student about a particular writing choice or thought process, the community recognizes we are on different, albeit equal ground. I am no longer the master of the second space; my curiosity reveals it. My questions indicate respect and that I, too, am learning. It is in the third space where students recognize the master as human, not unlike themselves. It is in moments like these where the greyness of the institution fades away, and we become an authentic community seeking to know. Mills and Comber (2013) refer to the third space as "A new area of negotiation of meaning and representation, where official and unofficial, formal and informal spaces become permeable and create the potential for new kinds of learning" (p. 3). The third space experience is palpable, and it is among the most rewarding of teaching experiences. It is my belief that third space interactions are encouraged as teachers seek common interests, and music is among the most available, easily accessible, and rich with literacy possibilities. Music appears at first neutral; then it summons a power difficult to explain to create a space where things change.

Teacher as Audience: Music as Literacy and Identity

I continue to encourage students into a musical third space, and occasionally, they invite me into one of their making. The assignment was simple: present an understanding of themes in Golding's (1954) *Lord of the Flies* and write a reflection of the process. Students were afforded agency to express their unique thoughts and ideas, which is supported by research; Mills (2010) found in a review of empirical literature that students' use of digital literacies was most effective when learning was directed by their interests. I did not stipulate a specific app or technology for the assignment. I knew that my students' abilities varied as some were more adept at digital production while others preferred to share their expertise in digital design. According to Curwood and Gibbons (2010), it is important for teachers who implement digital literacies to emphasize the process and product rather than trendy apps students may utilize. Student submissions were written, recorded, and uploaded to our district digital learning platform using mobile phones, tablets, and desktops. Among them were commercials for traveling to the island, an old-time radio hour with sound effects, and an original composition written and performed by a student-musician, who recorded the performance on a mobile phone and converted it to a digital file for submission. I listened to the composition before reading the reflection, and I played it again because the music drew me with its haunting tones, rising and falling in a crash of emotion. When I read the student's reflection, I listened again. The student captured the emotional essence of Simon's death without words, effectively conveying a message without paragraphs or topic sentences; Mills (2010) suggests that in the New Literacy Studies, "hybridization of texts" occurs when meaning is made through varying representations of texts, which could also include an original musical score (p. 256). I was astonished and moved by the creation. I messaged to let the student know the effect the composition had on me, and she replied with gratitude.

In our next virtual class meeting, most students appeared on their mobile phones, a few with open cameras, most with audio only. I had asked prior permission to share the piece, and the musician agreed. Together, the class and I complimented the work, expressing collective awe, and we moved to a third space of equality. I acknowledged the musician's expertise while admitting she holds skills I admire but do not personally possess (Benson, 2010). Here, the musician gained confidence, opening her camera feature to share her visual image with us. My student is a musician and a gifted composer; the audience's reaction supported that identity. Nash (2018) asserts that "the shift to allowing student choice and interests in composition [creates] space in many classrooms for students to explore and share aspects of their identities" (p. 351). Curwood and Gibbons (2010) agree, suggesting it is important for teachers to provide purposeful opportunities for students to express themselves and share identities with an audience. While I know this was the case with the musician, this was also unexpected, an organic shift in the assignment. My objective had been critical, creative thought to display understanding of the text. While I did not convey it, I had expected traditional products, and I was astonished at the freedoms students took to make the assignment individual, cultural, and unique to their purpose. The learning experience did not stop with one student; the reaction and confidence had a positive effect on others in the virtual meeting. Moran (2018) suggests that even as students emphasize individual strengths, the third space is a "shared space that [belongs]... to all of them" (p. 236). Again, the power of music as indicated by Saunders (2010) becomes a "vehicle through which pupils may explore both themselves (as parts of their identities) and others" (p. 70). Mobile phones afford students choice as well as access and agency to create, share, and learn. This assignment became a counter narrative for students. This experience could not have occurred in a school-based narrative, one-dimensional essay assignment (Curwood & Gibbons, 2010). And it was made possible because of technology. If students were faced with a single live-performance choice, I may not have realized their capabilities, and we might never have reached the third space. Countryman and Rose (2017) say it best in the spirit of John Dewey: "The moral ends of public schooling are to equip young people to be independent thinkers and actors, to free them from adults' care so that they might not only shape and direct an unfolding world, but also reimagine it. Freedom, empowerment, agency, self-reliance, one-another-ness–these are the moral ends of education" (p. 78). Digital literacies are part of students' independence and creative agency, and it is through unique and critical creations flowing to one and then another that students know and are known by audiences of their peers.

It's All About the Base, No Trouble: From Master Narrative to Narrative of the Self

In the years that mobile phones have gained stature among students, I have learned they also afford a strategic portal to their world. One afternoon, as my last class was entering the room, a student entered with flair, moving to the beat of the music emitted through wireless headphones. I was greeting students at the door, and as he got closer, he looked up and smiled at me as I mouthed the question, *Lil Baby*? I knew the artist's name, one of his favorites, because I had asked the first time I heard him singing the lyrics--*a cappella* because the music was his alone. This artist has had his share of problems and consequences, but his integrity is irrelevant to me. I am looking for a connection, and I am persistent in my search to find it.

That afternoon students were working collaboratively on constructed responses as we prepared for end-of-course tests. Students dislike the drill-and-kill type writing, and it is more difficult in the late afternoon, an hour before the final dismissal bell. As my co-teacher and I trudged through the formulaic lesson framed by the mandated acronym strategy, we moved from group to group where students were supposed to work collaboratively to accomplish the task. One student was sitting alone, which was unusual because he had a rep; he liked to hijack attention and create all manner of havoc during class. He was an adult student, and it troubled me to find him sitting in solitude outside classroom doors or alone in a study carrel serving in-school suspension. His struggles were not alleviated with an individual education plan; institutional control is difficult for older students, and most teachers are watchful, knowing that at any time they may walk away and never return. He was measured through a limited and ideological view of literacy which, as discussed by Mills and Comber (2013), speaks both socially and historically to patterns of marginalization. The tragedy is that while his Lexile scores might have indicated functional illiteracy, those tests did not measure his creativity or consider his evolving strengths in other, digital literacies (Perry, 2012). This was his second attempt at American Literature, and I wanted to make sure it would be his last.

I could see he was working diligently, tapping keys on his mobile phone, so I stopped to ask if he had any questions. He looked at me sheepishly, and I realized that he was writing song lyrics instead of practicing the writing strategy. I sat with him and asked about his music; he was a digital lyricist and music composer; I'd spoken to him before about his work. As we talked, he played his most recent self-publication, and I listened intently; he blushed as profanity rose with the music from his mobile phone. I ignored it and asked what he was working on at the time. He shared his vision, and the composition he was struggling to complete. His table-mate returned from a lengthy restroom break to complain that he had not helped her finish the assignment. I asked her how I might help, and we worked through the strategies I'd gone over many times in mini-lessons. When she was satisfied that she understood the assignment, she replaced her wired headphones, adjusted a playlist on her phone, and sealed herself away to her work.

I asked the young man if I could help him with his composition. He looked surprised at first, but then he eagerly explained to me what he was attempting; the theme was brokenness. Since we were studying *The Great Gatsby* (Fitzgerald, 1925), I asked if he could see similarities between his first-person lyrics and the experiences of the main character. He was puzzled at first. His writing occurred in his first, private space, and he had not considered that his personal interests might ever intersect with the second-space classroom. Lynch (2008) contends that as students "are encouraged to bring knowledge from familiar aspects of their lives into the classroom, there is the possibility that they will learn more deeply and in new ways" (p. 336). I asked to listen to the recording again to get a sense of his style and preferences; he hesitated at first, saying he was sorry for the profanity. I explained that expletives make us pause, and when well-placed, they become visual or visceral art, transmitting multiple meanings while evoking passions. Wide-eyed, he revealed his bewilderment but nodded in consensus. He wanted to see me as human, not just his cardigan-clad teacher. As I listened to the music, I found unity in his compositions, a resounding flow and urgency set to beats; they were carefully and lovingly crafted. I felt privileged that he'd shared with me. As we talked about his composition, I infused Fitzgerald's characterization of Jay Gatsby into the mix, and I asked him about Gatsby's love for Daisy, nudging him on until he found the place where Gatsby had broken himself. Daisy had not changed from the beginning; she is a static character, I explained. Gatsby, however, was alive and dynamic; he had choices, but he could not accept himself as whole and worthy without acceptance into Daisy's world. After a few moments, his eyes lit with knowing; he allowed the spaces to come together; it was a base, a foundation to build upon. In this moment, at the collision of his worlds, he was motivated because he identified learning relevant to his first space interests. This reaction is affirmed by research of multiliteracy practice; the New London Group (1996) asserts that it is difficult for people to learn when they are not driven by self-interests, inferring that learning should be authentic and situated in sociocultural context and identity.

We found what Sheey (1999, as cited in Mills & Comber, 2013) called an "in-between space," which equates to third space negotiation; I honored his first space interests, and he acknowledged the second space expectation (p. 4). He did not accomplish the objectives of the master narrative during that class, but he did engage in literacy of his choosing, and through personal narrative, he was able to create and share his story with an audience (Curwood & Gibbons, 2010). This unscripted, learning experience mimics what the New London Group (1996) identifies as "Transformed Practice" where the "student now has to both juxtapose and integrate (not without tension) two different discourses, or social identities" (p. 87). He identified first as a songwriter-composer, even while physically present in the second space classroom. His resistance to the authority of the second space created tensions which tugged at the freedom he needed to fully engage in his independent pursuits. The emergence of the third space provided relevancy, meaning, and perhaps new perspectives of opportunities and resources available for him in the second space.

He did eventually return to the mandates of the second space; he promised to stay for tutoring and finish the constructed response, which he did, and he passed the end-of-course test with two points to spare. He succumbed to the mandates and expectations of the second space, which he recognized had influence over his future. Perry (2012) asserts that it is important for teachers to accept a conceptualized literacy which is diverse in every context and multimodal definition, and we must begin to acknowledge and honor the ways students practice literacy in the real world. It is through understanding and valuing the cultures and life experiences students bring into our classrooms that we are able to release traditions and categorizations of normal (Chase, 2018). After that semester, he came back again and again, sharing new creations from a well-worn mobile phone, the screen cracked into webs. I used these visits to monitor his progress toward graduation. He was fortunate; his teachers were invested in his success. We knew what it meant to his family. He was a first generation American and a fifth-year senior, and he was determined to graduate, which he did the following spring to thunderous applause. It was his moment; he had found an audience in the virtual world, and with this accomplishment his worlds collided again as he achieved a physical audience to also celebrate him.

In a social media-driven world where identity is built through likes, comments, influence, and digital gestures, the concept of audience has become central to adolescents' interactions (Alvermann, 2008). The need for an audience is in effect the need for affirmation. The third space is dependent on affirmations of acceptance and respect. The search for Sheehy's (1999, as cited in Mills and Comber, 2013) "in-between spaces" requires a "[disruption] of the daily rhythms of the typical literacy economy classrooms" (p. 5). This is difficult for teachers who have been conditioned through mandates and observations to dance to scores of school narratives. But I am learning to hold loosely to the reins of the second space because a third space opportunity may arrive unexpectedly.

Expect It, Even When It is Unexpected: Space and Motility

He was playing "Stairway to Heaven" (Page & Plant, 1971), those first few chords everyone learns when they begin playing the guitar. He had written about learning to play in an assignment, and I asked him if he wanted to bring his guitar to class to play for us. As he played, the lyrics were audible in my mind: "There's a lady who's sure / All that glitters is gold / And she's buying a stairway to Heaven" (Page & Plant, 1971, lines 1-3). I cite this as a poem because I used these lines to connect to the poetry we were studying. Students were struggling with Longfellow's "The Tide Rises, The Tide Falls," and I related the song to the individual, sometimes ambiguous, meanings derived from poetry; songs are, after all, poetry set to music. I asked the student playing the guitar if he knew what the lyrics meant, and he said he only knew the chorus, which amounts to "Oh, oh, oh, she's buying a stairway to heaven...Ooh, it makes me wonder" (Plant & Page, 1971, 7,14). So, I challenged him to listen to the song, think about it and decide for himself what Jimmy Page and Robert Plant (1971) were trying to express. We played the music video, and everyone sang along (with the chorus). We discussed poetry in a new, engaging way with the lyrics on the big screen, which we froze as students marked ideas, meanings, and allusions; they took the lead in their learning, and the space was filled with their experience. Ehret & Hollett (2014) studied space as it relates to physical as well as virtual presence in the classroom when students are granted *motility*, that is, the right to move independently within the second, institutional space in the practice of literacies. The third space is born of struggle between second space, school tensions and students' rights to motility and authentic learning (Ehret & Hollett, 2014; Nixon, 2013).

Students continued to struggle with Longfellow, but it was a moment of cohesive engagement with everyone focused on one thing--a moment of teachers' daydreams. Lessons that go beyond the bounds of textbooks and copies of ancient texts do more than engage; this type of learning creates experience and retention (Cowles, 2019). Learning that evolves from students' interests while also incorporating multimodalities supports a new view of literacy. Students in my class that day did not know they were supporting research; multiliteracies create multilayered meanings where connections are made and remade based on the collective sharing of knowledge and experience (Nash, 2018). It was because of music, this time Page and Plant (1971), that my students gave Longfellow another try, and they found something different in those subsequent readings and discussions that were made possible by freedom of interest, a multiliteracy approach, and technology in our classroom. And, while we used the teacher computer and the big screen for the lesson, I am pretty sure a few students managed to use their mobile phones to circulate a Tik Tok or Snapchat likely captioned, "Look what we did in *English* today." Mobile phones create conversations, and even when initiated by sarcasm or indignation, virtual interactions employ literacy.

Can't Touch This: Respect the First Space

In the age before *hear* it--*want* it--*download* it, my music was sourced from television, and more often radio, FM--not broadband. Masters of popular music like MTV's Nina Blackwood and Martha Quinn, or Dick Clark of "American Bandstand," or Casey Kasem of "America's Top 40," gave the go-ahead before I spent hard-earned money to buy physical copies of recordings, most often in the form of vinyl record albums. That process seems burdensome and inconvenient compared to the current world where music--*any* music--is mobile and easily accessible. Those vinyl albums of my youth were the dinosaurs to digital downloads, iTunes Libraries, YouTube, and Spotify. Owning those albums was important to me in the first space of my youth. They were tangible and tactile; their covers made me an art collector. Even the turntable, guiding the needle to the first grooves on the vinyl became part of a visceral experience that has been replaced by a click or swipe. The grainy scratch-skips have given way to digital clarity made richer by noise-cancelling headphones. Students make up a modern audience that would never consider wasting time listening or storing filler songs, those before and after the hits on vinyl albums. Students are content to share music; they do not need to own it. They trust the music to be there when they choose to experience it, but choice is important. Students are territorial when it comes to their first space mobile phones, and it is among their most guarded traits.

In 2014, I had an iPhone, 6S-Plus. My students called it an iPad because of its robust nature; I called it practical because its size made it possible for me to see what I was doing. On September 9, 2014, my classroom was buzzing about a free album added to iTunes libraries. I had heard about the release on the news that morning, but I had not had a chance to see or listen to the gift Apple users had been afforded. My students' opinions varied, but most were indignant, suggesting that they did not want the age-old band on their phones. They were speaking of U2, and the band's lead singer-songwriter, Paul Hewson, better known by his stage name, Bono. I like U2, so I asked what was wrong with the album, and my students acted as if I had asked them what was wrong with kale--*we don't want it; that's the point.* Using their mobile phones, several students showed me the album cover, which is a bit provocative and elicited a few crude comments which I allayed with a teacher-look. A student played Hewson's (2014) lead track, "The Miracle" from their mobile phones, so I had a reference to the album. I knew the release must be related to publicity, but my students' reactions were emotional, decisive, even indignant, and I was perplexed. Reflecting on this now, it seems obvious that my students' reactions were related to their feelings of ownership of their first space--their mobile phones. Without permission, and by cover of night, Apple had entered, redecorated, and expected to be thanked for their invasion. When I asked what they would do with the album, most of my students said they'd already deleted it without listening to any of the songs. Others said they were holding it as evidence of their complaints against Apple; they felt violated. It is difficult to say if students' reactions were a result of their own beliefs or if peer pressure influenced their decisions; Walsh, White, and Young (2009) found that in addition to connectedness, adolescents' social identification and the need for social belonging was inherent to their mobile phone use. A third space is made possible by agreement and respect, a fact that Apple did not understand in 2014. I just checked my iTunes account, and *Songs of Innocence* is still there (Hewson, 2014). I could not bear to delete it, even in solidarity with my students; music is music, and as one accustomed to paying for albums, it's nice to get one for free.

CONCLUSION

The mobile phone is a literacy tool not entirely unlike the slate tablet of yesterday. Is it a problem with some students? Absolutely. Would I give it up? Some days, yes. But I also know that when used properly, mobile phones enhance students' learning experiences. While on one hand it is important to discuss the constraints of mobile phones in classrooms, on the other hand, it is a moot point. Mobile phones are not going anywhere, so teachers have two choices: draw a line of resistance with an awareness that the sand is shifting, or embrace the possibilities afforded by this powerful tool. When students arrive in our classrooms, they bring their first space with them where they may retreat at will--even during instruction. Music, existing in students' first space as well as the second space of the classroom, affords teachers an opportunity to establish a third space where collaboration and respect make new and authentic meaning.

But I get it. I continue to have reservations about mobile phones in the classroom. Avila and Pandya (2013) suggest that teachers are resistant to implement digital literacies through mobile phones in the classroom due to fears of criticism and judgment from colleagues and administrators. But, I also have to consider this: Curwood and Gibbons (2010), contend that resistance to other and digital literacies should be considered a bias as it amounts to complicity and the promotion of master narratives that deny possibilities of third space and authentic learning for all students. Mobile phones provide a convenient, easily accessible portal for digital literacy practice. According to Ehret and Hollett (2014), "one in four adolescents is a 'cell-mostly' Internet user, using a phone as his or her main conduit to the Internet" (p.

428). Students are spending vast amounts of time on the Internet in pursuit of digital literacies where they are creating, editing, and recreating by choice (Alvermann, 2008). Due in large part to the affordances of the mobile phone, society is redefining literacy to include virtual and digital spaces, so it is reasonable to assume that teachers must also redefine classrooms to support students' future literacy needs which go beyond traditional, school-based, test-driven curriculums (Mills, 2010). The conceptualization of literacy as action rather than skill is a starting point for educators to begin to question what it means to prepare for real-world contextual needs (Perry, 2012). Alvermann (2008) says it simply: "In a nutshell, adolescents with access to the Internet are developing the literacies that will serve them well in the years to come" (p.10). And finally, we must also reconsider conceptions of space, both physical and virtual, as we strive to prepare twenty-first century, global citizens. Mills and Comber (2013) assert that our students' habitations now and in the future will depend on their abilities to both navigate and participate in the varied purposes and pursuits of a universal economy, so our pedagogies should match the current and future needs of our students.

Kress (2003) speaks to the logic of progress, asserting that at the advent of the printing press, society did not reject technology while remaining fixed to practices that limited literacy opportunities; they applied their resources and understanding while embracing the new affordances the press provided. Those early scribes and scholars were privileged to witness history conceived in critical thought and raised in human ingenuity. We are also in a privileged position, and we should celebrate the efforts of researchers who continue to inspire and actualize the affordances of modern literacy. Thirty years ago, teachers might not have predicted that nearly every student in their classrooms would have immediate access to boundless literacy opportunities, but such a portal does exist, in a convenient, handheld device--the mobile phone.

REFERENCES

Alvermann, D. (2008). Why bother theorizing adolescents' online literacies for class-room practice and research? *Journal of Adolescent & Adult Literacy*, *52*(1), 8–19. doi:10.1598/JAAL.52.1.2

Avila, J., & Moore, M. (2012). Critical literacy, digital literacies, and Common Core State Standards: A workable union? *Theory into Practice*, *51*(1), 27–33. doi: 10.1080/00405841.2012.636332

Avila, J., & Pandya, J. (Eds.). (2012). *Critical digital literacies as social praxis: Intersections and challenges*. Peter Lang Publishing.

Benson, S. (2010). "I don't know if that'd be English or not:" Third space theory and literacy instruction. *Journal of Adolescent & Adult Literacy*, *53*(7), 555–563. doi:10.1598/JAAL.53.7.3

Bhabha, H. (1994). *The location of culture*. Routledge.

Bradstreet, A. (2008). To my dear and loving husband. In Glencoe literature: American literature (pp. 91-93). New York, NY: McGraw-Hill. (Original work published 1598).

Cain, J., Perry, S., & Schon, N. (1981). Don't stop believin' [Recorded by Journey]. On Escape [Record]. New York, NY: Columbia.

Carr, N. (2011). *The shallows: What the internet is doing to our brains*. W. W. Norton and Company.

Chase, E. (2018). Time, third space, and counternarratives of achievement for young mothers in high school. *Educational Studies*, *54*(3), 237–252. doi:10.1080/00131946.2017.1413371

Cook, M. (2005). A place of their own: Creating a classroom 'third space' to support a continuum of text construction between home and school. *Literacy*, *39*(2), 85–90. doi:10.1111/j.1741-4350.2005.00405.x

Countryman, J., & Rose, L. (2017). Wellbeing in the secondary music classroom: Ideas from hero's journeys and online gaming. *Philosophy of Music Education Review*, *25*(2), 128–149. doi:10.2979/philmusieducrevi.25.2.03

Cowles, M. (2019). Dot to dot: Lessons that are rich in arts are engaging, but how do you bring art into the classroom? *AMLE Magazine*, *7*(2), 5–6.

Curwood, J. S., & Gibbons, D. (2010). "Just like I have felt": Multimodal counternarratives in youth-produced digital media. *International Journal of Learning and Media*, *1*(4), 59–77. doi:10.1162/ijlm_a_00034

Ehret, C., & Hollett, T. (2014). Embodied composition in real virtualities: Adolescents' literacy practices and felt experiences moving with digital, mobile devices in school. *Research in the Teaching of English*, *48*(4), 428–452.

Emdin, C. (2013). Pursuing the pedagogical potential of the pillars of hip-hop through science mindedness. *The International Journal of Critical Pedagogy*, *4*(3), 83–99.

Fitzgerald, F. (1925). *The great Gatsby*. Charles Scribner's Sons.

Gabriel, P. (1986). In your eyes [Recorded by Peter Gabriel]. On So. [Record]. Santa Monica, CA: Geffen.

Gee, J. (2018). Affinity spaces: How young people live and learn online and out of school. *Phi Delta Kappan, 99*(6), 8–13. doi:10.1177/0031721718762416

Golding, W. (1954). *Lord of the Flies*. Penguin.

Griffiths, M. D. (2013). Adolescent mobile phone addiction: A cause for concern? *Education for Health, 31*(3), 76–78.

Gutiérrez, K. (2008). Developing a sociocritical literacy in the third space. *Reading Research Quarterly, 43*(2), 148–164. doi:10.1598/RRQ.43.2.3

Hensley, M. (2019). Getting freaky with the founders: Strategically implementing Hamilton: An American musical. *Social Studies Research & Practice, 14*(1), 28–39.

Hewson, P. (2014). The Miracle [Recorded by U2]. On Songs of Innocence [Digital Recording]. Santa Monica, CA: Island Interscope.

Hillocks, G., & Smith, M. W. (1995). *Teaching writing as reflective practice*. Teachers College.

Hrebik, J. (2019). Melodic expressions: Empowering first-year writers through songwriting. *CEA Forum, 48*(1), 268–289.

Kress, G. (2003). *Literacy in the New Media Age*. Routledge.

Leander, K., Phillips, N., & Taylor, K. (2010). The changing social spaces of learning: Mapping new mobilities. *Review of Research in Education, 34*(1), 329–394. doi:10.3102/0091732X09358129

Leem, J., & Sung, E. (2019). Teachers' beliefs and technology acceptance concerning smart mobile devices for SMART education in South Korea. *British Journal of Educational Technology, 50*(2), 601–613. doi:10.1111/bjet.12612

Lynch, T. L. (2008). Rereadings and literacy: How students' second readings might open third spaces. *Journal of Adolescent & Adult Literacy, 52*(4), 334–341. doi:10.1598/JAAL.52.4.6

Magraner, J., & Ramos, R. (2020). Instagram as a musical learning tool in secondary education and high school. *Revista de Comunicación. Vivat Academia, 151*, 25–44.

Mills, K. (2010). A Review of the "digital turn" in the New Literacy Studies. *Review of Educational Research, 80*(2), 246–271. doi:10.3102/0034654310364401

Mills, K., & Comber, B. (2013). Space, place and power: The spatial turn in literacy research. In K. Hall, T. Cremin, B. Comber, & L. Moll (Eds.), *International Handbook of Research in Children's Literacy, Learning and Culture*. Wiley-Blackwell Publishing, Inc. doi:10.1002/9781118323342.ch30

Moje, E., Ciechanowski, K., Kramer, K., Ellis, L., Carrillo, R., & Collazo, T. (2004). Working toward third space in content area literacy: An examination of everyday funds of knowledge and Discourse. *Reading Research Quarterly*, *39*(1), 38–70. doi:10.1598/RRQ.39.1.4

Moran, C. (2018). Learners without borders: Connected learning in a digital third space. *Contemporary Issues in Technology & Teacher Education*, *18*(2), 233–254.

Nash, B. (2018). Exploring multimodal writing in secondary English classrooms: A literature review. *English Teaching*, *17*(4), 342–356. doi:10.1108/ETPC-01-2018-0012

Nash-Ditzel, S., & Brown, T. (2012). Freedoms in the classroom: Cultivating a successful third space for literacy growth. *Language and Literacy: A Canadian Education Journal*, *14*(3), 95–111.

Nikolopoulou, K., & Gialamas, V. (2018). Mobile phone dependence: Secondary school pupils' attitudes. *Education and Information Technologies*, *23*(6), 2821–2839. doi:10.100710639-018-9743-1

Nixon, A. (2013). Engaging urban youth in meaningful dialogue through digital storytelling. In C. Lankshear & M. Knobel (Eds.), *A New literacies reader: Educational perspectives* (pp. 123–138). Peter Lang Publishing.

Page, J., & Plant, R. (1971). Stairway to heaven [Recorded by Led Zeppelin]. On Led Zeppelin IV [Record]. New York, NY: Atlantic.

Perry, K. (2012). What is literacy?—A Critical overview of sociocultural perspectives. *Journal of Language and Literacy Education*, *8*(1), 51–71.

Pew Research Center. (2020). *Mobile Phone Fact Sheet* [graph]. Retrieved from https://www.pewresearch.org/internet/fact-sheet/mobile/

Russo, C. J. (2018). Students and cell phones: Learning tools or learning distractions? *School Business Affairs*, *84*(3), 33–35.

Rutherford, J. (1990). The third space: Interview with Homi Bhabha. In *Identity: Community, culture, difference*. London, UK: Lawrence and Wishart.

Saunders, J. (2010). Identity in music: Adolescents and the music classroom. *Action, Criticism, and Theory for Music Education*, *9*(2), 70–78.

Strovas, S. (2011). Music in the first-year writing classroom. *CEA Forum*, *40*(2), 24-42.

The New London Group. (1996). A pedagogy of multiliteracies: Designing social futures. *Harvard Educational Review*, *1*(60).

Walsh, S., White, K., & Young, R. (2009). The phone connection: A Qualitative exploration of how belongingness and social identification relate to mobile phone use amongst Australian youth. *Journal of Community & Applied Social Psychology*, *19*(3), 225–240. doi:10.1002/casp.983

Yan, Z. (2018). Child and adolescent use of mobile phones: An unparalleled complex developmental Phenomenon. *Child Development*, *89*(1), 5–16. doi:10.1111/cdev.12821 PMID:28485017

Section 4
Mobile Phones in the Classroom

Chapter 9
Cell Phones and Classroom Management:
Minimizing the Distraction of Cell Phones in the Classroom to Ensure Student Success

Rachel V. Hagerman
International School of Aruba, Aruba

ABSTRACT

This chapter outlines and analyzes various classroom management strategies for teachers to regulate cell phone use. Beginning with the background of why cell phones are known to cause distractions in the classroom, the chapter then focuses on using both positive and negative reinforcement strategies for teachers to structure and encourage proper mobile phone usage. The author also includes the benefits and challenges imposed by various classroom management systems in order to guide teachers in making the right decisions regarding cell phone use in their classrooms.

INTRODUCTION

When teachers consider cell phones in the classroom, some view them as their worst nightmare, a pesky distraction which keeps students off task and interrupts instruction. Others see them as an opportunity for student engagement, as mobile phones provide numerous apps and tools which can be used for educational purposes. What these two types of teachers have in common is the goal to effectively engage students in learning and keep students focused in class. In order to achieve that goal,

DOI: 10.4018/978-1-7998-5805-8.ch009

teachers must implement strategic classroom management policies to regulate phone use and reduce time off task.

This chapter discusses best practices for managing cell phone misuse in the classroom, with specific suggestions for the English language arts (ELA) classroom. Beginning with the background of why cell phones are known to cause distractions in the classroom, the chapter then focuses on using both positive and negative reinforcement strategies for teachers to regulate proper mobile phone usage. The chapter also includes the benefits and challenges imposed by various classroom management systems in order to guide teachers in making the right decisions regarding cell phone use in their classrooms.

BACKGROUND

While there is new research to prove that there are benefits to mobile learning, cell phones have a reputation for creating distractions in the classroom. This has caused many schools to have a complete disallowance of cell phone use in the learning environment (Liu et al., 2014). An audible notification, for example, has the power to interrupt an entire lesson. Rumanyika & Mashenene (2015) wrote:

Generally, the most reported forms regarding mobile phones misuse in classrooms include: calling or receiving calls, texting, examination cheating, sexting, game playing, listening to music, interacting with social media and others. (p. 38)

A study by researchers at Sterling College stated that students are well-aware of how distracting cell phones can be (Froese et al., 2012). If a student is using his or her phone during classroom instruction, this also becomes a distraction for those in that student's near vicinity (Tindell & Bohlander, 2012).

However, students are still doing what they can to sneak around no-phone rules, sometimes in very creative and unsuspecting ways. Belastock (2019) wrote:

Students are often getting around cellphone restrictions or bans by carefully hiding their use through cordless earbuds, smart watches, Bluetooth speakers, or long hair paired with a hoodie. They are also using positional strategies such as putting their head in their hands, rummaging through their backpacks and using the restroom break as an opportunity to text. (para. 8)

While this may seem insignificant so long as students are completing their assignments, the truth is, students aren't nearly as good at multitasking as they think they are (Kowalski, 2016). When students multitask by switching their attention to and from their phones during class time, they lose out on valuable information: "We can't pay attention to two things simultaneously, such as reading a text string while listening to a teacher's instructions. Inevitably, something gets missed" (Berdik, 2018). When inappropriate cell phone usage is left unmonitored and unaddressed, it can have detrimental outcomes on student learning.

Despite these challenges, some schools have also recognized the benefits of mobile phones and have lifted cell phone bans in recent years. Thomas et al. (2013) wrote that: "the increased functionality and ubiquity of cell phones have many educators weighing their instructional benefits and re-evaluating the ban schools have on their use in the classroom" (Thomas et al., 2013). New York City, for example, repealed the ban in 2015, with one reason being that New York City Mayor Bill de Blasio thought it was important for parents to stay connected to their children during the school day through mobile communication (Hess, 2019). This is certainly not the only advantage to cell phones in the classroom. Cell phones can be used as replacements for other clunkier materials such as calculators or textbooks (Kowalski, 2016). Teachers can better differentiate learning by connecting students to various apps, educational websites, and other pathways. Cell phones provide more opportunities for student choice in terms of the creation of products to demonstrate learning. Mobile learning, or m-learning, also allows for more movement and physical activity than one would have when sitting at a desk or computer (Thomas & Munoz, 2016). Liu et al. (2014) compared studies of students across various grade levels to show that "students involved in m-learning had greater achievement than those who received traditional instruction and without mobile access." Furthermore, m-learning increases student engagement because students generally love being on their cell phones (Liu et al., 2014).

For schools who choose to embrace these benefits and allow cell phones, educators are left with the question of how to best regulate this new technology. While permitting and encouraging cell phone use in the classroom is a relatively new phenomenon, this isn't the first time educators have had to adapt teaching philosophies and practices to support new technology. Just as other technologies like calculators and computers have changed society and transformed education, cell phones are on the trajectory to do the same (Liu et al., 2014).

When computers were first introduced to the classroom, educators experienced both benefits, such as the ease of student research, and drawbacks, such as the ease of cheating and distraction. Sandholtz et al. (1992) wrote that teachers during the early 1990s felt unprepared to deal with student misbehaviors such as stealing work from other students' disks or ignoring teacher directions. This required educators to envision new classroom management policies specific to technology use. Many teachers who were well-established in the education field had to essentially relearn how to teach in order to have mastery over technology integration. Some had to step back and accept the fact that some of their students knew more about technology than they did, and allowed for these students to become leaders in the classroom (Sandholtz et al., 1992). According to Sandholtz et al. (1992): "As classroom contexts change, so do the classroom management issues" (p. 479). New innovations in the classroom require innovative ways of thinking about classroom management.

SUGGESTIONS FOR PRACTICE

Classroom Management with Positive and Negative Reinforcement

Creating a positive learning environment in which students engage in desirable behaviors begins with setting classroom expectations and procedures. No classroom is the same, so teachers should be sure to clearly communicate the classroom structure and norms they would like to set in place. Teachers should carefully craft and implement procedures for anything that might cause disruption or confusion during class time. Consistency is key, so teachers should be sure to enforce said procedures regularly and address behavioral concerns according to these set structures. Procedures and expectations should be justifiable to students so that students will buy in and adhere to classroom structures (Pedota, 2007). If not, teachers should resort to positive or negative reinforcement.

In order to persuade students to adhere to classroom rules and procedures, teachers either reward students for following directions, or punish students who do not comply. The act of adding things to encourage a certain type of behavior is known as positive reinforcement. The act of taking things away to discourage an undesirable behavior or to encourage a desired behavior is known as negative reinforcement. Behavioral psychologist Skinner both named this phenomenon and researched extensively the effectiveness of both positive and negative reinforcement. Unfortunately, the psychology of positive and negative reinforcement is foreign to many teachers, causing numerous educators to establish ineffective classroom management policies (Dad et al., 2010).

Negative reinforcement, or taking something away, can be effective when a number of criteria are met. Negative reinforcement does not necessarily mean punishment. If a student does something desirable, such as completing all course assignments, the teacher could remove something, such as exempting that student from taking the final exam (The IRIS Center, n.d.). In terms of negative reinforcement as punishment, according to Witting et al. (1984), punishment for an inappropriate behavior should be administered soon after the behavior occurs. This is to ensure the connection between the undesirable behavior and punishment. Punishment should be consistently administered whenever said inappropriate behavior should occur. As the severity of punishment increases, so does the likelihood that the negative behavior will cease (Witting et al., 1984). However, negative reinforcement can also have disadvantages, such as negative emotions which hinder relationships. Students can become bitter and resentful towards educators who resort to punishment. On its own, negative reinforcement is insufficient, and should be complemented with rewards and praise, or positive reinforcement (Dad et al., 2010).

In general, positive reinforcement has proven to be more successful in modifying and improving student behavior than negative reinforcement. Not only does effective positive reinforcement increase the likelihood of the desired behavior, but it is also more beneficial for teachers' and students' social and emotional health. Many students misbehave in order to gain attention from their teacher or fellow classmates. If teachers consistently direct positive attention towards students who are doing the right thing, then attention-seekers have less need to be disruptive. Furthermore, students are more likely to comply with directions if they feel their actions are appreciated (Rumfola, 2017).

There are different sub-categories for reinforcers, many of which can be part of positive reinforcement. CEHD (2016) describes natural and direct reinforcement, social reinforcers, activity reinforcers, tangible reinforcers, and token reinforcers. Natural and direct reinforcement does not require effort from the teacher, as the action itself has a natural consequence. For example, students who work well in group activities will likely be invited to join other group activities in the future. Social reinforcers are words and gestures of approval, such as saying "Good job!" when someone is doing the right thing. Teachers utilize activity reinforcers when they reward students with a desired activity, such as playing a game. Tangible reinforcers are prizes such as candy or stickers that students can earn for exhibiting a desired behavior. Lastly, token reinforcement is when students earn something like points or tickets which they can eventually trade for something valuable.

While each of these reinforcers can be used alone, CEHD (2016) recommends pairing all reinforcers with a social reinforcer, such as verbalizing how well a student performed on a task. CEHD (2016) noted that it is very important to move from less natural reinforcement (tokens, tangibles) to more natural reinforcement (social, direct and natural reinforcement). The goal is for natural and social consequences as well as intrinsic motivation to take over and for students to form desirable habits without the need for a prize.

Creating and Communicating Policies for Cell Phone Use

Direct communication is key when establishing new policies for cell phone use. When talking through and explaining general classroom procedures to students, teachers should include an explanation of appropriate technology use (Findley & Varble, 2006). Engel & Green (2011) wrote that clear policies must be in place that outline when, where, and how the devices can be used. Included in the policies must be the consequences for misuse of the devices. Educators should establish distinct expectations for mobile phone learning and effectively communicate these expectations to students.

Parental Buy-In

Getting buy-in from parents is crucial when implementing policies and procedures for cell phone use. This is true if cell phones are banned altogether or if they are banned only in cases of inappropriate use. Middle school ELA teacher Kerrigan Potter includes her cell phone policy on her course syllabus that students and parents must sign at the beginning of the school year. She does this in order to reduce potential backlash from parents when she enforces the policy (K. Potter, personal correspondence, 28 May 2020). Middle and high school teacher Ralitza Spassova also attributes the success of her classroom cell phone policy to the two-way communication she has established between herself and parents (R. Spassova, personal correspondence, 29 May 2020).

Parents don't want to be caught off guard if their child's phone is confiscated. They also don't want to be shocked if their child informs them of their frequent cell phone use in class. Engel & Green (2011) wrote that parents who have detailed information about who, when, where, and why the devices will be used are more likely to be in support of their use. Teachers may want to consider sending a letter home with students outlining the mobile phone policy. Most students' parents grew up in an age when cell phones were either not around or were not permitted in the classroom. Communicating why one's classroom policy *does* allow for cell phone use in class can add to parental support of said policy.

Student-Generated Cell Phone Policies

One strategy for teachers is enabling students to come up with their own classroom cell phone policy. Many teachers choose the student input approach for developing any of their classroom rules. Erwin (2004) said that taking into consideration the viewpoints of all students when developing classroom rules and expectations makes each student feel empowered and validated (Erwin, 2004). Tindell & Bohlander (2012) wrote that students can help set the rules for cell phone use and may be more likely to comply. This can also strengthen the student-teacher partnership in the classroom.

In the ELA classroom, providing students with the opportunity to design their own cell phone policy can reinforce the essential ELA content area skills of reading, writing, speaking, and listening. Erwin (2004) offers an outline for facilitating student-generated classroom policies. Students can start by individually brainstorming and writing down their own ideas for classroom policies, culture, and atmosphere. This doesn't necessarily need to be limited to cell phone related topics, but can span a range of classroom expectations. Next, each student can collaborate with one or two other classmates, share ideas, and use critical thinking to compromise on ideas with partners. Small groups or pairs can then articulate their ideas for cell phone policies and other class policies by presenting to the class. Once all groups have presented, the students can use their speaking, listening, collaboration, and persuasion skills to come to a final consensus about classroom guidelines and expectations (Erwin, 2004). Not only does this activity provide students with buy-in and a sense of ownership over their classroom policies, but it is a great starting off point for showcasing their ELA skillsets.

While this may seem risky, teachers may find that student-created cell phone policies are comparable to their own ideas. After all, many students also share concerns about disruptions and distractions caused by cell phones. Thomas & Muñoz (2016) wrote that students want to be allowed to use phones in the classroom, but they do not want phones to disrupt their learning or to be used inappropriately. This is evident in a student-generated cell-phone policy described by Engel & Green (2011). In one cell phone integrated classroom, students decided that cell phones should only be visible when needed to complete classroom activities. These students also determined consequences for not complying, which involved cell phone confiscation and parental notification. While this cell phone policy was developed by students, it is similar to policies that many teachers would determine on their own. The difference is, there is now ownership and buy-in from students (Engel & Green, 2011).

Negative Reinforcement: Keeping or Taking Phones Away

A popular method for managing cell phone use in the classroom is requiring students to keep their phones away, out of sight, and out of reach. Some teachers require students to place their phones in a designated container or area of the room. Teachers can implement this system as part of their standard classroom routines. For students who don't comply with required cell phone procedures, teachers may need to resort to negative reinforcement for those students, (e.g. taking their phones away for a longer period of time. This system can have benefits, such as reducing the distractions caused by cell phones, but it can also have drawbacks, such as damaging teacher relationships with students and/or their parents.

Phone Storage Systems: Ideas and Procedures

One fifth grade teacher, Dan Henderson (2019), created the classroom routine for students to place their phones in a clear plastic tub as soon as they entered the classroom. The transparency of the tub allowed students to still keep an eye on their phones. If students didn't abide by the cell phone jail rule, they would get detention (Henderson, 2019).

Belastock (2019) wrote about how teachers can use affordable containers such as calculator caddies, shoe organizers or freezer bags to store student phones. As a suggestion for classroom procedures, Belatock (2019) wrote, "Students turn off or put their cell phones into airplane mode, place them in these organizers and retrieve them at the end of class" (para. 10). The idea is that when students get into the habit of placing their phones in these specific places, they will be less tempted to use their cell phones inappropriately in class.

Middle and high school teacher Ralitza Spassova introduced a firm no cell phone policy at the beginning of the 2019-2020 school year and used designated containers and confiscation to enforce the rule. Her first step in implementing this policy was clear structure and communication with both students and parents. She required students to immediately place their phones in a calculator caddy labeled "Cell Phone Bunk Beds" upon entering the classroom. For those who did not comply and used their phones without permission while in her classroom, she would confiscate their phone, securing it in a locked container labeled "Cell Phone Jail" until the rest of the day. For second offenders, she would hold their phones in custody for twenty-four hours. For third offenders, she would keep the phone for two days, continuing to increase the length with each reoccurring offense. Whenever she would confiscate a child's phone, she would contact home (R. Spassova, personal correspondence, 29 May 2020).

Another system used to keep cell phones nearby yet out of reach in the classroom is a device created by the company Yondr. Yondr produces magnetic cell-phone pockets which can be used in classroom settings. This system allows individuals to maintain possession of their phones without the ability to view the screen or utilize it. Phones stay safely locked away in the Yondr pouch. At one high school who used Yondr, students were expected to enclose their phones in these pouches as soon as they entered the classroom. In some classes, teachers would even let students keep the pouches atop their desks. At the end of the class period, students were allowed to unlock their phones from the pouches using a special instrument with a metal pin. The advantage to this system is that students will not actually be separated from their phones (Orenstein, 2019).

Benefits to Phone Storage Systems

Keeping cell phones away and out of reach for students reduces the temptation for students to check their phones. Kevin Brown (2020), an English professor at Lee University, supports taking away students' cell phones if the devices will be used inappropriately in class. He wrote that "the students who most suffer from being distracted by their phones are the ones who can least afford to be distracted" (Brown, 2020). In her case, Spassova found that the rigid structure of this system was straightforward enough for students and parents to understand and did not leave any gray areas for potential confusion or excuses. It also succeeded in eliminating the distractions caused by cell phones in the classroom (R. Spassova, personal correspondence, 29 May 2020).

Drawbacks and Challenges of Phone Storage Systems

There are some drawbacks to cell phone storage stations or containers in classrooms. In the case of Yondr pouches or other similar models, there is the initial start-up cost of paying for all of the pouches and equipment. At one high school that tried Yondr, some complained that the funds to cover Yondr materials could have been redirected to other more necessary school supplies (Orenstein 2019). For teachers and schools with financial limitations, another less costly system such as a calculator caddy might be more feasible.

While not all cell phone storage systems are costly, a disadvantage for any cell phone storage system is that students have to hurry to unlock or retrieve their phones at the end of class. This is why middle school teacher Lauren Jones has chosen not to use a cell phone locker or cubby system in her classroom. She said: "Students will scramble to collect their phones at the end of class time, which will cause them to be late to their next class" (L. Jones, personal correspondence, 28 May 2020). When implementing a similar system, teachers should be sure to accommodate for student cell phone retrieval by ending their instruction time a minute or two early.

Further Challenges and Complications

While some teachers have systems that allow students to retrieve their phones at the end of the class period or the end of the school day, others maintain possession of students' phones overnight or until a parent comes to retrieve it. The motivation behind this strategy is to deter inappropriate phone use by negative reinforcement. However, this strategy can bring about problems for student-teacher relationships and can lead to backlash from parents. To top it off, this doesn't always succeed in getting to the root of the problem.

Cell phones are often students' most prized possessions, so when teachers confiscate the devices, many students respond with extremely negative emotions directed towards the teacher. Fifth grade teacher Dan Henderson (2017) wrote about what happened when he tried to confiscate the cell phone of a student. It led to defensive arguing, crying, and ultimately ended with a Facetime call to the student's mom (Henderson, 2017). "Students tend to talk back and get angry when I take their phones," noted middle school teacher Lauren Jones (L. Jones, personal correspondence, 28 May 2020). This anger and resentment is problematic, as positive student-teacher relationships are essential in ensuring students' academic success. (Boynton & Boynton, 2005).

While some teachers receive parental support when implementing cell phone confiscation policies, others are faced with criticism. Parents are concerned about reaching their children during emergencies, whether the emergency happens at school, on the bus, or after the child returns home. Some parents panic that they may not be able to contact their children in the event of an emergency, such as a school shooting. Older children may return home from school to empty houses, and parents want to make sure they can check in on them. Other parents feel that they should be able to communicate with their children all throughout the school day, "even if it means texting them in class" (Klein, 2019). For cell phone confiscation policies, it is crucial to communicate and come to an agreement with parents as well.

Taking away a student's phone as a deterrent for future inappropriate cell phone use in class does not always have the desired effect. Teacher Carly Cockerham experienced this firsthand when she worked at a high poverty high school. Students frequently used their phones without permission. The school's policy was for teachers to confiscate cell phones if students used them in class. Then, teachers were required to turn these phones in at the main office. Students could only get their phones back if their parents came to the school to retrieve them. Alternatively, if students refused to hand over their phones, they would be suspended for a day. Many of the students' parents worked long hours or did not have the means to drive to the school to collect their child's confiscated phone. Knowing this, Cockerham's students usually chose a day of suspension rather than giving up their phones indefinitely (C. Cockerham, personal correspondence, 15 May 2020). If the goal of taking phones is truly to reduce students' distractions and enable students to be successful academically, this method of negative reinforcement becomes extremely counterproductive, as it can cause students to miss out on more instructional time.

Using Positive Reinforcement and Incentives to Regulate Phone Use

While taking away students' phones keeps the distraction away, it can be harmful for students' emotional health and teacher-student relationships. This is where positive reinforcement becomes a desirable option for regulating phone use. Rewards and special privileges can serve as powerful motivators for students to refrain from mobile phone misuse and class.

Pocket Points

One way to encourage students to keep their phones away during instructional time is to use phone usage tracking apps like Pocket Points. This free app tracks student phone use data on its own, so teachers don't have to waste their energy constantly monitoring if students have their phones out. Pocket Points allows students to earn points for the amount of time they spend *not* using their phones. With these points, students can earn incentives and prizes designed by the classroom teacher. Students can also limit their cell phone use outside of class to earn points and win rewards from businesses, such as free food from participating restaurants (Copper, 2019).

The Pocket Points website provides ideas for both individual and group rewards for students. While students can monitor their own personal progress for individual rewards, they can also encourage their classmates to stay off their phones so that the class can work towards a group reward. In order to set up Pocket Points for a group reward, teachers should decide what percentage of the class needs to reach the time goal for the entire class to earn the reward.

The website also discloses a variety of reward ideas sorted by "Grade Related," "Free," and "Not Free." Some suggestions for grade-related rewards are: "drop your lowest quiz/assignment score" or "ask the teacher a yes or no question on a test." For the ELA classroom, "reduced word count on essay" may be a desirable prize. Some free rewards, which could also double as group rewards, are: "choose your own seats", and "play a game in class". Finally, some rewards which would cost teachers money are: "pizza party", "school supplies", and "choose from the prize box." The possibilities are endless.

Since many students get distracted during long periods of sustained reading, ELA teachers could implement Pocket Points during reading units to encourage student focus. High school English teacher Jenna Copper tested out the Pocket Points system in her twelfth grade English class. For her reading unit, she calculated that given her forty-four minute class periods, students would spend approximately fourteen hours working through the unit. Rather than requiring students to *never* check their phones in class, she set the goal at eleven hours of phone-free focused class time.

Students who reached this goal would earn extra points on their final project score. Due to the opportunities to earn incentives, Copper (2019) reported that there was great buy-in for using Pocket Points from her students. Copper (2019) wrote:

Though I gave them the option to participate or not, every single student decided to try it out. One thing I observed was that it became a class culture in which students reminded each other to stay off of their phones. Many even reported that they started using it for homework and out-of-school time too. (para. 6)

Pocket Points incentivizes refraining from cell phone use rather than punishing cell phone use which makes it more appealing for students and educators.

No solution is perfect, so when implementing Pocket Points, it is important to prepare for any problems or controversies which may arise. If multiple teachers at the same school are utilizing Pocket Points for example, students may notice that one teacher offers higher rewards for a lower number of points (Gaines, 2017). Teachers may need to collaborate and come to an agreement about which types of prizes a certain number of points can earn. There also may be students who do not have a cell phone capable of downloading the app. For Copper (2019), although not every student had a properly working cell phone, she was able to modify her rewards system on those students' behalf. For example, one student's phone would not correctly track the data, so Copper (2019) allowed this student to record his phone-free minutes on paper.

Lottery Tickets

Another classroom management strategy that can be used to deter inappropriate or distracting cell phone usage is a class ticket or lottery system. This system uses positive reinforcement and the excitement of chance to motivate students to display desirable behaviors. When students demonstrate the desired behavior, such as refraining from cell phone usage, they earn a ticket. Periodically, teachers will hold a lottery drawing, and students with the most lottery tickets have the highest chance of winning the reward.

Teacher blogger JoEllen described how she uses the ticket reward system in her elementary classroom to reinforce positive habits in her students. JoEllen (2014) wrote that she would state a behavioral goal, then use raffle tickets to reinforce the desired behavior. The goals for students were not outlandish, but rather focused on habits and procedures that students should already be practicing. JoEllen would hand out raffle tickets to students throughout the week as she noticed them achieving these behavior goals. At the end of the week, she would hold a raffle drawing for students to earn prizes (JoEllen, 2014).

In my own field experience teaching middle school ELA, I established my own version of the ticket reward and lottery system. Rather than having students earn lottery tickets for positive behaviors, students would lose tickets for failing to comply with these goals. Students would begin the week with three hypothetical tickets, which I would document and track on my own. At the start of the week, I would announce the habit we would be working on for that week, something that I noticed some students were not already doing. Throughout the week, I would monitor students' behavior and let students know when they had lost a ticket. On Fridays, I would actually hand out the physical raffle tickets to students, based on however many they still possessed, given their weekly behaviors, and hold the lottery drawing. As prizes, I used classroom incentives such as bonus points or choosing your seat. Specifically for the ELA classroom, another prize was for the power to choose a creative writing prompt for the rest of the class to answer. I also used tangible rewards such as candy or snacks.

While I eventually focused on a variety of positive classroom habits such as completing assignments on time and actively participating in discussions, one area I chose to address with the lottery system was curbing student phone usage during class. My students were having difficulties keeping their phones away throughout the period. Some would keep their phones face down in the corners of their desks, or insist that they needed to have their phones out to charge, only to check their text messages or social media when they thought I wasn't looking. It had become a major distraction from learning. One of my weekly lottery requirements was for students to keep their phones away during class. If I so much as saw the phone, the owner of the phone would lose a ticket. This proved to be very effective at limiting phone distractions in class. Students did not complain because they were more focused on the reward aspect of the lottery and the chance to earn prizes if they complied.

Each week I would up the ante as we built upon these positive habits. For instance, one week I required students to be in their seats when class started in order to keep their tickets. For the next week, students not only had to be in their seats when class started, but also needed to have their phones away. For the third week, students had to be in their seats, phones away, and have necessary materials out when class time started. Because I built upon each goal and procedure, it did not become too overwhelming for students. Students began to follow these guidelines out of habit rather than out of conscious decision-making.

Classroom Management Strategies for Allowing Phones in the Classroom

Not all teachers choose to prohibit cell phone use entirely. In fact, some ELA teachers feel that in order to promote student literacy, teachers should ensure students are also technologically literate (Pope & Golub, 2000). Furthermore, in order to best prepare students for an ever-adapting society, ELA teachers should set aside preconceived ideas of language and communication and be open to new modes of discourse (Gutiérrez et al., 1997). Today, this could mean permitting and even encouraging cell phone use in class.

When cell phone use is permitted during class time, even if that phone use is minimal, teachers will need to employ new strategies for classroom management. These strategies will ensure that students are staying on task and are not losing focus from important classroom instruction. Some ideas that have proven successful for some educators are proper monitoring, enforcing clear procedures, and encouraging students' own reasoning skills about proper cell phone use.

Establishing Structures for Phone Allowance and Disallowance

Teachers who allow some cell phone use in their classrooms recognize that these devices are not necessary in all learning activities. For example, phones may be permitted during a class competition, but prohibited during direct instruction or while taking an exam. Establishing and communicating clear structures for when students can use their phones is necessary.

One suggestion is to use a stoplight system. With this strategy, students can easily recognize whether or not they should be using their phones. Klein's (2019) system involves the teacher setting a color (red=no phones allowed; yellow=phones can be out if there is no new content; and green=phones out for the lesson). This color-coded system leaves no gray area for student confusion.

Monitoring Academic Cell Phone Use

There are many engaging cell phone apps and tools that can be incorporated into classroom instruction. There are also many tempting social media platforms and distracting apps with pop-up notifications. While schools can equip student laptops with monitoring software and restrict websites, they do not have the same power over students' personal cell phones. The question then becomes: How can teachers ensure students are not distracted when using their phones for academic purposes?

A best practice for classroom management, which is especially important for cell phone use, is effectively monitoring all students and encouraging participation. Generally speaking, it is effective for teachers to circulate the room, keep an eye on students' behavior, and intervene whenever there is a problem (Sieberer-Nagler, 2015). Teachers can also use verbal communication, such as saying students' names, and nonverbal communication, such as eye contact, to increase student focus. This method not only helps build rapport with students, but can diminish the urge for students to text in class (Froese et al., 2012).

Another suggestion is to create fast-paced and time-sensitive learning tasks. The idea is that students will be so focused on the excitement of the task that they will forget to worry about Instagram or Snapchat. Henderson (2017) wrote:

Instead of taking away the privilege of using cell phones use this technology to your advantage. Set up a trivia competition or research topic that requires them to use information from the internet. The biggest problem with this is off task cell phone usage. Try controlling students' cell phone searches by placing the classroom in teams and setting up timed competitions. When you make the internet entertaining to find sources or to answer trivia questions you help minimize status updates. (para. 3)

Specifically in the ELA classroom, teachers could facilitate fast-paced competitions with questions pertaining to a class novel study or vocabulary terms. Not only is a time-sensitive competition a good practice for minimizing off-topic cell phone usage, but it creates an engaging learning environment. Teachers will not need to constantly check over each student's shoulder if the lesson moves at a fast pace. Teachers could also send messages to students directly to their phones throughout class time. Rather than text-messaging, teachers could utilize apps like Remind to send the messages. A simple pop-up message reminding students to stay focused or alerting them about the amount of time remaining to complete an assignment can pull a student back on task. Loveless (n.d.) noted that even if instructional activities allow for cell phone use, teachers still need to monitor students and make sure they aren't simply idling on their phones.

When it comes to technology in the classroom, trust is also important. Not all students can be trusted to use their cell phones appropriately in class. Some may not be able to handle the temptations and potential distractions available on their personal devices. For these students, a laptop may be more conducive for learning. Middle school ELA teacher Kerrigan Potter only permits students who have proven themselves to be trustworthy to complete learning activities on their phones. Phone use then becomes a positive reinforcer for honorable behavior (K. Potter, personal correspondence, 28 May 2020).

Allowing Limited Cell Phone Use to Increase Focus

While cell phones have a reputation for being distracting and disruptive in the classroom, they can also be used to *increase* student focus when used effectively. In some cases, students can be *more* focused on their classwork when provided certain opportunities to use their mobile devices. Two methods for using cell phones to increase student focus are allowing students to listen to their own music during class, and scheduling cell phone breaks throughout class time. These strategies employ positive reinforcement techniques, as teachers are providing students with the opportunity to use cell phones in class, contingent on students' positive behavior and completion of learning tasks. Teachers should establish clear ground rules and structures before allowing phone use in order to be successful.

Potter allows her students to listen to music from their cell phones during class time as long as it is keeping them on task. She has found that students become much more focused on their independent work when they can tune out other distractions, such as talking to a friend. In her past experience, Potter has found cell phones to be a nuisance in the classroom. However, she has developed a procedure for managing mobile phone use for music which has proven successful for her:

Whenever students want to listen to music, it has to be during independent work time. They need to already have a playlist prepared so they aren't scrolling through their phones picking songs. As soon as they start the music, their phones need to be face down on their desks so they won't be tempted to look at their screens. If their speaker volume is too loud, I will tap them once on the shoulder as a warning. If they don't turn down their music after the first tap, they lose the privilege of using their cell phone in class that day. (K. Potter, personal correspondence, 28 May 2020)

This system not only appeals to students, as they get the privilege of using their phones in class, but it can effectively manage noise levels in the classroom and maintain student focus.

Another method is to allow for cell phone breaks, or "tech breaks" during class time. Teachers can schedule short breaks for students to pull out their cell phones and check their messages or social media before returning their focus to classroom instruction. One study found that students' anxiety from being away from technology decreases when told they would be allowed to use their devices again at a certain time in the near future (Berdik, 2018). Kliff Kingsbury, football coach for the Arizona Cardinals, has allowed his players to spend short amounts of time on their phones during every hour. Belastock (2019) wrote that Kingsbury allows players a 10-minute tech break every hour to check their phones. This short break cut down on distractions and reduced players' anxiety. Like professional football players, students' thoughts may be consumed with the prospect of a pending text message or comment on a social media post. If given the chance to check their phones periodically, students' anxiety will lessen, thereby enabling them to focus on other things, such as their schoolwork.

Self-Regulation

Another strategy, known as self-regulation, involves encouraging students to build up their own skills of cell phone manners and responsible cell phone use. These skills are not just limited to the classroom, but can be applied to any other setting. Burns & Lohenry (2010) wrote about how in nonacademic settings, such as places of worship, cinemas, and restaurants, people are generally aware of how distracting and embarrassing it can be for one's phone to ring or otherwise be in use. Moreover, apologies for inappropriate phone use in these settings don't actually make up for the distraction and annoyance caused. Inherent cell phone etiquette is necessary to prevent the distraction from occurring. Burns & Lohenry (2010) suggested that teaching and reinforcing proper manners in regards to mobile phones is imperative for educators.

In self-regulated classrooms, students are responsible for determining appropriate times to use their cell phones. To guide students' thinking, educators may ask students the question: "Do you think this is the best time to check your phone?" (Belastock, 2019). Teachers can also offer personal examples to bridge the connection between the classroom and other social settings. Potter said: "I tell kids that whenever I am talking with a friend while scrolling through my phone, I hear only half of what my friend is saying. It isn't fair to my friend that I am not giving her my full attention" (K. Potter, personal correspondence, 28 May 2020). The goal is for students to use empathy and reasoning to make the right decisions regarding cell phone use.

Critics of self-regulation cell phone policies say that it sounds good in theory, but when a student uses his or her cell phone during class time, other nearby students become distracted. It does not just affect the individual using the phone. Brown (2020) wrote that other students try to peek at their neighbor's phone while they are playing a game, texting or watching a movie, causing them to miss important material or instructions. This tends to happen in higher education, since most colleges do not have blanket policies about cell phone usage in lectures and classrooms. A 2012 survey of college students reported that not only do most of them use their phones during class, but most believe their professors are unaware of the extent of student cell phone use in class. Whenever the professor is aware of students' phone use in class, it can be distracting for both the students and the professor. This may lead to further disruption of instruction (Tindell & Bohlander, 2012). In short, if one student in the class is not properly self-regulating, it can be enough to distract others nearby, including the teacher.

CONCLUSION

The prevalence of cell phones in schools requires careful thought, consideration, and planning for educators. Structures for regulating phone use in classrooms are most effective when they are consistent and clearly communicated. Buy-in from students and their parents is essential in order to maintain these cell phone management systems and preserve healthy relationships. Positive and negative reinforcement strategies can motivate students to adhere to classroom policies regarding cell phones and encourage responsible cell phone use. While research shows that positive reinforcement is generally more effective than negative reinforcement, numerous teachers have had success using negative reinforcement policies to manage cell phone misuse.

To conclude, there is no single right or wrong way to manage cell phone use in class. When developing a cell phone policy, teachers should prioritize students' classroom engagement and academic success over any other factor. If educators look at the big picture and put students' needs first, they will make the right call about the management of cell phone use in their classrooms.

REFERENCES

Barshay, J. (2011, November 8). *How a "tech break" can help students refocus.* https://hechingerreport.org/how-a-tech-break-can-help-students-refocus/

Belastock, E. (2019, May 14). How should teachers manage smartphone distractions in the classroom? *Scoop News Group.* https://edscoop.com/how-should-teachers-manage-smartphones-distractions-in-the-classroom/

Berdik, C. (2018, January 22). To ban or not to ban: Teachers grapple with forcing students to disconnect from technology. *The Washington Post.* https://www.washingtonpost.com/news/grade-point/wp/2018/01/22/to-ban-or-not-to-ban-teachers-cope-with-students-driven-to-distraction-by-technology/

Boynton, M., & Boynton, C. (2005). The educators guide to preventing and solving discipline problems. Alexandria, VA: Association for Supervision and Curriculum Development.

Brown, K. (2020, January 28). Why I take students' cellphones. *Inside Higher Ed.* https://www.insidehighered.com/advice/2020/01/28/professor-gives-three-reasons-why-he-doesnt-allow-cellphones-his-classes-opinion

Burns, S. M., & Lohenry, K. (2010, September). Cellular phone use in class: Implications for teaching and learning a pilot study. *College Student Journal*, *44*(3), 805–810.

CEHD. (2016, December 2). *Positive reinforcement in the classroom: Tips for teachers*. https://cehdvision2020.umn.edu/blog/positive-reinforcement-teacher-tips/

Copper, J. (2019, April 2). A real solution to deal with cell phones in the classroom. *Doc Cop Teaching*. http://doccopteaching.com/2019/04/02/a-real-solution-to-deal-with-cell-phones-in-the-classroom/

Dad, H., Ali, R., Janjua, M. Z. Q., Shahzad, S., & Khan, M. S. (2010). Comparison of the frequency and effectiveness of positive and negative reinforcement practices in schools. *Contemporary Issues in Education Research*, *3*(1), 127–136. doi:10.19030/cier.v3i1.169

Engel, G., & Green, T. (2011). Cell phones in the classroom: Are we dialing up disaster? *TechTrends*, *55*(2), 39–45. doi:10.100711528-011-0482-z

Erwin, J. C. (2004). Power in the classroom: Creating the environment. In *The Classroom of Choice*. Association for Supervision and Curriculum Development.

Findley, B., & Varble, D. (2006). Creating a conducive classroom environment: Classroom management is the key. *College Teaching Methods & Styles Journal*, *2*(3), 1–6. doi:10.19030/ctms.v2i3.5262

Froese, A. D., Carpenter, C. N., Inman, D. A., Schooley, J. R., Barnes, R. B., Brecht, P. W., & Chacon, J. D. (2012). Effects of classroom cell phone use on expected and actual learning. *College Student Journal*.

Gaines, T. (2017, November 8). Pocket Points app leads to less smart phone usage. *The Eagle Eye*. https://eagleeye.news/news/pocket-points-app-leads-less-smartphone-usage

Gutiérrez, K., Gutiérrez, K. D., Baquedano-López, P., & Turner, M. G. (1997). Putting language back into language arts: When the radical middle meets the third space. *Language Arts*, *74*(5), 368–378.

Henderson, D. (2017, August 20). How can teachers control cell phones in their class? *Teachthought*. https://teachthought.com/technology/can-teachers-control-cell-phones-class/

Hess, A. (2019, January 19). Research continually shows how distracting cell phones are---so some schools want to ban them. *CNBC*. https://www.cnbc.com/2019/01/18/research-shows-that-cell-phones-distract-students--so-france-banned-them-in-school--.html

Irick, L. (2020a). *Class Wide Rewards*. https://intercom.help/portal-c4c52318881b/en/articles/3160848-class-widerewards

Irick, L. (2020b). *Huge List of Reward Ideas*. https://intercom.help/portal-c4c52318881b/en/articles/2535064-huge-list-ofreward-ideas

JoEllen. (2014, October 6). Using rewards in a classroom. *Cuppacocoa*. http://www.cuppacocoa.com/rewards-in-a-classroom/

Klein, A. (2019). Schools say no to cellphones in class. But is it a smart move? *Education Week*, *39*(4), 10–11. https://www.edweek.org/ew/articles/2019/09/11/schools-say-no-to-cellphones-in-class.html

Kowalski, K. (2016, March 3). When smartphones go to school. *Science News for Students*. https://www.sciencenewsforstudents.org/article/when-smartphones-go-school

Liu, M., Scordino, R., Geurtz, R., Navarrete, C., Ko, Y., & Lim, M. (2014, August 13). A look at research on mobile learning in K–12 education from 2007 to the present. *Journal of Research on Technology in Education*, *46*(4), 325–372. doi:10.1080/15391523.2014.925681

Loveless, B. (n.d.) Using cell phones as learning tools. *Education Corner*. https://www.educationcorner.com/cell-phones-learning-tools.html

Orenstein, N. (2019, October 8). Berkeley High takes students' phones away - sort of. *Berkleyside.com*. https://www.berkeleyside.com/2019/10/08/berkeley-high-takes-students-phones-away-sort-of

Pedota, P. (2007). Strategies for effective classroom management in the secondary setting. *The Clearing House: A Journal of Educational Strategies, Issues and Ideas*, *80*(4), 163–168. doi:10.3200/TCHS.80.4.163-168

Pope, C., & Golub, J. (2000). Preparing tomorrow's English language arts teachers today: Principles and practices for infusing technology. *Contemporary Issues in Technology & Teacher Education*, *1*(1), 89–97.

Rumanyika, J. D., & Mashenene, R. G. (2015, April 29). Mobile phone technology adoption and classroom management in higher learning institutions in Tanzania: Challenges and implications. *International Journal of Information Technology and Business Management, 36*(1), 34–51.

Rumfola, L. M. (2017). Positive reinforcement positively helps students in the classroom. *Education and Human Development Master's Theses, 286*, 1–53.

Sandholtz, J. H., Ringstaff, C., & Dwyer, D. C. (1992). *Teaching in high-tech environments: Classroom management revisited*. Apple Computer, Inc. doi:10.2190/Y5NE-V9RQ-FD63-WC2N

Sieberer-Nagler, K. (2015, December 14). Effective classroom-management & positive teaching. *English Language Teaching, 9*(1), 163–172. doi:10.5539/elt.v9n1p163

The IRIS Center. (n.d.). *Reinforcement: Positive versus negative*. Vanderbilt University. https://iris.peabody.vanderbilt.edu/wp-content/uploads/pdf_activities/independent/IA_Reinforcement_Positive_versus_Negative.pdf

Thomas, K., & Muñoz, M. A. (2016). Hold the phone! High school students' perceptions of mobile phone integration in the classroom. *American Secondary Education, 44*(3), 19–37.

Thomas, K. M., O'Bannon, B. W., & Bolton, N. (2013, December 11). Cell phones in the classroom: Teachers' perspectives of inclusion, benefits, and barriers. *Computers in the Schools, 30*(4), 295–308. doi:10.1080/07380569.2013.844637

Tindell, D. R., & Bohlander, R. W. (2012). The use and abuse of cell phones and text messaging in the classroom: A survey of college students. *College Teaching, 60*(1), 1–9. doi:10.1080/87567555.2011.604802

Witting, A. F., William, G. W., David, S. T., & Wagley, S. (1984). Study guide to accompany psychology: an introduction. McGraw-Hill.

Chapter 10
The New Normal Is Cell Phones in the Classroom:
A Twenty-Year Retrospective

Cynthia D. White
Georgia Public Schools, USA

ABSTRACT

This chapter seeks to compare and contrast a classroom without student cell phone use in 2000 to the ubiquitous use of cell phones in today's classroom and society. Cell phone use and how to include them in today's classroom is a hot topic in school systems and teacher education programs in America and therefore relevant to establishing instructional guidelines for cell phone inclusion in the classroom. The author will share lived classroom experience in the 20 years from cell phone infancy to usage by more than 90% of students in today's classroom. The author will share effective use of cell phones in the classroom and pitfalls to allowing cell phones in the class without a well-planned instruction basis for cell phone use.

INTRODUCTION

When I entered my first classroom in 2000, the technology consisted of a VCR/TV combo, access to an overhead projector from the library and the only computer in the class was my teacher's desktop. We had a book room with class sets of canonical texts and books on tape--which was considered an advancement. Cell phone use in the student body was sporadic. As a teacher I had a cell phone primarily as an emergency use tool. My cell phone had a QWERTY keypad, limited Internet, and a screen less than half the size of the cell phone itself. These early cell phones

DOI: 10.4018/978-1-7998-5805-8.ch010

were nothing like the powerful, capable and connected devices that students now use some with 5 inch screens. When 911 occurred, my students were called from class, via the intercom, by the front office when their parents came to the school to check them out.

We were kept informed about the days' events through the intercom and from teachers who escaped to the lounge to watch CNN. They returned with news which was whispered in front of partially closed doors while students waited for updates. No one pulled out a cell phone to watch the news in real time. Cell phones were contraband and, if used during class, I was to take them and send them to the office and a parent would have to pick the phone up after school. On that day, we were locked down with our first period class the entire day, and in this class, two students had cell phones on them and were unable to connect to the Internet to provide more information about the events of the day. Today, I keep my cell phone face down on my desk, set to vibrate and check and use it frequently, sometimes during class. In 2000, it was in my purse, in a locked closet. The wide-spread use of cell phones has changed in lock step with their usefulness and connectedness to all the parts of modern life. My sophomores sat quietly talking among themselves and occasionally asked questions that could not be answered: *Are we going to war? Why would they attack America? Are the attacks over?* I responded to student fears and angst and released them when they were summoned. We were back the next day.

Contrast this rather teacher-led, top-down moment, where most of the information came from the front office and other professionals in the building, to the day COVID-19 arrived in my school district with a teacher who had tested positive. When COVID-19 shut down schools, I found out from students who read the news on their cell phones as the school board tweeted and sent emails out in response to the pandemic. Almost every student held and watched a cell phone, yelling information as they retrieved it about what we all assumed would be an unscheduled three-day weekend. At the end of the day a meeting was held in the auditorium, confirming what we already knew, and asking us to vacate the building by four o'clock. This was Friday March 13, 2020 and we never returned. I left papers in the bins, sticky note collages on the white board, and agenda topics scribbled in dry-erase.

Teachers in the United States are grappling with the ways in which technology has changed the classroom. Students record each other and teachers on their cell phones. The struggle over the use and control of student access to their cell phones is one that creates division that did not exist 20 years ago. Then, technological incursion in the classroom was unheard of and teacher's like me wanted more useful technology in the classroom. The day every student would have a device like a tablet or laptop and not just a clunky computer lab, was the dream of every teacher I knew.

Cell phones grew in popularity but were not the primary source of classroom distraction, although naturally, distractions existed. Students were distracted by one another. I often caught students writing notes or writing rap lyrics, passing them back and forth during class. During my time at the high school, I never confiscated a cell phone the way I did candy, gum, or the occasional small knife--also contraband. There were arguments and fights, destruction of property, car accidents, deaths and suicides just like in today's schools. In my first years as a teacher, the students were more interested in one another, and much more likely to participate and engage. The classroom was teacher-centered with students as passive, if not captive, participants. The outside world was held at bay once the door shut. Today's classroom is composed of students whose relationships, self-value and community exists largely outside of the classroom--even the school building-- and is held together by their cell phones.

Pros for Cell Phone Inclusion: Lose the Battle and Win the War

Fast forward 20 years, and I decided to attend graduate school and complete a Master's in Teaching English. After more than seventeen years, I was back in the classroom, first as a student teacher and then as a new hire at an urban high school outside of Atlanta in 2020, replacing a teacher who retired and took a job working with a content company. As a student teacher, when asked by the lead teacher my preference for cell phone usage in the class, I explained that I felt it was better to allow the devices than ban them. Because there was no plan to utilize the cell phones as part of content delivery or assessments the phones quickly became problematic and were banned by the lead teacher. It then became a task to monitor student use of cell phones and divvy out corrections. I learned from this experience that students would have their phones, we just needed a way to make them part of the lesson.

My new senior-level classes had experienced over a month of various subs who had come and gone. I walked into a room where the students used their phones openly and continually during class, many sharing videos and texting, but not working on class curriculum or activities. It became apparent to me that restricting use all together would not be a feasible plan as the students accessed the audio for the class novel via a pdf or Youtube video with live read-alouds. Simply banning the phones was not a practical option. I had no time to engage in a prolonged fight to ban cell phones that students relied on to access class content. Rather than focus on banning phones, I gave the students rules of use. I created and posted a daily agenda such that class time was segmented into different work times and activities and when cell phones were appropriate was clearly delineated and when they were not to be used was also clearly outlined. At no time were students allowed to make or receive calls. Cell phones could be out but had to be face down on their desks. If I walked by a student and they were off-task, I warned them. If the inappropriate use was repeated, I would ask them to put the device away.

What turned the tide and allowed me to reign in control of the use of the devices was the counter intuitive step of including cell phone use in instruction. I begin using platforms and applications like Quizzez, Kahoot!, and even Google search as part of instruction and assessment, not just allowing students to read and access the text via their phones. Students earned *real* points for *real* grades when they used their phones to complete and engage in classwork and assessments. They did this by logging in to apps and using their phones or tablets to access teacher-approved sites and platforms. Inclusion of cell phones and tablets in the instruction and assessment meant that student performance could be tracked. A high percentage of failure on a reading quiz, allowed me to reinforce learning and offer support. Rather than using their phones individually to troll the internet, their phones became tools for classroom use which strengthened the understanding of our texts, helped students navigate new applications, and gain technical and academic skills which supported learning. Of course, managing the classroom was still paramount as students used their cell phones and redirecting off-task behavior is part of the work of teaching in any classroom. Students who refused to comply with the cell phone rules lost participation points, information needed on later assignments or skills they could later leverage into success on course work and student collaborations.

The more meaningful and directed their cell phone use was in class, I discovered, the less I had to police their use and the less time cell phone use stole from instruction. They soon learned that they *needed* to participate for maximum success. Cell phone use was limited by design to no more than 20 minutes of a 90-minute block. Although every student had a cell phone, plans, access and speed are not equal. Students could access all content and classwork via school provided tablets if cell phone access was an issue. Most students, however, like the familiarity and comfort of their cell phones. They are objects of affection not just devices. Students who refused to comply were referred to the assistant principal down the hall and soon got on board. By week two students were coming in and getting to work, putting cell phones away when asked.

Cell phones add value to learning. Students gain the ability to work with and in various learning contexts (Burden et.al., 2019). Best practice with cell phone usage is designed instruction with cell phones at the onset. In other words, cell phones must be considered when designing lesson plans and activities. To prohibit cell phones, especially for a student body that relies on them for all types of communication and wellbeing "may cause a missed opportunity for educators to relate to students, encourage their participation, and bring up-to-the-minute facts to the classroom activities" (Tessier, 2013, p. 25).

Educator and writer, Robert Sterner in his article *4 Things You'll Miss by Banning Cell Phones in Your Classroom,* likens banning cell phones in the classroom to a teacher snatching "a tangible symbol of teens' independence" and at the onset setting up a conflict, and failing to recognize that "its power with [our] students makes it a useful instrument for getting the behavior needed in class." It is tantamount to removing the white board because some students cannot help but write on it. Sterner cautions educators to "[r]emember everything about that cell phone in your student's pocket is vastly more powerful than the computer used by Neil Armstrong to land on the moon. Take advantage of that power!" (Sterner, 2015, p. 57). An educator is fighting a hard--losing--battle to keep cell phones out. The better course is to plan and use them. Put the cell phones in the hands of learners rather than off-task students.

The COVID-19 shut down demonstrated that simply having a cell phone and access to a computer/tablet does not mean that students are computer literate. I was shocked by the number of students who were unable to access the school's online platforms, effectively upload and download material and communicate concerns and questions via the platforms. Yet, each student is a daily cell phone and computer user. Like with reading literacy, students must be equipped to relate to and respond with many different types of media on their cell phones, laptops and other devices and platforms. When we relegate cell phones to back pockets and backpacks, we are communicating to our learners that there is no connection between it and the education they are undertaking which is far from the truth. This 'digital literacy' therefore must "involve not just being able to 'operate' tools like computers and mobile phones, but also the ability to adapt the affordances and constraints of these tools to *particular* circumstances" (Jones and Hafner, 2012, p. 13). A student should be taught to recognize the power of the device in an educational context in the same way they understand its use in a private, personal context. This new literacy is a way of "breaking down boundaries that have traditionally defined our literacy practices" (Jones and Hafner, 2012, p. 13).

As part of an interview for a new teaching position, I was asked what my take away from COVID-19 was and it is this: students must be taught how to use every application, platform and standard technology a school requests they use and more. As educators, we cannot assume that because this is the age of information students are well versed in the use of pertinent technology. Banning cell phones is a stumbling block to the technical education and literacy of students. Before implementing use, I will need to educate my students in how-to and purpose-driven uses of the educational technology at their disposal. Were a shutdown to occur again, or even a snow day, students would know how to access the school's technology and use it to continue learning. Many of my fellow educators lost almost half of their student population when schools went online, never hearing from the student or parent again. In my case, I was overwhelmed with emails from parents and students asking how to access class information and instruction. Some students had never logged on to their school provided accounts.

The Equity of Cell Phones

A surprising change for sixth grade teacher Jennifer McKelvey, during the school closing was the number of English Language Learners who responded well to online learning. Suddenly, according to McKelvey, these students became "more responsive and engaged than they had been in the classroom" (McKelvey 2020). As we discussed this change in some of her ELLs, she noted that her students who had been reluctant to speak in front of their classmates, found liberation online, "commenting and writing in ways they never had in class" (personal correspondence, McKelvey, 2020).

Can using devices like cell phones bridge gaps with language acquisition and provide safe space for speakers and writers to openly and fluently communicate? It happened for this educator. In addition, as many schools sought to provide laptops, students still struggled to find the necessary Wi-Fi connection to use the computers. Cell phones come with a data plan, allowing 24/7 access to internet and mobile device capable platforms and applications. Cell phones, in many ways, break down socioeconomic barriers to access. However, teachers will have to recognize the different devices available to students and plan curriculum accordingly.

Cell Phones as Part of Structured Learning

As with any work or task, extensive and unsupervised time may lead to distraction or off-task behavior. I learned to take control of the class time by not only meeting my students at the door, but shutting the door and then promptly directing students to the warmup. The message is clear: we have work to do.

During the first ten minutes of a warm-up, either via worksheet, writing prompt or grammar review is the first task and does not require a cell phone. In this way, students are required to get busy and put cell phones aside. Next, I review the daily agenda and expectations and we review the warmup as a class activity. With the warmup completed, the next segment is a review of our topic with teacher instruction and/or information. During this time, I present new information, continue instruction or present new ideas and themes from the novel, *The Hate U Give* (Thomas, 2017). As we study the novel, a Tupac song is presented and, as a class, we examine his music and lyrics through the lens of the novels' social protest and other themes revolving around racial conflict. After class discussion and feedback, students are free to use their cell phones to access the novel and read. Students may listen to the audio book or watch the novel read by various Youtubers. When and how cell phones are used as part of the classroom activities and instruction is planned in the same manner use of texts and journals are planned for use.

Clearly, Including, rather than banning cell phones in classrooms creates "positive benefits for learners, such as greater student agency, choice and opportunities to work in more seamless and varied contexts. Therefore, we conclude that there is a need to support teachers and pre-service teachers in designing similar mobile pedagogical activities" (Burden et.al., 2019 p.19). Students are going to use their cell phones to be sure, weaving them into academics and practical assessments means they will be using them during class to assist with learning new skills and literacies. Therefore, the design of pedagogical activities must be in keeping with building student understanding of concepts and cognitive developments for future learning. A United Kingdom study demonstrated that in using cell phones in the classroom, "[t]he relationship between students and teachers was more democratic than normal" and ". . . the mobile device bridged the boundaries between these contexts, potentially making learning more authentic and meaningful" (Burden et.al., 2019, p. 17-18).

But this is not revolutionary. When I began teaching, worksheets were the thing, with many teachers relying on them to deliver context and meaning. Just as a worksheet can numb young minds, so can extensive and random use of cell phones in class. As with any tool, cell phone use must be practical and helpful--building literacy of one kind or another--not an opt out for poor planning and content.

Each reading section is teacher-led to ensure all students whether on phones or tablets were in the correct program or audio and I walked the class to be sure. Students on other applications or programs were redirected. There have to be consequences just like in the old days to distractions and off-task behavior. Taking a student's cell phone is what Sterner (2015) calls "a willpower test" (p. 57-58). We teach responsibility and modify behavior when we remove any roadblock to student learning in our classrooms. By discerning which of our students are cell phone distracted teachers "can help students work to build willpower . . . But by having a growth mindset—or instilling one—students can learn to increase their willpower and task persistence" (Sterner, 2015, p. 58). After all these students will go to college and then on to work and careers where choices will be limited and technology/device use restricted.

Clearly, teacher led activities are necessary even with cell phones. Students who are continually off task will not be permitted to use their cell phones and will have to use their county provided tablets or borrow a teacher-provided, old-fashioned book. Teachers must plan for dead cell phones, power outages and system crashes.

The Case for Restriction in Traditional Classrooms

Of course, cell phones can be of use in the classroom. Incorporating cell phones into every assignment or instructional segment can drain their effectiveness. Some days, students need to sit quietly and listen or take notes. They will need to work with and listen to each other to gain new literacies. This learned forbearance allows for the active learner stage which comes later. In today's classroom wonder and excitement can still be had by teaching students to use and develop technical skills. Most students have no problem opening TikTok and scrolling through numerous short videos, but can they create a video for the classroom exploring the use of animal myths in early Native American folklore? Such challenges move students from passive users to active creators. Similarly, we may challenge students to use Instagram to create dialogue as a class about globing warming or Shakespeare's theme of betrayal in the characters Iago and Brutus from *Othello* and *Julius Caesar* respectively. Such an assignment would require that students learn to upload and download images and snips of video. It requires feedback and continuing the thematic thread beyond the snips on Instagram or TikTok. They need to learn to write headers and create links to more material and information. These are projects and concepts that require more than just whipping out a cell phone. Students will need to use laptops and tablets and work collaboratively. An innovative and skill-based classroom requires more than just cell phone use. Back in the old days we worked the tech into the teaching not the teaching into the tech.

In the past, when students broke pencils and threw paper, there were consequences. Now, students need to understand that cell phone use comes with certain rules of engagement and consequences for misuse. "Teachers need to be bold and persistent with helping students regulate their cell phone use, while communicating honestly about the impacts of cell phones" (Gillmore, 2019, p. 21). There will be days when the cell phone will need to be put away and students will have to engage with teachers and cohorts without them. Clearly, we need to teach students how to have proper and appropriate discourse and to connect with others. Often, as one teacher noted, the student who cannot afford to be on their phone during class is the one who cannot resist and "It becomes an addiction, and at that point it becomes really hard to get a kid back and re-engage them in education. A lot of them see more value in the interactions with phones than the interactions with whatever's going on in the class,'" (Gillmore, 2019, p. 21). When I first started teaching students understood implicitly that their focus and attention were *required* as part of being a successful student. Nearly twenty years later, I walked into my class and the students who soon followed were under the impression that neither were necessary and were disgruntled by my demands for their focus and attention. They fully expected to be given an assignment and let loose to do as they pleased, largely on their cell phones. I ended this and the class became a better, more open place as we discussed *The Hate U Give* in a whole class setting and small group work activities. If the cell phone had continued unchecked, the poignant moments of learning would have been missed.

The Future is Now: Cell Phones as Connection

One thing the pandemic made clear is that education and how it is delivered have changed. The rush to online was met with faulty hardware, crashing servers and many students disappearing all together. Page (2020) reported that one in five teachers did not plan to return to the classroom after 2020. Truthfully, many teachers I know report that they are out of the profession and glad for it. As states are faced with budget cuts and an uncertain future, teachers are feeling the brunt of possible increases in workload and responsibilities as the classroom in the wake of COVID-19 changes. In New York, a state hard hit by the pandemic, teachers' unions and advocacy groups worried about protecting teachers who were immunocompromised or over the age of fifty (Sorkin, 2020). Whether schools come up with hybrid or online learning plans, cell phones are certain to be a part of the student response to accessing school content and curriculum.

SUGGESTIONS FOR PRACTICE

The first thing to do in a newly opened school is cell phone data collection. Many school systems are offering hybrid or virtual/online options for students.

1. Verifying phone numbers and emails for parents and students, including school issued emails, is a necessary first step. Lines of open and constant communication must be accessed and used. As the economic impact of COVID-19 continues, many students may move in and out of districts with few methods of tracking them. Because so many American students have cell phones, these devices may not only offer tracking and delivery of services point-of-contact, but will more than likely be used to deliver course content and assessments as well.
2. Parents and students may need to accept responsibility to sign on and use school data and technology to meet curriculum and content delivery needs. Failure to login and be present online if a virtual option is chosen, will have the same consequences as absenteeism from physical buildings. Cell phones will be a part of this process and can be used to login to school-based resources.
3. Schools may need to demand that creators of school platforms and software that deliver necessary content also develop cell phone friendly versions for students who do not have laptops, tablets or desktops at home but do have cell phones.
4. Districts and school systems need to clearly delineate acceptable use of cell phones for curriculum in the classroom and at home in hybrid, virtual and brick

and mortar school scenarios. School buildings should remove any blocking or firewalls that keep students from accessing important sites, such as YouTube.

5. Cell phone policies may need to be included in student resource guides, codes of conduct and online toolkits. Like teachers, students need to know what is acceptable use of cell phones in class or when accessing school-based technology or content.
6. Student privacy rights are also important and schools need to be clear about where a student's right to privacy is protected or not as they utilize their cell phones to access and use school technology and content.
7. Schools will also have to develop technology to prevent overreach of parents and stakeholders in completing student work or tasks by mandating some face-to-face interventions, even when parents and students have opted for virtual or online-only learning.
8. Text applications like Remind 101 and similar applications will continue to help teachers help students and parents with meeting deadlines and turning in assignments. This information is sent directly to students and parents, and it can be an invaluable tool in delivering needed information and resources. Teachers will also want to use student cell phones to deliver information immediately and directly about their classes.

CONCLUSION

Schools and educators that attempt to ban cell phone use are facing an uphill battle, especially after prolonged time off and away from school norms for most students in the United States. Rather than banning cell phones, educators should embrace them for the useful tools they are and use them in meaningful and deliberate ways to increase student learning. Right now, educators are planning to digitize more and more learning using cell phone friendly apps that students can easily access. It is hopeful that more innovative school-friendly platforms similar to Zoom and Schoology will be developed and made cost effective for schools and educators. No matter what the classroom looks like, cell phones will be part of instruction and delivery of content. The new normal is to use them and continue shaping young minds. The dreams of 20 years ago are now realized. Students and teachers have a wealth of computer power at our fingertips. The cell phones in our students' pockets are another way to reach and teach diverse learners where they are.

REFERENCES

Burden, K., Schuck, S., & Kearney, M. (2019). Is the use of mobile devices in schools really innovative? What does the evidence say? *Impact (Sydney)*, 16–19.

Gilmore, M. (2019). Restricted access: Banning cell phones in the classroom. *Teach*, 20-22.

Jones, R. H., & Hafner, C. A. (2012). *Understanding digital literacies: A practical introduction*. Routledge. doi:10.4324/9780203095317

Page, S. (2020, May 26). Back to school? 1 in 5 teachers are unlikely to return to reopened classroom this fall, poll says. *USA Today*.

Sorkin, A. D. (2020, June). Safer schools. *The New Yorker*, 11–12.

Sterner, R. (2015). 4 things you'll miss by banning cell phones in your classroom. *Education Digest*, *81*(2), 56–58.

Tessier, J. (2013). Student impressions of academic cell phone use in the classroom. *Journal of College Science Teaching*, *43*(1), 25–29. doi:10.2505/4/jcst13_043_01_25

Thomas, A. (2017). *The hate u give*. Harper Collins.

Compilation of References

Abrams, S. S. (2017). Emotionally crafted experiences: Layering literacies in Minecraft. *The Reading Teacher, 70*(4), 501–506. doi:10.1002/trtr.1515

Agawu, K. (2001). African Music as Text. *Research in African Literatures, 32*(2), 8–16. doi:10.2979/RAL.2001.32.2.8

Agu, Z. (2019). *Teachers salary structure in Nigeria in 2019.* https://www.legit.ng/1215762-teachers-salary-structure-nigeria-2019.html

Ajayi, H. O. (2006). Correlates of primary school pupils reading proficiency. *International Journal of Applied Psychology and Human Performance, 1*, 207–215.

Alvermann, D. E. (2008). Why bother theorizing adolescents' online literacies for classroom practice and research? *Journal of Adolescent & Adult Literacy, 52*(1), 8–19. doi:10.1598/JAAL.52.1.2

Alvermann, D. E., & Harrison, C. (2016). Blowin in the wind. *Journal of Adolescent & Adult Literacy, 60*(1), 91–93. doi:10.1002/jaal.566

Anderson, M., & Jiang, J. (2018). *Teens, social media & technology 2018.* Retrieved from https://www.pewinternet.org/2018/05/31/teens-social-media-technology-2018/

Anderson, M., & Jiang, J. (2020, May 30). *Teens, social media & Technology 2018.* Retrieved from https://www.pewresearch.org/internet/ 2018/05/31/teens-social-media-technology-2018

Asikhia, O. A. (2010). Students and teachers' perception of the causes of poor academic performance in Ogun state secondary schools in Nigeria: Implications for counseling for national development. *European Journal of Soil Science, 13*(2), 229–242.

Atalay, A., & Topuz, A. C. (2018). What is being played in the world: Mobile eSport Applications. *University Journal of Educational Research, 6*(6), 1243–1251. doi:10.13189/ujer.2018.060615

August, D., & Shanahan, T. (Eds.). (2006). *Developing literacy in second-language learners: A report of the National Literacy Panel on Language-Minority Children and Youth.* Lawrence Erlbaum Associates. doi:10.1080/10862960903340165

Auxier, B., & Anderson, M. (2020, May 31). *As schools close due to the coronavirus, some U.S. students face a Digital 'HOMEWORK GAP'*. Retrieved from https://www.pewresearch.org/fact-tank/2020/03/16/as-schools-close-due-to-the-coronavirus-some-u-s-students-face-a-digital-homework-gap/

Auxier, B., Anderson, M., & Kumar, M. (2019, December 20). 10 tech-related trends that shaped the decade. *Fact Tank, News in the Numbers*. Pew Research Center. https://www.pewresearch.org/fact-tank/2019/12/20/10-tech-related-trends-that-shaped-the-decade/

Avila, J., & Moore, M. (2012). Critical literacy, digital literacies, and Common Core State Standards: A workable union? *Theory into Practice*, *51*(1), 27–33. doi:10.1080/00405841.2012.636332

Avila, J., & Pandya, J. (Eds.). (2012). *Critical digital literacies as social praxis: Intersections and challenges*. Peter Lang Publishing.

Ballantyne, J., & Retell, J. (2020). Teaching careers: Exploring links between well-being, burnout, self-efficacy, and Praxis shock. *Frontiers in Psychology*, *10*, 2255. doi:10.3389/fpsyg.2019.02255 PMID:32132940

Bambara, C. S., Harbour, C. P., Davies, T. G., & Athey, S. (2009). Delicate engagement: The lived experience of community college students enrolled in high-risk online courses. *Community College Review*, *36*(3), 219–238. doi:10.1177/0091552108327187

Barshay, J. (2011, November 8). *How a "tech break" can help students refocus*. https://hechingerreport.org/how-a-tech-break-can-help-students-refocus/

Barton, J., Peek, N., & Crocker, B. (n.d.). *The TechEds Program*. http://pauldingteched.weebly.com/the-techeds-program.html

Batchelor, G. (2017). *Far from noise*. George Batchelor.

Bawa, P. (2016). Retention in online courses: Exploring issues and solutions— a literature review. *SAGE Open*, *6*(1), 1–11. doi:10.1177/2158244015621777

Bawden, D. (2008). Origins and concepts of digital literacy. In C. Lankshear & M. Knobel (Eds.), *Digital literacies: Concepts, policies, and practices* (pp. 17–32). Peter Lang.

Beach, R., Hull, G., & O'Brien, D. (2011). Transforming English Language Arts in a Web 2.0 world. In D. Lapp & D. Fisher (Eds.), *Handbook of research on teaching the English Language Arts* (3rd ed., pp. 161–167). Routledge.

Bejba, S. (2019). The new point and shoot: Photography lessons using phones and scanners. In J. C. Castro (Ed.), *Mobile media in and outside of the art classroom: Attending to identity, spatiality, and materiality* (pp. 165–182). doi:10.1007/978-3-030-25316-5_8

Belastock, E. (2019, May 14). How should teachers manage smartphone distractions in the classroom? *Scoop News Group*. https://edscoop.com/how-should-teachers-manage-smartphones-distractions-in-the-classroom/

Benson, S. (2010). "I don't know if that'd be English or not:" Third space theory and literacy instruction. *Journal of Adolescent & Adult Literacy, 53*(7), 555–563. doi:10.1598/JAAL.53.7.3

Berdik, C. (2018, January 22). To ban or not to ban: Teachers grapple with forcing students to disconnect from technology. *The Washington Post*. https://www.washingtonpost.com/news/grade-point/wp/2018/01/22/to-ban-or-not-to-ban-teachers-cope-with-students-driven-to-distraction-by-technology/

Best Colleges. (2020). *Online education trends report*. Retrieved from https://res.cloudinary.com/highereducation/image/upload/v1584979511/BestColleges.com/edutrends/2020-Online-Trends-in-Education-Report-BestColleges.pdf

Bhabha, H. (1994). *The location of culture*. Routledge.

Bos, B., Wilder, L., Cook, M., & O'Donnell, R. (2014). iSTEM: Learning mathematics through minecraft. *Teaching Children Mathematics, 21*(1), 56–59. doi:10.5951/teacchilmath.21.1.0056

Boynton, M., & Boynton, C. (2005). The educators guide to preventing and solving discipline problems. Alexandria, VA: Association for Supervision and Curriculum Development.

Bradstreet, A. (2008). To my dear and loving husband. In Glencoe literature: American literature (pp. 91-93). New York, NY: McGraw-Hill. (Original work published 1598).

Brauer, L., & Clark, T. C. (2008). The trouble is English: Reframing English studies in secondary schools. *English Education*, (4), 293.

Briggs, S. (2014, September 20). *Students as creators: How to drive your students to be more than just consumers*. https://www.opencolleges.edu.au/informed/features/students-as-creators/

Broken Rules. (2017). *Old man's journey*. Broken Rules.

Brown, K. (2020, January 28). Why I take students' cellphones. *Inside Higher Ed.* https://www.insidehighered.com/advice/2020/01/28/professor-gives-three-reasons-why-he-doesnt-allow-cellphones-his-classes-opinion

Brown, M. G. (2016). Blended instructional practice: A review of the empirical literature on instructors' adoption and use of online tools in face-to-face teaching. *Internet and Higher Education, 31*, 1–10. doi:10.1016/j.iheduc.2016.05.001

Bruder, P. (2014). Gadgets go to school: The benefits and risks of BYOD (Bring Your Own Device). *Education Digest, 80*(3), 15–18.

Brunzell, T., Stokes, H., & Waters, L. (2016). Trauma-informed positive education: Using positive psychology to strengthen vulnerable students. *Contemporary School Psychology, 20*(1), 63–83. doi:10.100740688-015-0070-x

Buonomo, I., Fatigante, M., & Fiorelli, C. (2017). Teacher burnout profiles: Risk and protective factors. *The Open Psychology Journal, 10*(1), 190–201. doi:10.2174/1874350101710010190

Burden, K., Schuck, S., & Kearney, M. (2019). Is the use of mobile devices in schools really innovative? What does the evidence say? *Impact (Sydney)*, 16–19.

Burns, M. (2018). *Tasks Before Apps: Designing rigorous learning in a tech-rich classroom*. ASCD.

Burns, S. M., & Lohenry, K. (2010, September). Cellular phone use in class: Implications for teaching and learning a pilot study. *College Student Journal*, *44*(3), 805–810.

Butler, D., Brown, M., & Criosta, G. (2016). Telling the story of mindrising: Minecraft, mindfulness and meaningful learning. *Proceedings from ITS, ICEduTECH, and STE '16: The International Conference on Internet Technologies & Society, Education Technologies, Sustainability, Technology, & Education.*

Cain, J., Perry, S., & Schon, N. (1981). Don't stop believin' [Recorded by Journey]. On Escape [Record]. New York, NY: Columbia.

Cakebread, C. (2017, November 15). Without mobile phones, hundreds of millions of people wouldn't have internet access. *Business Insider*. https://www.businessinsider.com/mobile-phones-only-connection-internet-developing-world-chart-2017-11

Camera, L. (2020). *Disconnected and disadvantaged: Schools race to give students access.* Retrieved from https://www.usnews.com/news/education-news/articles/2020-04-01/schools-rush-to-get-students-internet-access-during-coronavirus-pandemic#:~:text=According%20to%20the%20most%20recent,higher%2C%20at%2012%20million%20children

Canning, S., & Betrus, A. (2017). The culture of deep learning in eSports: An insider's perspective. *Educational Technology*, *57*(2), 65–69.

Carr, N. (2011). *The shallows: What the internet is doing to our brains*. W. W. Norton and Company.

CEHD. (2016, December 2). *Positive reinforcement in the classroom: Tips for teachers*. https://cehdvision2020.umn.edu/blog/positive-reinforcement-teacher-tips/

Cengage. (2017). *A study guide for Luigi Pirandello's 'A Day Goes By'*. Cengage.

Chai, C. S., Ling Koh, J. H., & Tsai, C. (2010). Facilitating preservice teachers' development of technological, pedagogical and content knowledge (TPACK). *Journal of Educational Technology & Society*, *13*(4), 63–73.

Chang, M. L. (2009). An approasial perspective of teacher burnout: Examining the emotional work of teachers. *Educational Psychology Review*, *21*(3), 193–218. doi:10.100710648-009-9106-y

Chase, E. (2018). Time, third space, and counternarratives of achievement for young mothers in high school. *Educational Studies*, *54*(3), 237–252. doi:10.1080/00131946.2017.1413371

Chbosky, S. (1999). *The Perks of Being a Wallflower*. Pocket Books.

Chen, G. (2018, August 06). Should public schools ban cell phones? *Public School Review*. https://www.publicschoolreview.com/blog/should-public-schools-ban-cell-phones

Cheong, P. H., Martin, J. N., & Macfadyen, L. (2012). Mediated intercultural communication matters: Understanding new media, dialectics and social change. In P. H. Cheong, J. N. Martin, & L. Macfadyen (Eds.), *New media and intercultural communication: Identity, community and politics* (pp. 1–20). Peter Lang.

Cheong, P. H., Shuter, R., & Suwinyattichaiporn, T. (2016). Managing student digital distractions and hyperconnectivity: Communication strategies and challenges for professorial authority. *Communication Education, 65*(3), 272–289. doi:10.1080/03634523.2016.1159317

Chukwuedo, S. O., & Nwachukwu, C. E. (2014). Maintenance practices in mobile phones for training prospective electronic technologists. *JORIND, 12*(1). www.transcampus.org/journals; www.ajol.info/journals/jorind

Cipollone, M., Schifter, C. C., & Moffat, R. A. (2014). Minecraft as a creative tool: A case study. *International Journal of Game-Based Learning, 4*(2), 1–14. doi:10.4018/ijgbl.2014040101

Cisneros, S. (1984). *The house on Mango Street*. Arte Público Press.

Collins, S. (2008). *The Hunger Games*. Scholastic.

Columbaro, C. H., & Monaghan, N. L. (2009). Employer perceptions of online degrees: A literature review. *Online Journal of Distance Learning Administration, 12*(1). https://www.westga.edu/~distance/ojdla/spring121/columbaro121.html

Connell, R. (1924). *The most dangerous game*. Collier's.

Cook, M. (2005). A place of their own: Creating a classroom 'third space' to support a continuum of text construction between home and school. *Literacy, 39*(2), 85–90. doi:10.1111/j.1741-4350.2005.00405.x

Cope, B., & Kalantzis, M. (2000). *Multiliteracies: Literacy learning and the design of social futures*. Routledge.

Copper, J. (2019, April 2). A real solution to deal with cell phones in the classroom. *Doc Cop Teaching*. http://doccopteaching.com/2019/04/02/a-real-solution-to-deal-with-cell-phones-in-the-classroom/

Countryman, J., & Rose, L. (2017). Wellbeing in the secondary music classroom: Ideas from hero's journeys and online gaming. *Philosophy of Music Education Review, 25*(2), 128–149. doi:10.2979/philmusieducrevi.25.2.03

Cowles, M. (2019). Dot to dot: Lessons that are rich in arts are engaging, but how do you bring art into the classroom? *AMLE Magazine, 7*(2), 5–6.

Craig, T., & Van Lom, M. (n.d.). Impact constructivist learning theory and mobile technology integration. In *Theories of Educational Technology*. EDTECH, Boise State University. https://sites.google.com/a/boisestate.edu/edtechtheories/craig_and_vanlom

Curwood, J. S., & Gibbons, D. (2010). "Just like I have felt": Multimodal counternarratives in youth-produced digital media. *International Journal of Learning and Media, 1*(4), 59–77. doi:10.1162/ijlm_a_00034

Dad, H., Ali, R., Janjua, M. Z. Q., Shahzad, S., & Khan, M. S. (2010). Comparison of the frequency and effectiveness of positive and negative reinforcement practices in schools. *Contemporary Issues in Education Research, 3*(1), 127–136. doi:10.19030/cier.v3i1.169

Daily Magic Productions. (2017). *Sender unknown: The woods*. Daily Magic Productions.

Darling-Hammond, L., Zielezinski, M. B., & Goldman, S. (2014). Using technology to support at-risk students' learning. *Stanford Center for Opportunity Policy in Education. Alliance for Excellent Education.* Retrieved from https://edpolicy.stanford.edu/sites/default/files/scope-pub-using-technology-report.pdf

Davis, V., & Lang, A. (2017, January 27). *How teachers can find time to innovate*. Bam Radio Network. https://www.bamradionetwork.com/track/nefields-exposed-kids-naive-adults/

Day, J. (2015). Academic continuity: Staying true to teaching values and objectives in the face of course interruptions. *Teaching & Learning Inquiry: The ISSOTL Journal, 3*(1), 75–89. doi:10.20343/teachlearninqu.3.1.75

Dewey, J. (2001). *Democracy and education*. Penn State Electronic Classics. (Original work published 1916)

Dewey, J. (2005). *Art as experience*. TarcherPerigree. (Original work published 1932)

Dodds, L. (2017, January). Students as social media content creators. *CSLA Journal, 40*(2), 13–16.

Domitrovich, C., Staley, K. C., Durlak, J. A., & Weissberg, R. P. (2017). Social-emotional competence: An essential factor for promoting positive adjustment and reducing risk in school children. *Child Development, 88*(2), 1–9. doi:10.1111/cdev.12739 PMID:28213889

Donham, J. (2013). Text sets, deep learning, and the common core. *School Library Monthly, 29*(6), 5–7.

Dontnod Entertainment. (2015). *Life is strange*. Dontnod Entertainment.

Echevarría, J., Short, D., & Vogt, M. E. (2013). *Making content comprehensible for English language learners: The SIOP Model* (4th ed.). Allyn & Bacon.

Ehret, C., & Hollett, T. (2014). Embodied composition in real virtualities: Adolescents' literacy practices and felt experiences moving with digital, mobile devices in school. *Research in the Teaching of English, 48*(4), 428–452.

Eisner, E. W. (2002). *The arts and the creation of mind*. Yale University Press.

Elgan, M. (2017, August 12). *Smart phones make people distracted and unproductive*. Computerworld. https://www.computerworld.com/article/3215276/smart phones-make-people-distracted-and-unproductive.html

Elish-Piper, L., Wold, L. S., & Schwingendorf, K. (2014). Scaffolding high school students' reading of complex texts using linked text sets. *Journal of Adolescent & Adult Literacy*, *57*(7), 565–574. doi:10.1002/jaal.292

Ellis, R., Tanaka, Y., & Yamazaki, A. (1994). Classroom Interaction, Comprehension and the Acquisition of Word Meanings. *Language Learning*, *44*(3), 449–491. doi:10.1111/j.1467-1770.1994.tb01114.x

Emdin, C. (2013). Pursuing the pedagogical potential of the pillars of hip-hop through science mindedness. *The International Journal of Critical Pedagogy*, *4*(3), 83–99.

Engel, G., & Green, T. (2011). Cell phones in the classroom: Are we dialing up disaster? *TechTrends*, *55*(2), 39–45. doi:10.100711528-011-0482-z

Engerman, J. A., & Hein, R. (2017). eSports gaming and you. *Educational Technology*, *57*(2), 62–64.

English Language Arts Georgia Standards of Excellence. (2020). Retrieved from https://www.georgiastandards.org/Georgia-Standards/ Documents/ ELA-Standards – Grades-9-12.pdf

English Language Arts Standards. (2020). *Reading: Literature: Grade 9-10*. Retrieved from http://www.corestandards.org/ELA-Literacy/RL/9-10/

Erwin, J. C. (2004). Power in the classroom: Creating the environment. In *The Classroom of Choice*. Association for Supervision and Curriculum Development.

Fabelo, T., Thompson, M. D., Plotkin, M., Carmichael, D., Marchbanks, M. P., III, & Booth, E. A. (2011, July). *Breaking Schools' Rules: A Statewide Study of How School Discipline Relates to Students' Success and Juvenile Justice Involvement*. The Justice Center. https://knowledgecenter.csg.org/kc/system/files/Breaking_School_Rules.pdf

Findley, B., & Varble, D. (2006). Creating a conducive classroom environment: Classroom management is the key. *College Teaching Methods & Styles Journal*, *2*(3), 1–6. doi:10.19030/ctms.v2i3.5262

Fitzgerald, F. (1925). *The great Gatsby*. Charles Scribner's Sons.

Flaherty, C. (2020). Zoom boom. *Inside Higher Ed*. Retrieved from https://www.insidehighered.com/news/2020/04/29/synchronous-instruction-hot-right-now-it-sustainable

Fond, C. (2018, October 9). *Turning kids from consumers to creators: How to boost student creativity in schools*. Medium. https://medium.com/the-edtech-world/boost-student-creativity-830bc68348c1

Forenbacher, I., Husnjak, S., Cvitić, I., & Jovović, I. (2019). Determinants of mobile phone ownership in Nigeria. *Telecommunications Policy*, *43*(7), 101812. doi:10.1016/j.telpol.2019.03.001

Frank, A. (1947). *The diary of Anne Frank*. Contact Publishing.

Froese, A. D., Carpenter, C. N., Inman, D. A., Schooley, J. R., Barnes, R. B., Brecht, P. W., & Chacon, J. D. (2012). Effects of classroom cell phone use on expected and actual learning. *College Student Journal*.

Fullbright Company. (2013). *Come Home*. Fullbright Company.

Gabriel, P. (1986). In your eyes [Recorded by Peter Gabriel]. On So. [Record]. Santa Monica, CA: Geffen.

Gaines, T. (2017, November 8). Pocket Points app leads to less smart phone usage. *The Eagle Eye*. https://eagleeye.news/news/pocket-points-app-leads-less-smartphone-usage

Gallagher, C. (2014). *Minecraft in the classroom: Ideas, inspiration, and student projects for teachers*. Peachpit Press.

Game Pressure. (2020). *Life is Strange*. https://guides.gamepressure.com/lifeisstrange/

Ganyaupfu, E. M. (2013). Teaching methods and students' academic performance. *International Journal of Humanities and Social Science Invention*, *2*(9), 29–35. http://www.ijhssi.org/papers/v2(9)/Version-2/E0292029035.pdf

Garcia, A. (2017, October 19). *Teens, teachers, and mobile tech*. Confessions of an Aca Fan. http://henryjenkins.org/blog/2017/9/7/an-interview-with-antero-garcia-part-two

Gay, G. (2010). *Culturally responsive teaching: Theory, research, and practice*. Teachers College Press.

Gee, J. P. (2010). A situated-sociocultural approach to literacy and technology. In E. A. Baker (Ed.), The new literacies: Multiple perspectives on research and practice (pp. 165–193). Academic Press.

Gee, J. (2018). Affinity spaces: How young people live and learn online and out of school. *Phi Delta Kappan*, *99*(6), 8–13. doi:10.1177/0031721718762416

Gee, J. P. (1996). *Social linguistics and literacies: Ideology in discourses* (2nd ed.). Falmer.

Gee, J. P. (2003). *What Video Games Have to Teach us About Learning and Literacy*. Palgrave MacMillan. doi:10.1145/950566.950595

Gee, J. P. (2017). Affinity spaces and 21st Century learning. *Educational Technology*, *57*(2), 27–31.

Gee, J. P., & Hayes, E. R. (2011). *Language and learning in the digital age*. Routledge. doi:10.4324/9780203830918

Genesee, F., Lindholm-Leary, K., Saunders, B., & Christian, D. (2006). *Educating English language learners: A synthesis of research evidence*. Cambridge University Press. doi:10.1017/CBO9780511499913

Gillwald, A., Odufuwa, F., & Mothobi, O. (2018). *The state of ICT in Nigeria. Policy paper series (5): After access of ICT in Nigeria*. Retrieved from: http://extensia-ltd.com/wp-content/uploads/2018/11/After-Access-Nigeria-State-of-ICT-2017.pdf

Gilmore, M. (2019). Restricted access: Banning cell phones in the classroom. *Teach*, 20-22.

Glazier, R. A., & Harris, H. S. (2020). *Common traits of the best online and face-to-face classes: Evidence from student surveys*. Retrieved from https://preprints.apsanet.org/engage/api-gateway/apsa/assets/orp/resource/item/5e2f9610cd361a001afed294/original/common-traits-of-the-best-online-and-face-to-face-classes-evidence-from-student-surveys.pdf

Golding, W. (1954). *Lord of the Flies*. Penguin.

Goldstein, D., Popescu, A., & Hannah-Jones, N. (2020, April 6). *As school moves online, many students stay logged out*. Retrieved from https://www.nytimes.com/ 2020/ 04/06/us/ coronavirus-schools-attendance-absent.html

Graham, E. (n.d.). *Using smart phones in the classroom*. National Education Association. https://www.nea.org/tools/56274.htm

Griffiths, M. D. (2013). Adolescent mobile phone addiction: A cause for concern? *Education for Health*, *31*(3), 76–78.

GSM Association. (2017). *The mobile economy – Sub-Sahara Africa 2017*. Retrieved from: https://www.gsma.com/subsaharaafrica/wp-content/uploads2018/11/2017-07-11-7bf3592e6d750144e58dcfac6adfab.pdf

GSM Association. (2018). *The mobile economy – West Africa 2018*. Retrieved from: https://www.gsmaintelligence.com/research/?file=e568fe9e710ec776d82c04e9f6760adb&download

Guloba, M. M., Wokadala, J., & Bategeka, L. (2010). *Does teaching methods and availability of teaching resources influence pupils' performance: Evidence from four districts in Uganda*. Research series No. 77, Economic Policy Research Centre. http://citeseerx.ist.psu.edu/viewdoc/download;jsessionid=C3A254921E07B006282B85561A749D92?doi=10.1.1.670.7103&rep=rep1&type=pdf

Gutiérrez, K. (2008). Developing a sociocritical literacy in the third space. *Reading Research Quarterly*, *43*(2), 148–164. doi:10.1598/RRQ.43.2.3

Gutiérrez, K., Gutiérrez, K. D., Baquedano-López, P., & Turner, M. G. (1997). Putting language back into language arts: When the radical middle meets the third space. *Language Arts*, *74*(5), 368–378.

Hafner, A. (2015). Remix culture and English language teaching: The expression of learner voice in digital multimodal compositions. *TESOL Quarterly*, *49*(3), 486–509. doi:10.1002/tesq.238

Hancock, M. (1996, January 1). *What is a photojournalist?* http://markhancock.blogspot.com/1996/01/what-is-photojournalist.html

Handley, L. (2019, January 24). *Nearly three quarters of the world will use just their smart phones to access the internet by 2025*. CNBC. https://www.cnbc.com/2019/01/24/smart phones-72percent-of-people-will-use-only-mobile-for-internet-by-2025.html

Harasim, L. (2000). Shift happens: Online education as a new paradigm in learning. *The Internet and Higher Education*, *3*(1-2), 41–61. https://go.aws/341sDn7. doi:10.1016/S1096-7516(00)00032-4

Harvey, M. M., Deuel, A., & Marlatt, R. (2020). To be or not to be: Modernizing Shakespeare with multimodal learning stations. *Journal of Adolescent & Adult Literacy*, *63*(5), 559–568. doi:10.1002/jaal.1023

Heard, G. (2020, July 9). *Heart maps*. Retrieved from https://www.georgiaheard.com/heart-maps/

Heath, S. B. (2008). Vision for learning; History, Theory, and Affirmation. In J. Flood, S. B. Heath, & D. Lapp (Eds.), *Handbook of research on teaching literacy through the communicative and visual arts* (Vol. 2, pp. 3–12). Lawrence Erlbaum Associates.

Henderson, D. (2017, August 20). How can teachers control cell phones in their class? *Teachthought*. https://teachthought.com/technology/can-teachers-control-cell-phones-class/

Hensley, M. (2019). Getting freaky with the founders: Strategically implementing Hamilton: An American musical. *Social Studies Research & Practice*, *14*(1), 28–39.

Herrington, A., & Herrington, J. (2007) Authentic mobile learning in higher education. *AARE 2007 International Educational Research Conference*.

Hess, A. (2019, January 19). Research continually shows how distracting cell phones are---so some schools want to ban them. *CNBC*. https://www.cnbc.com/2019/01/18/research-shows-that-cell-phones-distract-students--so-france-banned-them-in-school--.html

Hess, A. (2019, January 19). *Research continually shows how distracting cell phones are—so some schools want to ban them*. CNBC. https://www.cnbc.com/2019/01/18/research-shows-that-cell-phones-distract-students--so-france-banned-them-in-school--.html

He, W. (2013). Examining students' online interaction in a live video streaming environment using data mining and text mining. *Computers in Human Behavior*, *29*(1), 90–102. doi:10.1016/j.chb.2012.07.020

Hewson, P. (2014). The Miracle [Recorded by U2]. On Songs of Innocence [Digital Recording]. Santa Monica, CA: Island Interscope.

Hicks, T. (2006). Expanding the Conversation: A Commentary Toward Revision of Swenson, Rezema, Young, McGrail, and Whitin. *Contemporary Issues in Technology & Teacher Education*, *6*(1), 46–65.

Hicks, T., & Turner, K. H. (2013). No longer a luxury: Digital literacy can't wait. *English Journal*, *102*(6), 58–65.

Hillocks, G., & Smith, M. W. (1995). *Teaching writing as reflective practice*. Teachers College.

Hinton, S. E. (1967). *The outsiders*. Viking Press.

Hobbs, R. (Ed.). (2016). *Exploring the roots of digital and media literacy through personal narrative*. Temple University Press. doi:10.2307/j.ctvrf898z

Hodges, C., Moore, S., Lockee, B., Trust, T., & Bond, A. (2020). The difference between emergency remote teaching and online learning. *Educause Review*. Retrieved from https://er.educause.edu/articles/2020/3/the-difference-between-emergency-remote-teaching-and-online-learning

Hodges, C., Moore, S., Lockee, B., Trust, T., & Bond, A. (2020, March 27). The difference between emergency remote teaching and online learning. *EDUCAUSEreview*. https://er.educause.edu/articles/2020/3/the-difference-between-emergency-remote-teaching-and-online-learning

Hogan, R. L., & McKnight, M. (2007). Exploring burnout among university online instructors: An initial investigation. *The Internet and Higher Education*, *10*(2), 117–124. doi:10.1016/j.iheduc.2007.03.001

Hookway, C. (2007). Short on Peirce's Early Theory of Signs. *Transactions of the Charles S. Peirce Society*, *43*(4), 619–625.

Horn, M. B. (2020). COVID-19s long term impacts on education in 2020 and beyond. *EdSurge*. https://www.edsurge.com/news/2020-03-23-covid-19-s-long-term-impacts-on-education-in-2020-and-beyond

Hotch, M. L., McCarty, R., Gurvitz, D., & Sitkoski, I. (2018). Five key principles: Guided inquiry with multimodal text sets. *The Reading Teacher*, *72*(6), 701–710. doi:10.1002/trtr.1781

Hrebik, J. (2019). Melodic expressions: Empowering first-year writers through songwriting. *CEA Forum*, *48*(1), 268–289.

Hwang, K. A., & Yang, C. H. (2009). Automated inattention and fatigue detection system in distance education for elementary school students. *Journal of Educational Technology & Society*, *12*(2), 22–35.

Ingraham, N., & Nuttall, S. (2016). The story of an arts integration school on English-language-learner development: A qualitative study of collaboration, integrity, and confidence. *International Journal of Education & the Arts*, *17*(28). http://www.ijea.org/v17n28/

Inkle. (2014). *80 days*. Inkle.

International Association for Mobile Learning. (n.d.). *Six learning theories for mobile learning*. https://iamlearning.pressbooks.com/chapter/six-learning-theories/

International Association for the Evaluation of Educational Achievement. (2018). *ICILS 2018 Results | IEA*. IEA. https://www.iea.nl/news-events/news/icils-2018-results

International Association for the Evaluation of Educational Achievement. (2018). *Preparing For Life In A Digital World IEA International Computer and Information Literacy Study 2018 International Report*. Springer Publishing. https://www.iea.nl/sites/default/files/2020-04/IEA%20International%20Computer%20and%20Information%20Literacy%20Study%202018%20International%20Report.pdf

International Literacy Association. (2018). Improving digital practices for literacy, learning, and justice: More than just tools [Literacy leadership brief]. Newark, DE: Author.

Irick, L. (2020a). *Class Wide Rewards*. https://intercom.help/portal-c4c52318881b/en/articles/3160848-class-widerewards

Irick, L. (2020b). *Huge List of Reward Ideas*. https://intercom.help/portal-c4c52318881b/en/articles/2535064-huge-list-ofreward-ideas

Ivey, G., & Johnston, P. H. (2013). Engagement with young adult literature: Outcomes and processes. *Reading Research Quarterly*, *48*(3), 255–275. doi:10.1002/rrq.46

Jaggars, S. S. (2014). Choosing between online and face-to-face courses: Community college student voices. *American Journal of Distance Education*, *28*(1), 27–38. doi:10.1080/08923647.2014.867697

Jiménez, F. (1997). *Cajas de Cartón*. University of New Mexico Press.

JoEllen. (2014, October 6). Using rewards in a classroom. *Cuppacocoa*. http://www.cuppacocoa.com/rewards-in-a-classroom/

Jones, R. (2012). *Understanding Digital Literacies: A Practical Introduction* (1st ed.). Routledge. doi:10.4324/9780203095317

Kajee, L. (2018). Teacher education students engaging with digital identity narratives. *South African Journal of Education*, *38*(2), 1–9.

Kamenetz, A. (2019, October 31). *It's a smartphone life: More than half of U.S. children now have one* [Radio Broadcast]. NPR. https://www.npr.org/2019/10/31/774838891/its-a-smartphone-life-more-than-half-of-u-s-children-now-have-one

Kang, G. Y. (2018). Playing with digital tools with explicit scaffolding. *The Reading Teacher*, *71*(6), 735–741. doi:10.1002/trtr.1672

Kareva, V., & Echevarria, J. (2013). Using the SIOP model for effective content teaching with second and foreign language learners. *Journal of Education and Training Studies*, *1*(2), 239–248. doi:10.11114/jets.v1i2.173

Kayaoğlu, M. N., Sağlamel, H., & Kobul, K. (2017). Learner perspectives on mobile phone integration for vocabulary development in translation classes. *Lublin Studies in Modern Languages and Literature, 41*(1), 191 – 214. http://www.lsmll.Umcs.Lublin.Pl

Kay, R. H., & Lauricella, S. (2011). Unstructured vs. structured use of laptops in higher education. *Journal of Information Technology Education: Innovations in Practice.*, *10*, 34–42. doi:10.28945/1363

Kenkel, D. (2015). Minecraft or mindcraft: Co-designing and co-learning in a virtual world. *Adminfo, 28*, 9–11. https://bcpvpa.bc.ca/wp-content/uploads/2015/12/Dec15Adminfo.pdf

Kennedy, D. M. (2014). M-learning to support English in a Hong Kong university. *Journal of Online Learning and Teaching*, *10*(4), 640–653.

Kieschnick, W. (2019, January 15). Supercharged literacy: Strategies and digital tools to support content area literacy [Video file]. *Brightcove.* Retrieved from https://players.brightcove.net/6834871900l/default_default/index.html?videoId=5993548059001&elqTrackId=bf82fa7e05804fdba2698866a043bda2&elqaid=4046&elqat=2

Kieschnick, W. (2017). *Bold school: Old school wisdom plus new school technologies equals blended learning that works.* International Center for Leadership in Education.

Kim, D., Rueckert, D., Kim, D. J., & Seo, D. (2013). Student perceptions and experiences of mobile learning. *Language Learning & Technology, 17*(3), 52–73. http://llt.msu.edu/issues/october2013/kimetal.pdf

Kim, V. (2018). Technology-Enhanced Feedback on Student Writing in the English-Medium Instruction Classroom. *English Teaching, 73*(4), 29–53. doi:10.15858/engtea.73.4.201812.29

Klein, A. (2019). Schools say no to cellphones in class. But is it a smart move? *Education Week, 39*(4), 10–11. https://www.edweek.org/ew/articles/2019/09/11/schools-say-no-to-cellphones-in-class.html

Knobel, M., & Lankshear, C. (2008). Remix: The art and craft of endless hybridization. *Journal of Adolescent & Adult Literacy, 52*(1), 22–33. doi:10.1598/JAAL.52.1.3

Koehler, M. J., & Mishra, P. (2005). What happens when teachers design educational technology? The development of technological pedagogical content knowledge. *Journal of Educational Computing Research, 32*(2), 131–152. doi:10.2190/0EW7-01WB-BKHL-QDYV

Koehler, M. J., Mishra, P., & Cain, W. (2013). What is technological pedagogical content knowledge (TPACK)? *Journal of Education, 193*(3), 13–19. doi:10.1177/002205741319300303

Kolb, L. (2019, February). Smart classroom-tech integration. *The Tech-Savvy School, 76*(5), 20-26. http://www.jite.org/documents/Vol10/JITEv10IIPp033-042Kay840.pdfhttp://www.ascd.org/publications/educational_leadership/feb19/vol76/num05/Smart_Classroom-Tech_Integration.aspx

Korkut, S., Dornberger, R., Diwanji, P., Simon, P., & Maerki, M. (2015). Success factors of online learning videos. *International Journal of Interactive Technologies, 10*(1), 116–182. doi:10.3991/ijim.v9i4.4460

Kowalski, K. (2016, March 3). When smartphones go to school. *Science News for Students.* https://www.sciencenewsforstudents.org/article/when-smartphones-go-school

Kress, G. (2003). *Literacy in the New Media Age.* Routledge.

Kress, G., & van Leeuwen, T. (2006). *Reading images: The grammar of visual images.* Routledge. doi:10.4324/9780203619728

Ladson-Billings, G. (1995). But that's just good teaching. The case for culturally relevant pedagogy. *Theory into Practice, 34*(3), 159–165. doi:10.1080/00405849509543675

Ladson-Billings, G. (1995). Toward a theory of culturally relevant pedagogy. *American Educational Research Journal*, *32*(3), 465–491. doi:10.3102/00028312032003465

LaFave, N. (2017, July 25). *Creative lessons with fake texts, tweets, Facebook pages, and more.* https://www.fractuslearning.com/get-creative-fake-texts-tweets-facebook-pages/

Lalonde, M. (2019). The connected image in mobile and social media: The visual instances of adolescents becoming. In J. C. Castro (Ed.), *Mobile media in and outside of the art classroom: Attending to identity, spatiality, and materiality* (pp. 27–46). doi:10.1007/978-3-030-25316-5_2

Langford, S., Narayan, A., & Von Glahn, N. (2016). Revisiting the Technology and Student Learning Debates: Critical Issues and Multiple Perspectives. *Transformative Dialogues: Teaching & Learning Journal*, *9*(2), 1–15.

Lankshear, C., & Knobel, K. (2008). Introduction: Digital literacies—concepts, policies, and practices. In C. Lankshear & M. Knobel (Eds.), *Digital literacies: Concepts, policies, and practices* (pp. 1–16). Peter Lang.

Lankshear, C., & Knobel, M. (2007). Sampling "the New" in new literacies. In M. Knobel & C. Lankshear (Eds.), *A New Literacies Sampler* (pp. 1–24). Peter Lang.

Leander, K., Phillips, N., & Taylor, K. (2010). The changing social spaces of learning: Mapping new mobilities. *Review of Research in Education*, *34*(1), 329–394. doi:10.3102/0091732X09358129

Lee, C. Y., Dickerson, J., & Winslow, J. (2012). An analysis of organizational approaches to online course structures. *Online Journal of Distance Learning Administration*, *15*(1).

Leem, J., & Sung, E. (2019). Teachers' beliefs and technology acceptance concerning smart mobile devices for SMART education in South Korea. *British Journal of Educational Technology*, *50*(2), 601–613. doi:10.1111/bjet.12612

Lehtinen, A., Nieminen, P., & Viiri, J. (2016). Preservice teachers' TPACK beliefs and attitudes toward simulations. *Contemporary Issues in Technology & Teacher Education*, *16*(2). https://citejournal.org/volume-16/issue-2-16/science/preservice-teachers-tpack-beliefs-and-attitudes-toward-simulations

Lessig, L. (2008). *Remix: Making art and commerce thrive in the hybrid economy*. Bloomsbury Academic. doi:10.5040/9781849662505

Lewis Ellison, T. (2017). Digital participation, agency, and choice: An African American youth's digital storytelling about Minecraft. *Journal of Adolescent & Adult Literacy*, *61*(1), 25–35. doi:10.1002/jaal.645

Lewis Ellison, T., & Evans, J. N. (2016). "Minecraft," teachers, parents, and learning: What they need to know and understand. *School Community Journal*, *26*(2), 25–43.

Lewis Ellison, T., & Solomon, M. (2018). Digital play as purposeful productive literacies in African American boys. *The Reading Teacher*, *71*(4), 495–500. doi:10.1002/trtr.1657

Leyden, A. (2018). *40 uses of smartphones in school.* https://www.goconqr.com/en/examtime/blog/40-uses-for-smartphones-in-school/

Lippincott, J. (2007, November/December). Student content creators: Convergence of literacies. *EDUCAUSE Review, 42*(6), 16–17.

Liu, M., Scordino, R., Geurtz, R., Navarrete, C., Ko, Y., & Lim, M. (2014, August 13). A look at research on mobile learning in K–12 education from 2007 to the present. *Journal of Research on Technology in Education, 46*(4), 325–372. doi:10.1080/15391523.2014.925681

Lorch, M., & Mills, J. (2016). How Minecraft could help teach chemistry's building blocks of Life. *Chemistry in Australia*, (Sep), 20–23.

Loveless, B. (n.d.) Using cell phones as learning tools. *Education Corner.* https://www.educationcorner.com/cell-phones-learning-tools.html

Lowry, L. (1993). *The giver*. Houghton Mifflin Harcourt.

Lupo, S. M., Strong, J., Lewis, W., Walpole, S., & McKenna, M. C. (2018). Building background knowledge through reading: Rethinking text sets. *Journal of Adolescent & Adult Literacy, 61*(4), 433–444. doi:10.1002/jaal.701

Lynch, T. L. (2008). Rereadings and literacy: How students' second readings might open third spaces. *Journal of Adolescent & Adult Literacy, 52*(4), 334–341. doi:10.1598/JAAL.52.4.6

Magraner, J., & Ramos, R. (2020). Instagram as a musical learning tool in secondary education and high school. *Revista de Comunicación. Vivat Academia, 151*, 25–44.

Mahdi, H. S. (2017). Effectiveness of mobile devices on vocabulary learning: A meta-analysis. *Journal of Educational Computing Research, 56*(1), 134–154. doi:10.1177/0735633117698826

Maloney, D. (2017, March 10). *The essential work of English Language Arts- and our ELA teachers- in our democracy.* NCTE. Https://Ncte.Org/Blog/2017/03/Essential-Work-English-Language-Arts-Ela-Teachers-Democracy/

Mann, M. D. (2017). Increasing student motivation to learn by making computer game technology more engaging: Measurable outcomes that determine success. *Contemporary Issues in Education Research, 10*(2), 117–120. doi:10.19030/cier.v10i2.9922

Marklund, B., & Taylor, A. (2016). Educational games in practice: The challenges involved in conducting a game-based curriculum. *Electronic Journal of e-Learning, 14*, 122-135.

Marlatt, R. (2018a). Get in the game: Promoting justice through a digitized literature study. *Multicultural Perspectives, 20*(4), 222–228. doi:10.1080/15210960.2018.1467769

Marlatt, R. (2018b). Literary analysis using Minecraft: An Asian American youth crafts her literacy identity. *Journal of Adolescent & Adult Literacy, 62*(1), 55–66. doi:10.1002/jaal.747

Marlatt, R. (2020). Capitalizing on the craze of Fortnite: Toward a conceptual framework for understanding how gamers construct communities of practice. *Journal of Education*, *200*(1), 3–11. doi:10.1177/0022057419864531

Martin, J. (2019). Building relationships and increasing engagement in the virtual classroom: Practical tools for the online instructor. *Journal of Educators Online*, *16*(1). Advance online publication. doi:10.9743/jeo.2019.16.1.9

McCarthy, E. (2015, November 17). *24 Things you might not have known about Hamilton*. Mental Floss. https://www.mentalfloss.com/article/71222/20-things-you-might-not-have-known-about-hamilton

McGrail, E. (2005). Teachers, technology, and change: English teachers' perspectives. *Journal of Technology and Teacher Education*, *13*(1), 5–24.

McGuire, G. (1984). How Arts Instruction Affects Reading and Language: Theory and Research. *The Reading Teacher*, *37*(9), 835–839.

McTigue, E. M., & Uppstad, P. H. (2018). Getting serious about serious games: Best practices for computer games in reading classrooms. *The Reading Teacher*, *72*(4), 453–461. doi:10.1002/trtr.1737

Mehta, D. (2017). *Excessive use of mobile phones in children*. https://www.lybrate.com/topic/excessive-use-of-mobile-phones-in children/cf8aa2d927af556f4a2f0b3741769eca

Meyer, L. (2016). 9 Strategies for managing BYOD in the classroom. *T.H.E. Journal*, *43*(6), 24–26.

Michielse, M., & Partti, H. (2015). Producing a meaningful difference: The significance of small creative acts in composing within online participatory remix practices. *International Journal of Community Music*, *8*(1), 27–40. doi:10.1386/ijcm.8.1.27_1

Miller, D., Sharp, C., Minnich, C., & Sokolowski, K. (2018). Digital tools you need to know. *Voices from the Middle*, *25*(4), 60–62. https://secure.ncte.org/library/NCTEFiles/Resources/Journals/VM/0254-may2018/VM0254Notes.pdf?_ga=2.235130433.1521800320.1594835033-855434546.1587059887

Mills, K. (2010). A Review of the "digital turn" in the New Literacy Studies. *Review of Educational Research*, *80*(2), 246–271. doi:10.3102/0034654310364401

Mills, K., & Comber, B. (2013). Space, place and power: The spatial turn in literacy research. In K. Hall, T. Cremin, B. Comber, & L. Moll (Eds.), *International Handbook of Research in Children's Literacy, Learning and Culture*. Wiley-Blackwell Publishing, Inc. doi:10.1002/9781118323342.ch30

Mills, K., & Exley, B. (2014). Research and Policy: Narrative and Multimodality in English Language Arts Curricula: A Tale of Two Nations. *Language Arts*, *92*(2), 136–143.

Mishra, P., & Koehler, M. J. (2006). Technological pedagogical content knowledge: A framework for teacher knowledge. *Teachers College Record, 108*(6), 1017–1054. doi:10.1111/j.1467-9620.2006.00684.x

Mojaye, E. M. (2015). Mobile phone usage among Nigerian university students and its impact on teaching and learning. *Global Journal of Arts Humanities and Social Sciences, 3*(1), 29-38, http://www.eajournals.org/wp-content/uploads/Mobile-Phone-Usage-among-Nigerian-University-Students-and-Its-Impact-On-Teaching-And-Learning.pdf

Moje, E., Ciechanowski, K., Kramer, K., Ellis, L., Carrillo, R., & Collazo, T. (2004). Working toward third space in content area literacy: An examination of everyday funds of knowledge and Discourse. *Reading Research Quarterly, 39*(1), 38–70. doi:10.1598/RRQ.39.1.4

Moran, C. M. (2019, March 1). *5 reasons why virtual reality belongs in every classroom.* https://corwin-connect.com/2019/03/5-reasons-why-virtual-reality-belongs-in-every-classroom/

Moran, C. (2018). Learners without borders: Connected learning in a digital third space. *Contemporary Issues in Technology & Teacher Education, 18*(2), 233–254.

Moran, C. M., & Woodall, M. (2019). "It was like I was there": Inspiring engagement through virtual reality. *English Journal, 109*(1), 90–96.

Morrell, E. (2012). 21st-Century literacies, critical media pedagogies, and language arts. *The Reading Teacher, 66*(4), 300–302. doi:10.1002/TRTR.01125

Mupinga, D. M. (2017). School-wide and Classroom Policies on the Use of Mobile Technologies: An Exploratory Study. *The Journal of Technology Studies, 43*(2), 70–79. doi:10.21061/jots.v43i2.a.2

MySalaryScale. (2017). *Salaries of Nigerian teachers and their perceived lack of competence.* https://www.mysalaryscale.com/blog/salaries-nigerian-teachers-perceived-lack-competence/

Nash, B. (2018). Exploring multimodal writing in secondary English classrooms: A literature review. *English Teaching, 17*(4), 342–356. doi:10.1108/ETPC-01-2018-0012

Nash-Ditzel, S., & Brown, T. (2012). Freedoms in the classroom: Cultivating a successful third space for literacy growth. *Language and Literacy: A Canadian Education Journal, 14*(3), 95–111.

National Center for Education Statistics. (2014). *Teacher attrition and mobility: Results from the 2012–13 teacher follow-up survey* (NCES 2014-077). Author.

National Council of Teachers of English. (2018). *Beliefs for integrating technology into the English Language Arts classroom.* https://ncte.org/statement/beliefs-technology-preparation-english-teachers/print/

National Council of Teachers of English. (2018). *Beliefs for integrating technology into the English Language Arts classroom.* Retrieved from https://ncte.org/statement/beliefs-technology-preparation-english-teachers/

National Governors Association Center for Best Practices and Council of Chief State School Officers. (2010). *Common Core State Standards English Language Arts*. National Governors Association Center for Best Practices, Council of Chief State School Officers. http://www.corestandards.org/ELA-Literacy/

NEA. (2012). *Preparing 21st century students for a global society: An educator's guide to the "Four Cs"*. National Education Association.

Nikolopoulou, K., & Gialamas, V. (2018). Mobile phone dependence: Secondary school pupils' attitudes. *Education and Information Technologies*, *23*(6), 2821–2839. doi:10.100710639-018-9743-1

Nixon, A. (2013). Engaging urban youth in meaningful dialogue through digital storytelling. In C. Lankshear & M. Knobel (Eds.), *A New literacies reader: Educational perspectives* (pp. 123–138). Peter Lang Publishing.

Njoroge, G. N., Changeiywo, J. M., & Ndirangu, M. (2014). Effects of inquiry-based teaching approach on secondary school students' achievement and motivation in physics in Nyeri County, Kenya. *International Journal of Academic Research in Education and Review.*, *2*(1), 1–16. doi:10.14662/IJARER2013.010

O'Byrne, W. I. (2014). Online content creation: Empowering students as readers and writers of online information. In K. E. Pytash & R. E. Ferdig (Eds.), *Exploring Technology for Writing and Writing Instruction* (pp. 276–297). IGI Global. doi:10.4018/978-1-4666-4341-3.ch016

Oddone, K., Hughes, H., & Lupton, M. (2019). Teachers as connected professionals: A model to support professional learning through personal learning networks. *International Review of Research in Open and Distributed Learning*, *20*(3). Advance online publication. doi:10.19173/irrodl.v20i4.4082

Okewole, J. O. (2016). *Comparative effects of literature circle, dialogic reading and self-selection vocabulary on lower primary school pupils' reading skills in South Western Nigeria* (Unpublished Ph.D. Thesis). Obafemi Awolowo University, Ile-Ife, Nigeria.

Okewole, J. O., Odejobi, C. O., & Ajayi, H. O. (2018). Effects of literature circles, dialogic reading and vocabulary self selection strategies on the reading comprehension skill of lower primary school in Osun State. *Journal of Education and Practice, IISTE*, *9*(5), 29–36.

Omeruo, K. (2009). *The impact of GSM mobile phones on Nigerians*. Retrieved from: http://techtrendsng.com/the-impact-of-gsm-mobile-phones-on-nigerians/

Orenstein, N. (2019, October 8). Berkeley High takes students' phones away - sort of. *Berkleyside.com.* https://www.berkeleyside.com/2019/10/08/berkeley-high-takes-students-phones-away-sort-of

Oris, A. (2020). *Integration - SAMR Matrix*. Integration - SAMR Matrix. https://sites.google.com/cftigers.org/techcoach

Orlando, J. (2014). Veteran teachers and technology: Change fatigue and knowledge insecurity practice. *Teachers and Teaching*, *20*(4), 437–439. doi:10.1080/13540602.2014.881644

Overby, A., & Jones, B. L. (2015). Virtual LEGOs: Incorporating Minecraft into the art education curriculum. *Art Education*, *68*(1), 21–27. doi:10.1080/00043125.2015.11519302

Page, J., & Plant, R. (1971). Stairway to heaven [Recorded by Led Zeppelin]. On Led Zeppelin IV [Record]. New York, NY: Atlantic.

Page, S. (2020, May 26). Back to school? 1 in 5 teachers are unlikely to return to reopened classroom this fall, poll says. *USA Today.*

Pando, M., & Aguirre-Muñoz, Z. (2019). Engaging English language learners in model-based science instruction. In L. C. de Oliveira, K. M. Obenchain, R. H. Kenney, & A. W. Oliveira (Eds.), *Teaching the content areas to English language learners in secondary schools* (pp. 215–230). Springer. doi:10.1007/978-3-030-02245-7_14

Paris, D. (2012). Culturally sustaining pedagogy: A needed change in stance, terminology, and practice. *Educational Researcher*, *41*(3), 93–97. doi:10.3102/0013189X12441244

Park, S. (2015). *Assessing students' digital multimodal compositions.* Retrieved from https://www.literacyworldwide.org/blog/literacy-now/2015/11/27/ assessing-students-digitalmultimodalcompositions#:~:text=Digital%20multimodal%20compositin%20refers%20to,examples%20of%20digital%20multimodal%20composition

Pedota, P. (2007). Strategies for effective classroom management in the secondary setting. *The Clearing House: A Journal of Educational Strategies, Issues and Ideas*, *80*(4), 163–168. doi:10.3200/TCHS.80.4.163-168

Perry, K. (2012). What is literacy?—A Critical overview of sociocultural perspectives. *Journal of Language and Literacy Education*, *8*(1), 51–71.

Persson, M. (2011). *Minecraft*. Mojang Studios.

Pew Research Center. (2020). *Mobile Phone Fact Sheet* [graph]. Retrieved from https://www.pewresearch.org/internet/fact-sheet/mobile/

Philip, R. T. (2006). *Engaging 'tweens and teens: A brain compatible approach to reading middle and high school students*. Corwin.

Philip, T. M., & Garcia, A. (2015). Schooling Mobile Phones: Assumptions About Proximal Benefits, the Challenges of Shifting Meanings, and the Politics of Teaching. *Educational Policy*, *29*(4), 676–707. doi:10.1177/0895904813518105

Pike, J., & Stuppy, J. (2015). *Use Minecraft to teach math.* http://www.iste.org/explore

Pilon, A. (2019). Integrating traditional art making processes and new technology in the high school curriculum. In J. C. Castro (Ed.), *Mobile media in and outside of the art classroom: Attending to identity, spatiality, and materiality* (pp. 151–226). doi:10.1007/978-3-030-25316-5_7

Pope, C., & Golub, J. (2000). Preparing tomorrow's English language arts teachers today: Principles and practices for infusing technology. *Contemporary Issues in Technology & Teacher Education, 1*(1), 89–97.

Porter, G. (2016). How mobile phones are disrupting teaching and learning in Africa. *The Conversation.* https://theconversation.com/how-mobile-phones-are-disrupting-teaching-and-learning-in-africa-59549

Portier, C., Friedrich, N., & Peterson, S. S. (2019). Play(ful) pedagogical practices for creative collaborative literacy. *The Reading Teacher, 73*(1), 17–27. doi:10.1002/trtr.1795

Prensky, M. (2012). *From digital natives to digital wisdom: Hopeful essays for 21st century education.* Corwin. doi:10.4135/9781483387765

Price, K. M., & Nelson, K. L. (2014). *Planning Effective Instruction: Diversity Responsive Methods and Management, 5th Edition.* Retrieved from https://bookshelf.vitalsource.com/#/books/9781285499918/

Price-Dennis, D., Holmes, K. A., & Smith, E. (2015). Exploring digital literacy practices in an inclusive classroom. *The Reading Teacher, 69*(2), 195–205. doi:10.1002/trtr.1398

Ravitch, D. (2014). *Reign of error: The hoax of the privatization movement and the danger to America's public school.* Vintage Books.

Reading Length. (2020). *The Perks of Being a Wallflower.* https://www.readinglength.com/book/isbn-1451696191

Regan, K., Ermenova, A., Baker, P., Jerome, M. K., Spencer, V., Lawson, H., & Werner, T. (2012). Experiences of instructors in online environments: Identity and regulating emotions. *Internet and Higher Education, 15*(3), 204–212. doi:10.1016/j.iheduc.2011.12.001

Rezaiyan, A., Mohammadi, E., & Fallah, P. A. (2007). Effect of computer game intervention on the attention capacity of mentally retarded children. *International Journal of Nursing Practice, 13*(5), 284–288. doi:10.1111/j.1440-172X.2007.00639.x PMID:17883714

Risberg, C. (2015). More than just a video game: Tips for using Minecraft to personal- ize the curriculum and promote creativity, collaboration, and problem solving. Illinois Association for Gifted Children Journal, 44–48.

Robinson, K. (2013, April 23). *The dynamics of creativity.* http://sirkenrobinson.com/the-dynamics-of-creativity/

Rosenblatt, L. (1988). *Writing and reading: The transactional theory.* Bolt, Beranek, & Newman, Inc.

Rosenblatt, L. M. (1978). *The reader, the text, the poem: The transactional theory of the literary work.* Southern Illinois University Press.

Rowsell, J., Burke, A., Flewitt, R., Liao, H.-T., Lin, A., Marsh, J., Mills, K., Prinsloo, M., Rowe, D., & Wohlwend, K. (2016). Humanizing digital literacies: A road trip in search of wisdom and insight. Digital Literacy Column. *The Reading Teacher, 70*(1), 121–129. doi:10.1002/trtr.1501

Rumanyika, J. D., & Mashenene, R. G. (2015, April 29). Mobile phone technology adoption and classroom management in higher learning institutions in Tanzania: Challenges and implications. *International Journal of Information Technology and Business Management, 36*(1), 34–51.

Rumfola, L. M. (2017). Positive reinforcement positively helps students in the classroom. *Education and Human Development Master's Theses, 286*, 1–53.

Russell, D. (2018). Controlling smartphone use in schools. *Teacher Bulletin.* https://www.teachermagazine.com.au/articles/controlling-smartphone-use-in-schools

Russell, D. (2018). Mobile phones in the classroom – what does the research say? *Teacher Bulletin.* https://www.teachermagazine.com.au/articles/mobile-phones-in-the-classroom-what-does-the-research-say

Russo, C. J. (2018). Students and cell phones: Learning tools or learning distractions? *School Business Affairs, 84*(3), 33–35.

Rutherford, J. (1990). The third space: Interview with Homi Bhabha. In *Identity: Community, culture, difference.* London, UK: Lawrence and Wishart.

Rutkin, A. (2016). *How Minecraft is helping children with autism make new friends.* https://www.newscientist.com/article/mg23030713-100-how-is-helping-children-with-autism-make-new-friends/

Rybakova, K. (2020). Humanizing online assessment: Using screencasting as a multimedia feedback tool for first generation college students. In J. Lantz (Ed.), *Handbook of research on integrating digital technology with literacy pedagogies.* doi:10.4018/978-1-7998-0246-4.ch022

Rybakova, K., Rice, M., Moran, C., Zucker, L., McGrail, E., Mcdermott, M., Loomis, S., Gerber, H., Piotrowski, A., Garcia, M., Gibbons, T., & Marlatt, R. (2019). A long arc bending towards equity: Tracing almost 20 years of ELA teaching trends inCITE. *Contemporary Issues in Technology & Teacher Education, 19*(4).

Rybakova, K., Rice, M., Moran, C., Zucker, L., McGrail, W., Mcdermott, M., Loomis, S., Piotrowski, A., Garcia, M., Gerber, H., Marlatt, R., & Gibbons, T. (2019). A long arc bending towards equity: Tracing almost 20 years of ELA teaching trends in CITE. *Contemporary Issues in Technology & Teacher Education, 19*(4).

Saez-Lopez, J. M., Miller, T., Vasquez-Cano, E., & Dominquez-Garrido, M. C. (2015). Exploring application, attitudes, and integration of video games: MinecraftEDU in middle school. *Journal of Educational Technology & Society, 18*(3), 114–128.

Saheed, U. (2018). Factors affecting the teaching and learning of English language in primary school Nigeria. *Myschooltrick.* https://www.myschooltrick.com/2018/07/factor-affecting-the-teaching-and-learning-of-english-language-in-primary-school-nigeria.html

Salami, J. O. (2019). Effects of two instructional strategies on the acquisition of English basic phonology and morphology by lower primary school pupils in Ile – Ife, Osun State (Unpublished Master of Arts in Education). Obafemi Awolowo University, Ile-Ife, Nigeria.

Sandholtz, J. H., Ringstaff, C., & Dwyer, D. C. (1992). *Teaching in high-tech environments: Classroom management revisited*. Apple Computer, Inc. doi:10.2190/Y5NE-V9RQ-FD63-WC2N

Saunders, J. (2010). Identity in music: Adolescents and the music classroom. *Action, Criticism, and Theory for Music Education*, *9*(2), 70–78.

Schaeffer, K. (2019, August 23). *Most U.S. teens who use cellphones do it to pass time, connect with others, learn new things*. Pew Research Center. https://www.pewresearch.org/fact-tank/2019/08/23/most-u-s-teens-who-use-cellphones-do-it-to-pass-time-connect-with-others-learn-new-things/

Scheg, A. G. (2014). *Reforming teacher education for online pedagogy development*. IGI Global. doi:10.4018/978-1-4666-5055-8

Schifter, C., Cipollone, M., & Moffat, F. (2013). *Piaget, Inhelder and Minecraft. Proceedings from*. The International Association for Development of the Information Society.

Schrage, M. (2001). *The relationship revolution*. Retrieved from seedwiki.com/wiki/YiTan/TheRelationshipRevolution.html

Scott, L. A., Temple, P., & Marshall, D. (2015). UDL in online college coursework: Insights of infusion and educator preparedness. *Online Learning*, *19*(5), 99–119. doi:10.24059/olj.v19i5.623

Serafini, F., & Gee, E. (Eds.). (2017). *Remixing multiliteracies: Theory and practice from New London and new times*. Teachers College Press.

Shoffner, M., de Oliveira, L. C., & Angus, R. (2010). Multiliteracies in the secondary English classroom: Becoming literate in the 21st century. *English Teaching*, *9*(3), 75–89.

Short, D. (2012). Teaching scientific concepts using a virtual world—Minecraft. *Teaching Science*, *58*(3), 55–58.

Shulman, L. S. (1986). Those who understand: Knowledge growth in teaching. *Educational Researcher*, *15*(2), 4–14. doi:10.3102/0013189X015002004

Sieberer-Nagler, K. (2015, December 14). Effective classroom-management & positive teaching. *English Language Teaching*, *9*(1), 163–172. doi:10.5539/elt.v9n1p163

Silver, L., Smith, A., Johnson, C., Jiang, J., Anderson, M., & Raine, L. (2019, March 7). *Use of smart phones and social media is common across most emerging economies*. Pew Research Center. https://www.pewresearch.org/internet/2019/03/07/use-of-smart phones-and-social-media-is-common-across-most-emerging-economies/

Simplicio, J. (2015). How to effectively use social media as in-class teaching tools. *Reading Improvement*, *52*(4), 142.

Sleeter, C. E. (2005). *Un-standardizing curriculum: Multicultural teaching in the standards-based classrooms*. Teachers College Press.

Smart phones won. VSCO officially abandons personal computers to focus on the mobile application. (2018, December). https://www.xiaomist.com/2018/12/smart phones-won-vsco-officially.html

Smith, A. (2015). US Smartphone use in 2015. *Pew Research Group*. Retrieved from https://www.pewresearch.org/internet/2015/04/01/us-smartphone-use-in-2015/

Smith, T. (2020). *The invisible blizzard and the importance of e-learning*. Retrieved from https://thehill.com/blogs/congress-blog/education/489752-the-invisible-blizzard-and-the-importance-of-e-learning

Smith, B. E. (2017). Composing across modes: A comparative analysis of adolescents' multimodal composing processes. *Learning, Media and Technology*, *42*(3), 259–278. doi:10.1080/17439884.2016.1182924

Sorkin, A. D. (2020, June). Safer schools. *The New Yorker*, 11–12.

Stanovich, K. E. (1986). Matthew effects in reading: Some consequences of individual differences in the acquisition of literacy. *Reading Research Quarterly*, *21*(4), 360–406. doi:10.1598/RRQ.21.4.1

Sterner, R. (2015). 4 things you'll miss by banning cell phones in your classroom. *Education Digest*, *81*(2), 56–58.

Stewart, J. (2017, June 20). *The history of photojournalism. How photography changed the way we receive news*. https://mymodernmet.com/photojournalism-history/

Strovas, S. (2011). Music in the first-year writing classroom. *CEA Forum*, *40*(2), 24-42.

Supiano, B. (2020). 'Zoomed out:' Why live teaching isn't always the best. *The Chronicle*. Retrieved from https://www.chronicle.com/article/Zoomed-Out-Why/248401

Swier, R. (2014). Tasks for easily modifiable virtual environments. *The JALT CALL Journal*, *10*(3), 203–219. doi:10.29140/jaltcall.v10n3.176

Tessier, J. (2013). Student impressions of academic cell phone use in the classroom. *Journal of College Science Teaching*, *43*(1), 25–29. doi:10.2505/4/jcst13_043_01_25

The IRIS Center. (n.d.). *Reinforcement: Positive versus negative*. Vanderbilt University. https://iris.peabody.vanderbilt.edu/wp-content/uploads/pdf_activities/independent/IA_Reinforcement_Positive_versus_Negative.pdf

The New London Group. (1996). A pedagogy of multiliteracies: Designing social futures. *Harvard Educational Review*, *1*(60).

Thomas, A. (2017). *The hate u give*. Harper Collins.

Thomas, K. M., O'Bannon, B. W., & Bolton, N. (2013). Cell Phones in the Classroom: Teachers' Perspectives of Inclusion, Benefits, and Barriers. *Computers in the Schools*, *30*(4), 295–308. doi:10.1080/07380569.2013.844637

Thomas, K., & Munoz, M. A. (2016). Hold the phone! High school students' perceptions of mobile phone integration in the classroom. *American Secondary Education*, *44*(3), 19.

Thorton, P., & Houser, C. (2004). *Using mobile phones in education.* Retrieved from https://www.it.iitb.ac.in/~vijaya/ticet/dokuwiki/media/01281326.pdf

Time to Beat. (2020). *Life is Strange*. https://howlongtobeat.com/game?id=21702

Tindell, D., & Bohlander, R. (2011). The use and abuse of cell phones and text messaging in the classroom: A survey of college students. *College Teaching*, *60*(1), 1–9. doi:10.1080/87567555.2011.604802

Tondeur, J., Scherer, R., Siddiq, F., & Baran, E. (2017). A comprehensive investigation of TPACK within preservice teachers' ICT profiles: Mind the gap! *Australasian Journal of Educational Technology*, *33*(3), 46–60. doi:10.14742/ajet.3504

Tondeur, J., Scherer, R., Siddiq, F., & Baran, E. (2019). Strategies to prepare pre- service teachers for Technological Pedagogical Content Knowledge (TPACK): A mixed-method study. *Educational Technology Research and Development*. Advance online publication. doi:10.100711423-019-09692-1

Trekles, A. M. (2012). Creative writing, problem-based learning, and game-based learning principles. *Proceedings of the International Society for Technology in Education.* https://pdfs.semanticscholar.org/730f/5b706aeb0ae26b4eb12e348ce004733557e2.pdf

Tromba, P. (2013). Building engagement and knowledge one block at a time with Minecraft. *Learning and Leading with Technology*, 20–23.

U.S. Department of Education, National Center for Homeless Education. (2019). *Federal data summary: School years 2016-2017.* Retrieved from https://nche.ed.gov/wp-content/uploads/2019/02/Federal-Data-Summary-SY-16.17-Final published-2.12.19.pdf

Uribe, M., & Nathenson-Mejía, S. (2008). *Literacy essentials for English language learners: Successful transitions*. Teacher's College Press.

Valtonen, T., Sointu, E., Kukkonen, J., Kontkanen, S., Lambert, M. C., & Makitalo-Seigl, K. (2017). TPACK updated to measure pre-service teachers' twenty-first century skills. *Australasian Journal of Educational Technology*, *33*(3), 15–31. doi:10.14742/ajet.3518

Vasquez, H. (2020). What if we...don't return to school as usual. *National Equity Project.* Retrieved from https://medium.com/national-equity-project/what-if-we-dont-return-to-school-as-usual-4aceb5227df5

Vendantam, S. (2019, September 6). *The distracting draw of smart phones* [Radio Broadcast]. https://www.npr.org/2019/09/06/758199383/the-distracting-draw-of-smartphones

Verne, J. (2014). *Around the world in 80 days*. Black & White Classics.

Wagner, P., & Sawyer, W. (2018, June). *States of Incarceration: The Global Context 2018*. Prison Policy Initiative. https://www.prisonpolicy.org/global/2018.html

Waldman, B. (2020). Game, set…graduate! Schools diving into gaming as a source of education, not diversion. *Winnipeg Free Press*. https://www.winnipegfreepress.com/arts-and-life/life/sci_tech/front-hed-game-set-graduate-inside-hed-ready-to-learn-just-hit-play-567660792.html

Walsh, S., White, K., & Young, R. (2009). The phone connection: A Qualitative exploration of how belongingness and social identification relate to mobile phone use amongst Australian youth. *Journal of Community & Applied Social Psychology*, *19*(3), 225–240. doi:10.1002/casp.983

Ward, F. (2016). Integrating technology and literacy. *Classroom Technology*. https://www.edutopia.org/blog/integrating-technology-and-literacy-frank-ward

Wernholm, M., & Vigmo, S. (2015). Capturing children's knowledge-making dialogues in Minecraft. *International Journal of Research & Method in Education*, *38*(3), 230–246. doi:10.1080/1743727X.2015.1033392

Whillier, S., & Lystad, R. P. (2012). The effect of face-to-face teaching on student knowledge and satisfaction in an undergraduate neuroanatomy course. *Anatomical Sciences Education*, *6*(4), 239–245. doi:10.1002/ase.1338 PMID:23225606

White, M. (2017, April 12). Why everyone needs to make playlists. *The Odyssey Online*. https://www.theodysseyonline.com/everyone-needs-make-playlists

WhoSampled.com. (n.d.). https://www.whosampled.com/The-Notorious-B.I.G./Ten-Crack-Commandments/

Wilson, S. (2018). On digital otherness: Being 'of art' in the age of the internet. *International Journal of Contemporary Humanities*, *3*(1), 1–11. https://www.researchgate.net/publication/329625846_On_Digital_Otherness_Being_%27of_Art%27_in_the_Age_of_the_Internet

Windschitl, M. (2002). Framing constructivism as the negotiation of dilemmas: An analysis of the conceptual, pedagogical, cultural, and political challenges facing teachers. *Review of Educational Research*, *72*(2), 131–175. doi:10.3102/00346543072002131

Witting, A. F., William, G. W., David, S. T., & Wagley, S. (1984). Study guide to accompany psychology: an introduction. McGraw-Hill.

Wong Fillmore, L. (1992). Learning a language from learners. In C. Kramsch & S. McConnel-Ginnet (Eds.), *Text and context: Cross-disciplinary perspectives on language study* (pp. 44–66). Heath.

Woo, E. (2019, August 19). *Sick of distracted students? Some schools have started locking up their phones*. The Mercury News. https://www.mercurynews.com/2019/08/19/sick-of-distracted-students-some-schools-have-started-locking-up-their-phones/

Woodson, J. (2014). *Brown girl dreaming*. Penguin Group.

Wormell, R. (2015). *Moving students from passive consumers to active creators*. Association for Middle Level Educators. https://www.amle.org/BrowsebyTopic/WhatsNew/WNDet/TabId/270/ArtMID/888/ArticleID/526/Moving-Students-from-Passive-Consumers-to-Active-Creators.aspx

Yan, Z. (2018). Child and adolescent use of mobile phones: An unparalleled complex developmental Phenomenon. *Child Development*, *89*(1), 5–16. doi:10.1111/cdev.12821 PMID:28485017

Young, C. A., & Bush, J. (2004). Teaching the English language arts with technology: A critical approach and pedagogical framework. *Contemporary Issues in Technology & Teacher Education*, *4*(1), 1–22.

Zamarvide, N. L. (2019, March 29). *Fake social media generators- Ideas for the classroom*. https://natalialzam.wordpress.com/2019/03/29/fake-social-media-generators-ideas-for-the-classroom/

Zoch, M., Myers, J., & Belcher, J. (2016). Teachers' engagement with new literacies: Support for implementing technology in the English/Language Arts classroom. *Contemporary Issues in Technology & Teacher Education*, *17*(1). https://citejournal.org/proofing/teachers-engagement-with-new-literacies-support-for-implementing-technology-in-the-englishlanguage-arts-classroom/

Zoss, M. (2009). Visual arts and literacy. In L. Christenbury, R. Bomer, & P. Smagorinsky (Eds.), *Handbook of Adolescent Literacy Research* (pp. 183–196). The Guilford Press.

Zucker, A. (2012). *Using Digital Tools to Help Transform Schools*. AdvancedEd Source. https://www.advanc-ed.org/source/using-digital-tools-help-transform-schools

About the Contributors

Clarice M. Moran is a former journalist and English teacher. She currently is an Assistant Professor of English Education at Appalachian State University in Boone, North Carolina. Her research focuses on the integration of digital technologies into the English language arts curriculum, as well as teacher preparation and critical pedagogies. She presents regularly at national conferences and is the co-editor of Applying the Flipped Classroom Model to English Language Arts (IGI Global). She also has published numerous articles in newspapers and magazines, as well as scholarly work in peer-reviewed journals and books.

* * *

Hannah O. Ajayi, PhD, is an Associate Professor of Early Childhood Education, in the Institute of Education, Obafemi Awolowo University, Ile - Ife, Nigeria. She teaches Early Childhood Education and English Language Arts courses to postgraduate levels. She has published many of her works in national and international journals of high repute. She has attended many national and international conferences to present her research works. She belongs to national and international associations.

Cameron Bigelow is a current junior at Thomas College. He is currently earning a bachelors degree in Secondary Education in Social Studies. He hopes to attend graduate school, teach at the high school level, and continue to further study pedagogical theory.

Rachel Hagerman is a middle school English and social studies teacher residing in North Carolina. Rachel has experience teaching overseas in both Thailand and Aruba.

Miles Harvey is a literacy teacher educator and middle school ELA teacher and esports coach in Albuquerque, New Mexico. His research interests include gaming culture, game-based learning, esports, and digital literacies. The middle school esports team he founded is the first of its kind in New Mexico.

Stephanie Loomis is currently a Visiting Assistant Professor in Teaching and Learning at the University of Nevada, Las Vegas. Her research interests include teaching composition, teacher education, multimodal texts, and remix as a form of literacy.

Rick Marlatt is an assistant professor of English language arts and literacy at New Mexico State University. His work bridges the fields of English education, creative writing, digital literacies, literature study, and sociocultural theory. His recent interests include the cultivation of critical digital pedagogy in secondary English, incorporation of poetry writing into preservice teacher education, and the implementation of video games and virtual reality technology to enhance literature study and literacy identities for adolescents.

Monica Morall is an English Language Arts (ELA) instructor at Phoenix High School, a nontraditional school outside of Atlanta, Georgia. Over the past 24 years, she has taught students at every level from Honors/Pre-AP, to College Preparation, and Special Education in a Collaborative Setting. She holds a M.Ed in Curriculum and Instruction from Georgia Southern University and an Ed.S. in Secondary Education English from Kennesaw State University. Her current research interests are in social justice education and how culturally responsive education impacts engagement and empowerment in marginalized students.

Johnson O. Okewole, PhD, is a Senior Lecturer in the Institute of Education. He is an Early Childhood Education specialist with bias in Literacy and Social Studies. He teaches Early Childhood courses to the post graduate levels. He has published many of his works in reputable journals both at national and international levels, He has also attended several conferences to present his works. He belongs to many professional associations at national and international levels.

Magdalena Pando is an assistant professor of Bilingual Education and Teaching English to Speakers of Other Languages (TESOL) at New Mexico State University. She specializes in second language teaching methods in science for teachers of English language learners in K-12 grades. Her research interests include, STEM education for English language learners, second language pedagogies, and Systemic Functional Linguistics. Her work specializes in investigating the language of schooling applying sociocultural, sociolinguistic, culturally and linguistically responsive, and culturally sustaining theoretical frameworks to increase access for English language learners.

Glenn Rhoades teaches 10th grade Language Arts at Central Gwinnett High School in Gwinnett County, Georgia's largest public school system. He loves his students, and their cell phones. He lives with his partner, their three-year-old, two dogs, 1 ball python, 3 tarantulas, and a fat tailed gecko.

Katie Rybakova is an Assistant Professor of education at Thomas College and the current Executive Director of the Maine Association for Middle Level Education. She earned her Ph.D. from Florida State University in Curriculum and Instruction and studies digital literacies, young adult literature, and practical applications of pedagogy that help support the preservice and inservice teachers she works with.

Joshua O. Salami is a doctoral student of Early Childhood Education and a graduate assistant in the Institute of Education, Obafemi Awolowo, Ile -Ife, Nigeria. He has published some articles at the national and international levels. His bias is English Language. He belongs to national and international professional association.

Angela Tudor received an M.A.T. in Secondary English Education from Piedmont College in Demorest, Georgia, and an Ed.S. in English Education from Kennesaw State University. She has worked as a Secondary English Teacher for the last fourteen years, and her research interests include the effectiveness of sociocultural learning and the implementation of multiliteracy instruction for adolescents and young adults.

Cynthia White lives in the Atlanta area and teaches English.

Maya Woodall is a middle school language arts teacher as well as the language arts department head at Austin Middle School in Paulding County, Georgia. She is a doctoral student in the Language and Literacy Unit in the College of Education and Human Development at Georgia State University.

Index

F

H

I

K

L

M

N

O

P

Index

www.ingramcontent.com/pod-product-compliance
Lightning Source LLC
LaVergne TN
LVHW061536290926
849162LV00004B/805
* 9 7 8 1 7 9 9 8 5 8 0 5 8 *